# NEA
# MOTO

## Affordable Alternatives to Service Stations

(10th Edition)

by

**Hugh Cantlie**

Over 200 pubs, restaurants, hotels and places of interest just 5 minutes off a motorway junction.

Published by Cheviot Books

| | | | |
|---|---|---|---|
| 1st Edition | Sep 2001 | Reprint | Jan 2002 |
| 2nd Edition | Sep 2002 | 3rd Edition | Oct 2003 |
| 4th Edition | Oct 2004 | 5th Edition | Jan 2006 |
| 6th Edition | Feb 2007 | 7th Edition | Feb 2008 |
| 8th Edition | Apr 2010 | Reprint | Sep 2010 |
| 2nd Reprint | Nov 2010 | 3rd Reprint | Dec 2010 |
| 9th Edition | Oct 2011 | 10th Edition | Mar 2012 |


Illustrations Hugh Cantlie



A catalogue copy is held by the British Library.

Cheviot Books
e-mail: info@cheviotbooks.co.uk
website: www.cheviotbooks.com

ISBN 978-09539920-9-6

Printed by Potts Print (UK), Cramlington

# The Motorway Network

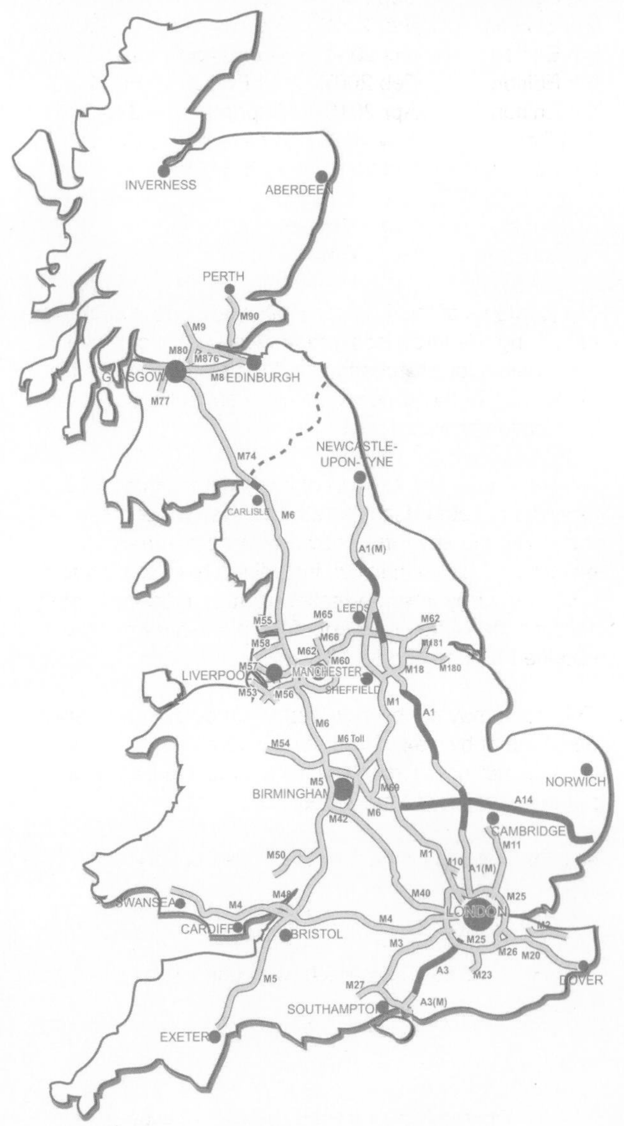

# Contents


| | |
|---|---|
| **Contents** | iv |
| **Foreword** | vi |
| **How to use your guide** | vi |
| **Deletions** | viii |
| **Additions** | ix |

**England and Wales**

| | |
|---|---|
| A1 | 1 |
| A3 | 39 |
| A14 | 43 |
| A19 | 61 |
| M1 | 67 |
| M2 | 87 |
| M3 | 93 |
| M4 | 101 |
| M5 | 123 |
| M6 | 149 |
| M11 | 173 |
| M18 | 182 |
| M20 | 185 |
| M23 | 193 |
| M25 | 197 |
| M26 | 204 |
| M27 | 207 |
| M40 | 211 |
| M42 | 223 |
| M48 | 227 |
| M50 | 231 |
| M53 | 237 |
| M54 | 241 |
| M56 | 245 |
| M61 | 249 |
| M62 | 253 |
| M65 | 261 |
| M66 | 264 |
| M69 | 267 |

**Scotland**

| | |
|---|---|
| Intro | 271 |
| M9 | 273 |
| M74 | 277 |
| M90 | 283 |

| | |
|---|---|
| **Notes** | 287 |
| **Alphabetical Index** | 289 |
| **Index by motorway** | 295 |
| **Places of Interest** | 299 |
| **Readers' suggestions** | 305 |

# Foreword

Why another edition? Well may you ask, as it is an enormous labour for everyone involved.

Apart from keeping it up to date this past year has been different as some fifteen of the thirty four deleted entries from last year have ceased to trade entirely.
A chilling reminder of the times we live in.

Another reason is that villagers went to the Local for a puff, a pint and politics. Politics is still discussed but a pint has been banned as we are apparently no longer responsible for our own actions. What has been the final straw for the pub trade is the banning of smoking anywhere in the premises. May all the do-gooders have a long and healthy life but they are destroying the well being of the local communities.

The good news is that of the ten Best Pubs of the Year Awards, three of them are already in the guide.

Thanks are due to those who have helped with the production of this edition. Merry Wadlow had been a great support in contacting the entries as well as help with the IT. Antony Duke has efficiently provided accurate maps and plans. Rollo de Walden now lives in Finland but his previous efforts are the basis for this edition. Potts Printers have not only done the printing but have also moulded the raw material into shape.

My thanks to all those entries who have been more than supportive and helpful for this edition in marked contrast to the many others who relied on my crystal ball to know the times for serving food or any other details.

Lastly thank you all who told me of their experiences and have made suggestions for any inclusions in the future.

Happier motoring

Hugh Cantlie

# How to use your guide

We have tried to make it easy to follow by arranging it in the same numerical order as the Motorways, starting with the main A roads and ending at Perth on the M90.

Each page will show the Motorway number in larger letters and then the Junction numbers as they would be seen from the Motorway with the names of the towns and road numbers. At one time these would have differed depending on the direction of travel but this seems now to be better.

There is then a description on how to find the entry in case your Satnav has let you down or your map, if you have remembered to bring it, is on too small a scale.

The plan, which shows any Filling Stations, should be redundant but is there to test your map-reading skills.

The letter in the roundel should correspond with that on the plan but it is human to err. The rest is easy. Name of the entry: the address and then the post code for Satnav purposes. The next line has the telephone number so you can book a table or confirm times of serving food. The Website is below, if there is one, for further details and the e-mail in case of need.

The symbols should be understandable and show the number of bedrooms; an eggcup for breakfasts; cup for a coffee break; a wheelchair for disabled; a table for outside seating; children for being children friendly and a paw for dogs allowed.

On the same line to the right is a £ or £s to indicate the price range.

There is then a brief write-up to give a feeling of what to expect and above all whether it is friendly and has a good ambiance.

The watercolours are apparently flattering but The Fighting Temeraire by Turner probably did the same.

# Deletions

There have been 34 deletions from the previous edition which means that since the 7th edition there have been some 130 changes from the average number of over 200 entries.

| | | |
|---|---|---|
| **A1** | 16 | Black Horse |
| | - | Wheatsheaf |
| | - | Robin Hood |
| | 45 | Piccolino |
| | - | Old Oak Tree Ye Olde |
| | 65 | Bowes Incline Hotel |
| **A14** | 17 | Green Man |
| | 20 | Mermaid |
| | 48 | Kings Arms |
| **A19** | - | Carpenters Arms |
| | - | Bay Horse |
| **M1** | 12 | Angel |
| | 13 | Birch |
| | 29 | Famous Shoulder |
| | 37 | Spencer Arms |
| **M3** | 9 | Flower Pots |
| **M4** | 13 | Tally Ho |
| **M5** | 30 | Bridge Inn |
| **M6** | 18 | Fox & Hounds |
| | 29 | Olde Hob Inn |
| | 35 | Eagles Head |
| | 44 | Crosby Lodge Hotel |
| | 45 | Gretna Chase Hotel |
| **M20** | 8 | Windmill |
| **M27** | 1 | Sir John Barleycorn |
| | 8 | The Bugle |
| **M40** | 6 | Sir Charles Napier |
| | 6 | Half Moon |
| **M42** | 14 | Holly Bush |
| **M50** | 1 | Jockey |
| | 3 | Penny Farthing |
| **M58** | 3 | Quattros |
| | 3 | Sandpiper |

# Additions

There are 40 new entries some of which have been suggested by fellow motorists to whom we thank.

| Road | Junction | Entry | Suggested by |
|---|---|---|---|
| **A1** | 9 | Three Horseshoes | |
| | - | George Brasserie | |
| | 16 | Stilton Cheese | Linda Moore |
| | 34 | White Swan | |
| | 48 | Ye Olde Punchbowl | Tim O'Connor-Fenton |
| | 51 | Green Dragon | |
| | - | Greyhound | |
| | 65 | Angel View Inn | |
| **A14** | 35 | Hole in the Wall | |
| **M1** | 12 | Carpenters Arms | |
| | 16 | Bliss Tearoom | Mark Wrigley |
| | 16 | White Hart | Jane Russell-Parsons |
| | 24 | Falcon | Helen Knuckle |
| | 38 | Old Post Office | Mike Dods |
| **M4** | 13 | Langley Hall Inn | |
| | 13 | Red House | |
| | 17 | Jolly Huntsman | |
| **M5** | 7 | Swan | |
| | 7 | Talbot | |
| | 13 | Frombridge Mill | Stuart Hamilton |
| | 18 | The Priory | |
| | 27 | Old Well | |
| | 30 | Greendale Farmshop | |
| **M6** | 19 | Windmill | David Shore |
| | 27 | White Lion | |
| | 38 | Cross Keys | |
| | 38 | Old School Tearoom | Roger Smith |
| | 38 | Kennedys Fine Chocolates | M. Bowman-Vaughan |
| | 44 | The Stag | |
| **M20** | 10 | Honest Miller | Jenny Ratcliffe |
| **M27** | 1 | Bell Hotel | |
| | 1 | Green Dragon | |
| | 1 | White Hart | |
| **M60** | 6 | Cherry Tree | |
| | 11 | New Inn | |
| | 13/14 | Leopard | |
| **M42** | 14 | Three Horseshoes | John Jolliffe |
| **M50** | 3 | Kilcot Inn | |
| **M74** | 13 | Abington Hotel | |
| | 14 | Black Bull Hotel | |

# A1(M)

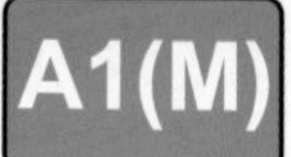

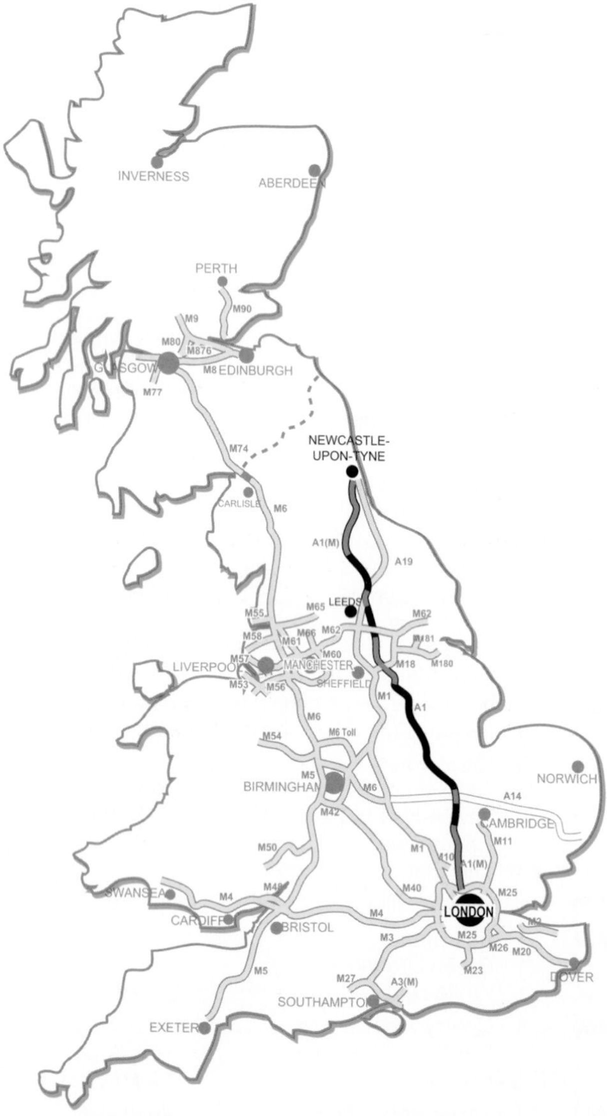


## A1(M) London to Newcastle

# JUNCTIONS 6 TO 65

The A1 is the old Great North Road from London to Edinburgh and for much of its length it still uses the routes of the old Roman roads.

Due to the increase in traffic on the M1 it is slowly being upgraded to motorway standard especially on the northern sections

Over the past few years this has happened from the junction with the M62 at Ferrybridge to the junction with the A19 north of Boroughbridge.

Work has now started on the section north of Boroughbridge to Leeming which is due to be finished in 2012.

It was planned to continue from Leeming to Scotch Corner to be finished in 2014 but this has been shelved for the time being due to lack of funding.

As a result of these continuing roadworks I have decided to include the A19 from Thirsk to the Tyne Tunnel which is a dual-carriageway alternative to the A1 as far as Newcastle. The A19 does not have numbered junctions.

However, there are stretches of dual carriageway still to be upgraded such as from Baldock to Huntingdon and the long section from Peterborough to south of Doncaster. These have been included although the turn-offs are not numbered and only have names of the villages or towns.

For ease of use I have divided the A1 into five different sections. The first is from Hatfield to the junction with the A14 at Huntingdon; the second from Huntingdon to Grantham; the next is from Grantham to the M62 at Ferrybridge and then the section from there to Scotch Corner. The last section is the motorway to Newcastle.

# HATFIELD TO HUNTINGDON

## TO INCLUDE JUNCTIONS  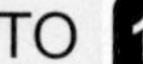 

6 TO 13

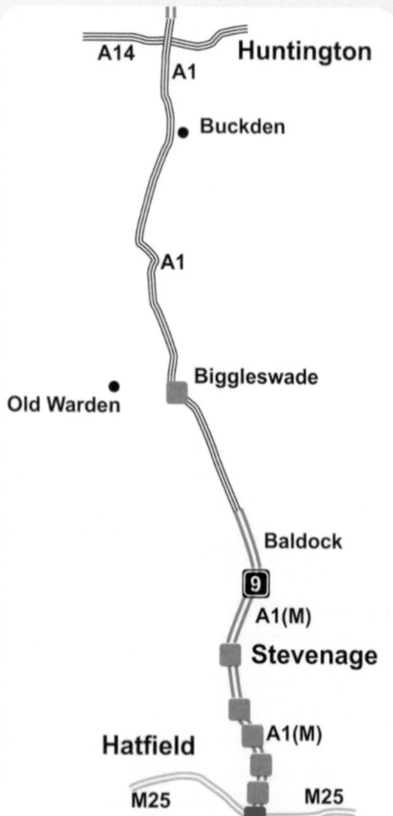


From the junction with the M25 at South Mimms, it is a motorway until north of Baldock. Hatfield is bypassed by going underneath it through a tunnel.

Welwyn Garden City was the first of the conceptual towns to be designed to bring the country to the town in the 1920s. It is still a surpris-ingly pleasant town to live in.

Stevenage was the first of the post-Second World War new towns. Apparently the brother of the Minister responsible for the concept had happened to have bought some of the farms surrounding Stevenage shortly before the details of the intended new town had been published.

Knebworth House, the home of the Lytton family since 1490, is to the west of the motorway by Stevenage. North of Baldock, the A1 continues as a well-maintained dual carriageway until the A14 at Huntingdon.

After coming off the motorway, take the first left on a modern road layout signposted Willian. Head for the church in the centre of the village and the Fox is facing it. The Three Horseshoes on the way into the village is a cheerful locals' pub.

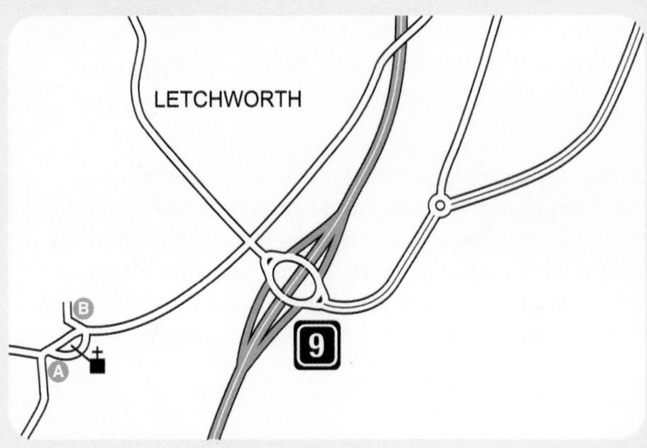


## Ⓐ The Fox at Willian

Baldock Lane, Willian, Herts.

01462 480 233

www.foxatwillian.co.uk
info@foxatwillian.co.uk

Satnav
**SG6 2AE**

**Orders for food:** Weekdays: Noon to 2.00pm and 6.30 pm to 9.15pm. Saturdays: Noon to 9.15pm. Sundays: Noon to 3.00pm.

££

A restaurant-cum-pub which has been refurbished so is now bare floors with wooden tables. Clean, bright and airy with a cheerful and friendly staff.

## B The Three Horseshoes

Satnav
**SG6 2AE**

Baldock Road, Willian, Herts
01462 685 713

threehorseshoes@yahoo.co.uk

**Orders for food:** Monday to Saturdays: Noon to 2.00pm. 6.00pm – 9.00pm. Sundays: Noon – 4.00pm

A friendly locals' pub with low beams, pewter mugs hanging from the ceiling and horse brasses along the walls. In addition there is a large coloured print of the Grand National at Bechers Brook, first time round, in 1969. That was many years after I was there at Canal Turn with six other cars, having a leisurely picnic.

By Biggleswade there is a roundabout by a supermarket. Take the B658 marked Old Warden and brown-signed for the Shuttleworth Collection. Straight on at the first roundabout and pass the Shuttleworth Collection and Swiss Garden on the left. The Hare and Hounds is 3.5 miles further on to your left as you come into the village of Old Warden.

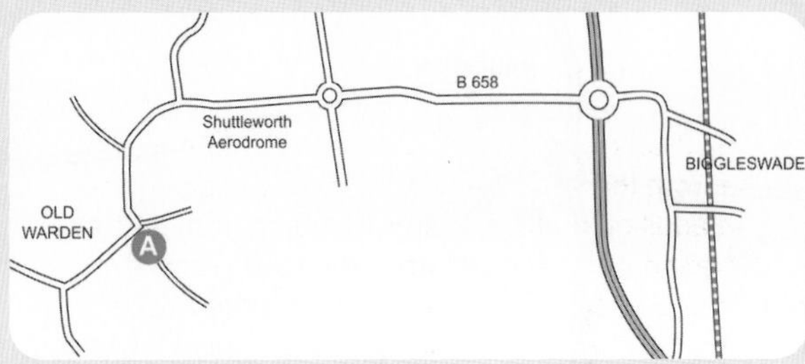


**Places of interest**

**Shuttleworth Collection of Historic Aircraft - 2 miles**

## Ⓐ The Hare and Hounds

Satnav **SG18 9HQ**

Main Street, Old Warden, Beds.
01767 627 225

www.hare&houndsoldwarden.co.uk
thehareandhounds@hotmail.co.uk

**Orders for food**: Tuesday to Saturday: Noon to 2.00pm and 6.30pm to 9.00pm. Sundays: Noon to 3.30pm. Closed Mondays.

££

A privately owned, comfortable wayside pub-cum-restaurant which specialises in local game from the nearby Shuttleworth estate, as well as Scottish beef. There are three separate dining rooms served by attentive and friendly staff. Just the place if you have left London rather later than planned.

Buckden is just off the A1 – by a Shell garage on a roundabout on its southern edge. As an alternative, the George Hotel and Brasserie is opposite and is modernised, light and spacious.

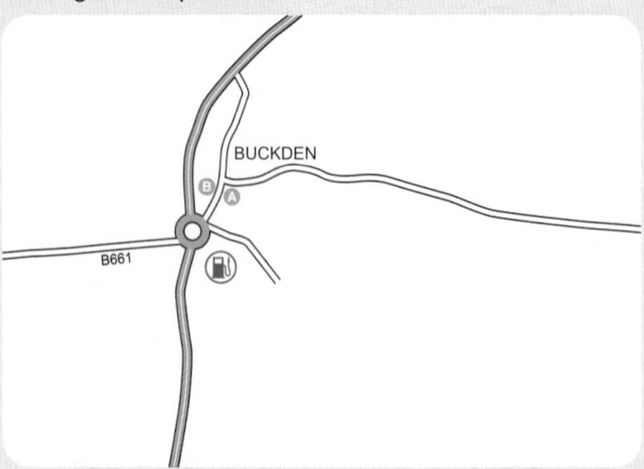


## Ⓐ The Lion Hotel

Satnav
**PE19 5XA**

High Street, Buckden, Cambs.
01480 810 313
www.thelionbuckden.co.uk
reception@thelionbuckden.co.uk

**Orders for food:** Daily: Noon to 2.30pm and 6.30pm to 9.00pm.

It was built in 1492 as a guest house for the new Bishop of Lincoln's Palace next door where Henry VIII's wife Catherine of Aragon spent some time. Extended in Georgian times, it was converted into a hotel and is an example of a bygone age with personal service and a homely feeling. Meals served in the bar or in the restaurant.

## B The George Brasserie

Satnav **PE19 5XA**

High Street, Buckden, Cambs
01480 812 300
www.thegeorgebuckden.com
mail@thegeorgebuckden.com

**Orders for food**: Daily: Noon to 2.30pm and 7.00pm to 9.30pm. Sundays: Noon to 3.30pm and 7.00pm to 9.30pm.

Originally a Georgian coaching inn, it is now a smart efficient brasserie which serves breakfasts, light lunches, teas and dinners. The bedrooms are all named after a George, such as Handel, Orwell or Shaw. The owners also own a range of boutique shops in the building in case it is raining!

# HUNTINGDON TO GRANTHAM

## TO INCLUDE JUNCTIONS 13 TO 17

The first stretch, after crossing over the A14, is a four-lane motorway until Peterborough and then dual-carriageway to Grantham.

Stamford is a remarkable town for being in a time warp. It should be congratulated for turning down the government's offer of a grant to have hanging baskets, daily street markets and no parking. The George Hotel in Stamford is world famous.

Grantham is now known for being the birthplace of Margaret Thatcher.

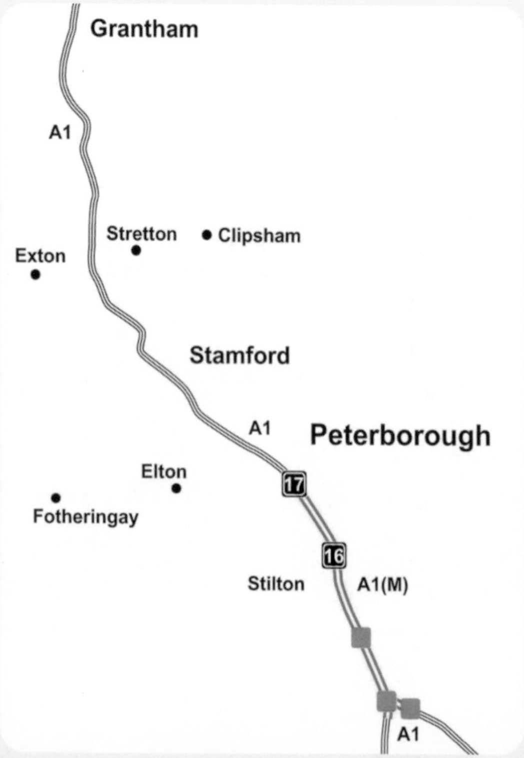

Take the B1043 south, and then almost immediately bear right to Stilton. Those looking for the home of Stilton Cheese could be disappointed, as it is actually made in Melton Mowbray. Nevertheless all five varieties of Stilton are served at the Bell Inn Hotel.

**Places of interest**
Peterborough Cathedral – 4 miles

## Ⓐ Bell Inn Hotel

Satnav
**PE7 3RA**

Great North Road, Stilton, Cambs.
01733 241 066
www.thebellstilton.co.uk
reception@thebellstilton.co.uk
**Orders for food:** Monday to Saturday: Noon to 2.30pm and 6.00pm to 9.30pm. Sundays: Noon to 3.00pm and 6.00pm to 9pm.

£££

A 16th-century coaching inn and now a privately owned well-furnished hotel with two bars, a bistro and a galleried restaurant on two levels under beamed ceilings. There is outside seating in an enclosed garden and courtyard, as well as private parking. Dick Turpin's room, where he rested between nefarious operations, is still in use as the resident's lounge.

## B The Stilton Cheese Inn

Satnav
**PE7 3RP**

24 North Street, Stilton, Cambs
01733 240 546

www.thestiltoncheesepublichouse.co.uk

**Orders for food:** Weekdays: Noon to 2.00pm and 6.00pm to 9.30pm. Sundays: Noon to 2.00pm.

A village pub which was recommended by a reader who found it to be friendly, not expensive and with delicious food with lots of fish specialities. There is outside seating when the weather improves and nearby shops for those seeking a well known brand of cheese.

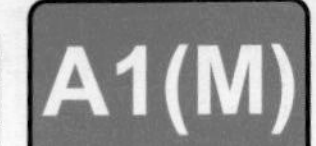


Take the A605 to Oundle. After 4 miles turn right signed Elton. Pass the house and grounds of Elton Hall and the Black Horse is on the left before the church. The Crown is further on, but bear to the right. You can reach The Falcon by taking a left at the end of the village.

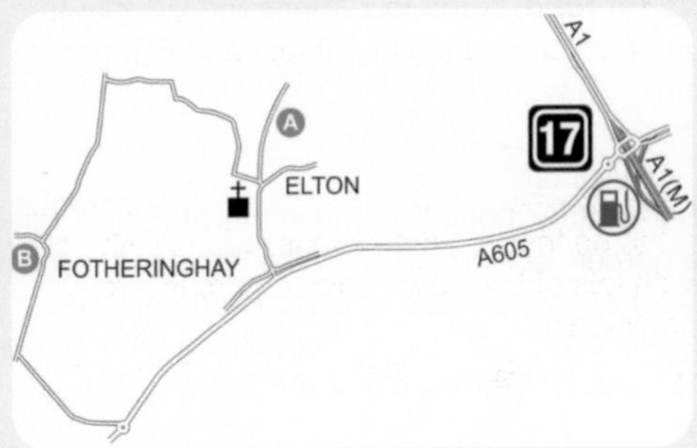

Elton Hall and Garden (15th & 17thC) HHA - 3 miles

## A Crown Inn

Satnav
**PE8 6RQ**

8 Duck Street, Elton Cambridgeshire
01832 280 232
www.thecrowninn.org
inncrown@googlemail.com

**Orders for food:** Weekdays: Noon to 2.00pm and 6.30pm to 8.00pm. Sundays: Noon to 3.00pm

££

A comfortably furnished hostelry with bedrooms in a Cotswold style old village. A friendly welcome even after arriving too late for lunch as they will make up a plate of something fulfilling. A good atmosphere.

## B The Falcon

Satnav
**PE8 5HZ**

Main Street, Fotheringhay, Northants.
01832 226 254
www.thefalcon-inn.co.uk
info@thefalcon-inn.co.uk

**Orders for food:** Noon to 2.15pm and 6.15pm to 9.00pm. Sundays: Noon to 3.00pm and 6.15pm to 8.30pm.

An 18th-century stone-built inn in this attractive village with a garden looking out on to the church. It is full of character and is run with efficiency and personality. There is a locals' bar and a smart dining room as well as a conservatory. Serves a modern British menu.

The Wheatsheaf is on the left as you come into Greetham. For the other two, take the road to Stretton where the Jackson Stops is signed from the road. The Olive Branch is in the next village of Clipsham, on the left by a sharp bend.

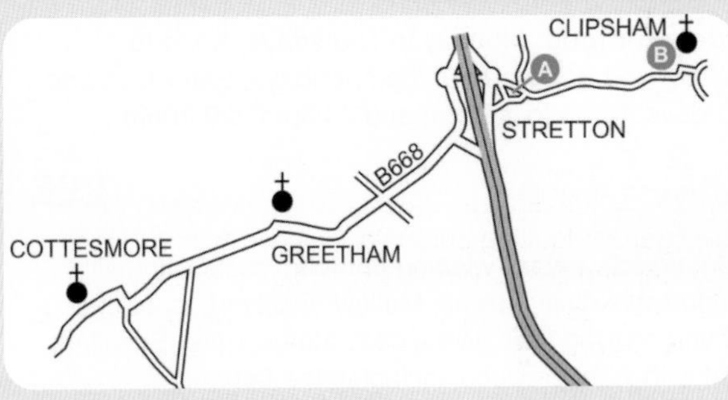


## Ⓐ Jackson Stops

Satnav
**LE15 7RA**

Rookery Road, Stretton, Rutland
01780 410 237
www.thejacksonstops.com

**Orders for food:** Weekdays: Noon to 2.30pm and 6.30pm to 9.00pm. Sundays: Noon to 2.30pm. Mondays: Closed.

££

This privately owned pub-cum-restaurant has changed hands and now has a good standard, with the traditional fare being home cooked, using fresh local produce.

## Ⓑ The Olive Branch

Satnav
**LE15 7SH**

Main Street, Clipsham, Leics.
01780 410 355

www.theolivebranchpub.com
info@theolivebranchpub.com

**Orders for food:** Monday to Thursdays: Noon to 2.00pm and 6.30pm to 9.30pm. Fridays, Saturdays and Sundays: Noon to 3.00pm and 7.00pm to 9.30pm.

£££

A deservedly award-winning pub-cum-restaurant with comfortable dining areas. Mellow brickwork, subdued lighting and log fires give a cosy atmosphere. Excellent food with local produce, including the famous Lincolnshire sausages. A well-tended garden, so outside eating in the evening.

# GRANTHAM TO FERRYBRIDGE

## TO INCLUDE JUNCTIONS 34 TO 38

This part has a short section of motorway near Doncaster but otherwise it is dual carriageway throughout. From Grantham, it is flat open countryside. At Newark, you will cross over the River Trent, the historical divide between North and South England.

North of Doncaster, by the side of the road, is Robin Hood's Well, designed by Sir John Vanbrugh in 1710, which must have been his smallest building commission.

The condensing towers of the Ferrybridge Power Station have been a familiar landmark for generations.

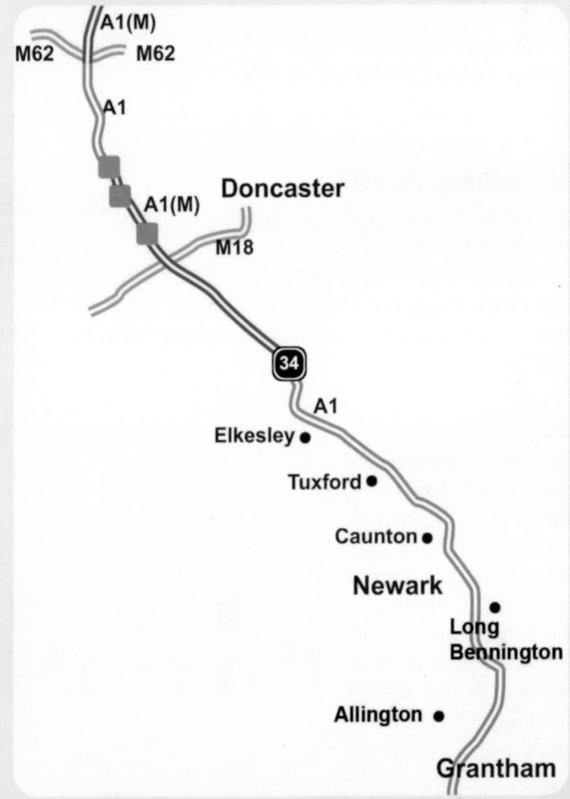

Coming from the south take the road to the left marked Allington at the bottom of the hill north of Grantham.

From the north after Long Bennington opposite Foston the road to Allington is marked.

**Places of interest**

Belton House (17thC) NT - 6 miles 

## A Welby Arms

Satnav
**NG32 2EA**

On the Green, Allington, Lincolnshire
01400 281 361
www.welbyarmsallington.com

**Orders for food:** Mondays to Saturdays: Noon to 2.00pm and 6.00pm to 9.00pm. Sundays: Noon to 8.30pm.

££

A locals' hostelry as the owner's wife Anna comes from the village. A friendly, cheerful place with a large terrace with umbrellas at the rear and fields nearby. The owner, Matt Rose, was trimming the ivy when I was there on a hot sunny day.

.

Long Bennington is still an attractive village as the new brick built houses are well designed and fit in sympathetically. Once it was on the Great North Road but it is now bypassed so is a haven of peace from the noise of traffic.

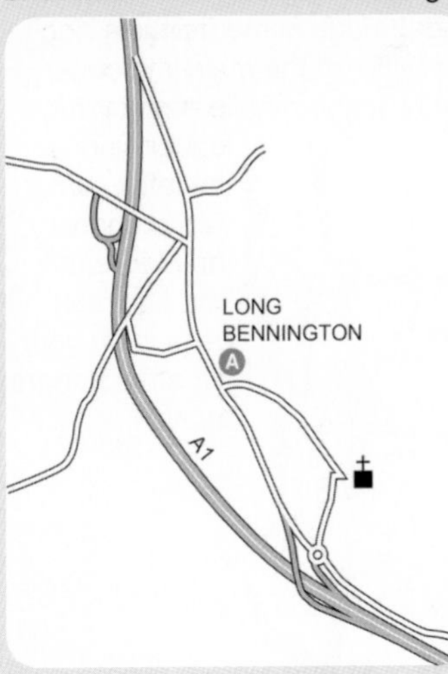


## Ⓐ Reindeer Inn

Satnav
**NG23 5EH**

22 Main Road, Long Bennington, Nottinghamshire
01400 281 382
www.reindeerinn.co.uk
janet@reindeerinn.co.uk

**Orders for food:** Mondays to Saturdays: Noon to 2.00pm and 6.30pm to 9.00pm. No food on Sundays.

££

A friendly welcome in this family-owned inn, with a continental feel to the outside seating at the front of the house. Good atmosphere and a cheerful service coupled with a good menu.

North of Newark there is a sign saying Caunton which is easy to use from both directions. Caunton is 3 miles to the west on a narrow road through some uninteresting countryside. The level crossing on the main line could add minutes to your journey. In the middle of the village is a turning to the left by what was probably the blacksmith. The Caunton Beck is on your left after a sharp bend.

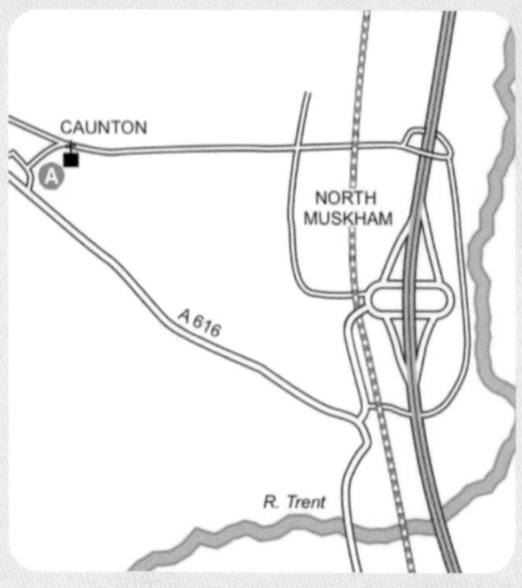


## Ⓐ Caunton Beck

Satnav
**NG23 6AB**

Main Street, Caunton, Notts.
01636 636 793
www.wigandmitre.com
email@cauntonbeck.com

**Orders for food:** Daily: 9.00am to 10.00pm.
Sundays: 9.00am to 9.30pm.

A brick-built range of buildings using old materials, it is now a comfortable restaurant with a bar. A cheerful atmosphere with a range of dining areas. Good wine list and traditional food with efficient and helpful service, especially after I had mislaid my mobile telephone.

The roundabout has been updated and rebuilt. Take the B1164 to Tuxford, and the Mussel and Crab is 600 yards on the right.

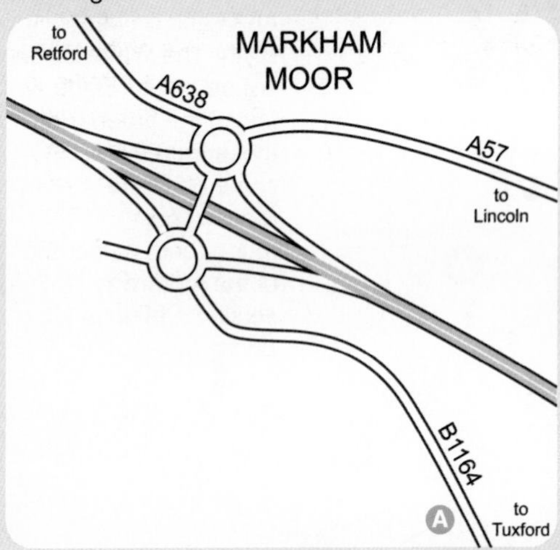


## Ⓐ Mussel and Crab

Satnav
**NG22 0PJ**

Sibthorpe Hill, Tuxford, Notts.
01777 870 491
www.musselandcrab.com
musselandcrab@hotmail.com

**Orders for food:** Monday to Saturday: 11.30am to 2.20pm and 6.00pm to 10.00pm. Sundays: Noon to 2.45pm and 6.00pm to 9.00pm.

£££

A privately owned country restaurant in a converted farmhouse. On entering you will be treated to the sound of the sea and in the WC, goldfish swim in water. There are several dining areas, in a modern style, and traditional bar meals can also be had. Al fresco also possible. Friendly, efficient service and excellent fish dishes.

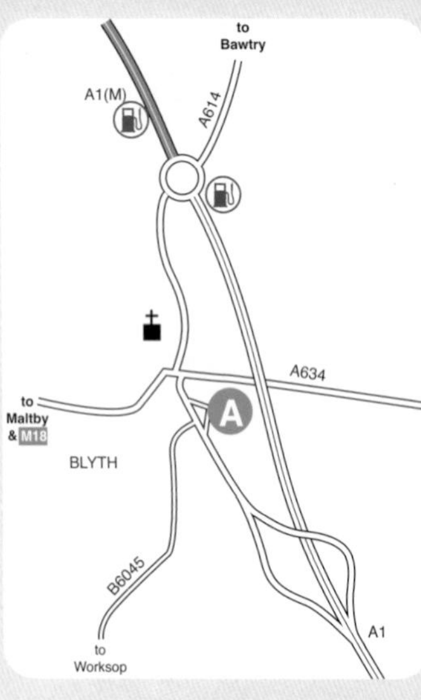


For those driving up from the south turn off where marked Maltby A634 and on into Blyth. The White Swan will be to your right facing the green. For those from the north come off at the recently built roundabout at the end of the motorway section and drive into Blyth.

## Ⓐ White Swan at Blyth

Satnav
**S81 8EQ**

High Street, Blyth, Notts.
01909 591 222
www.whiteswanatblyth.co.uk
info@whiteswanatblyth.co.uk

**Orders for food:** Mondays to Saturdays: Noon to 2.00pm and 5.30pm to 8.30pm. Sundays: Noon to 2.30pm.

££

The White Swan used to be in the guide but the whiff of vinegar was getting so pervasive that I took it out. It has recently changed hands and Richard and Claire have made it into a congenial and comfortable stopping off place with a menu to suit. It has been awarded Best Newcomer Pub in the British Pub Awards.

Wentbridge is so named as it was the bridge over the River Went. Easy to reach from the A1 but it is at the bottom of a hill, so check the brakes.

## Ⓐ Blue Bell Inn

Satnav
**WF8 3JP**

Great North Road, Wentbridge, W. Yorksire
01977 620 697
www.bluebellwentbridge.co.uk
info@bluebellwentbridge.co.uk

**Orders for food:** Daily: Noon to 2.30pm and 5.00pm to 9.00pm. Sundays: Noon to 7.00pm.

££

The original pub sign is still on view from the time it was renovated in 1633. It has since been updated and is now a comfortable, beamed and cheerful locals' pub with dining areas. The food is cooked to order so not instant. Two beer gardens outside.

# FERRYBRIDGE TO SCOTCH CORNER

## TO INCLUDE JUNCTIONS 41 TO 51

This section has now been upgraded to motorway standard from Ferrybridge to Dishforth. The stretch from Dishforth to Leeming is now being upgraded and will be finished in 2012. It was going to be upgraded from there north to Scotch Corner, but this has been deferred for the time being.

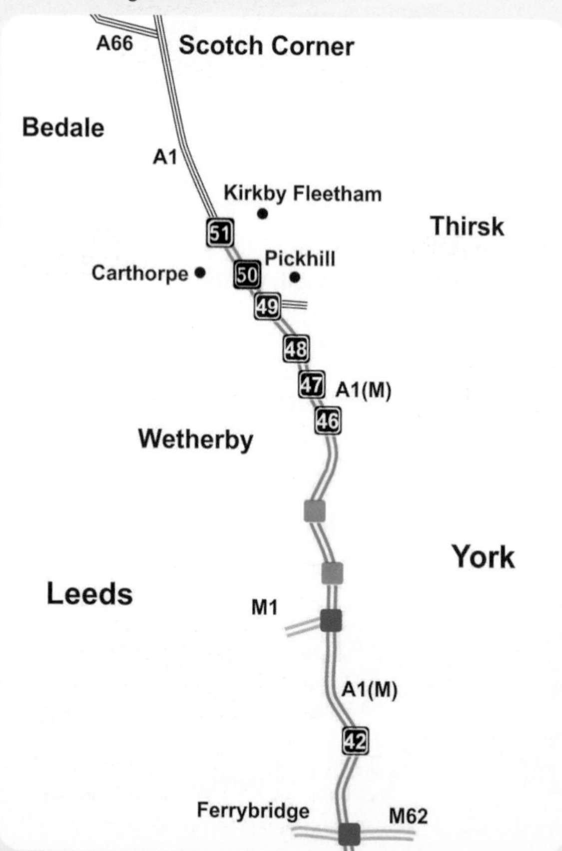

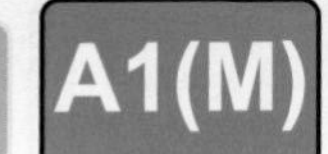


The approach to Ledsham has been altered since the upgrading of this section to a motorway. It is easier to find as there are feeder roads coming off the A1(M) in both directions.

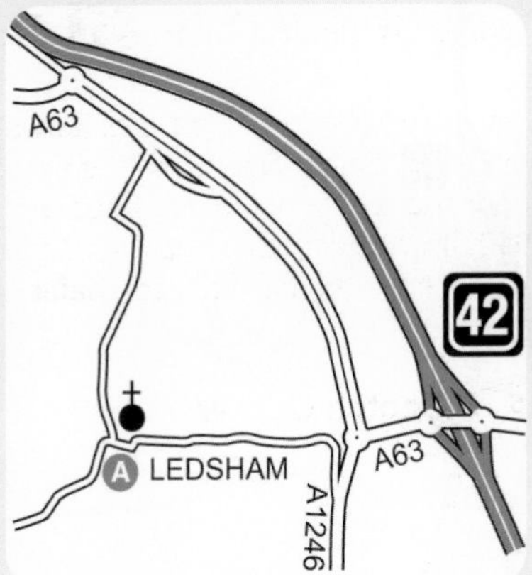


## Ⓐ Chequers Inn

Satnav
**LS25 5LP**

Main Street, Ledsham, S.Yorks.
01977 683 135
www.chequersinn.com
c.j.wraith@btconnect.com

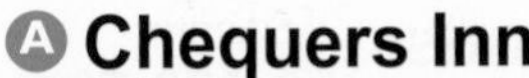

**Orders for food:** Monday to Saturday: Noon to 9.15pm.
Sundays: Closed.

££

A Free House in the middle of this estate village. It is closed all day on Sunday because the lady of the manor in 1830 was abused on her way to church by estate workers pouring out of the pub. Bar meals downstairs and a comfortable restaurant above. The two chefs cook to order from an imaginative menu; the steak pie and lamb shanks are in demand.

For the Fox and Hounds turn right before Bickerton and then left at the T-junction in Walton. The pub is to the left on a sharp left-hand bend.

## Ⓐ The Fox and Hounds

Satnav
**LS23 7DQ**

Hall Park Road, Walton, W.Yorks.
01937 2 192
www.thefoxandhoundswalton.com
basil@thefoxandhoundswalton.com

**Orders for food:** Monday to Saturday: Noon to 2.00pm and 5.30pm to 9.00pm. Sundays: Noon to 3.00pm and 5.00pm to 7.00pm.

££

A thoroughly agreeable pub-cum-restaurant with friendly and efficient service. My crab soup with home-baked bread was good. Car park at rear, but take care coming out with a blind corner on the left, especially after such a good meal. It has changed hands, so comments please.

Take the A59 towards Knaresborough. After half a mile turn right to Coneythorpe. The Tiger is on your right as you come into the village.

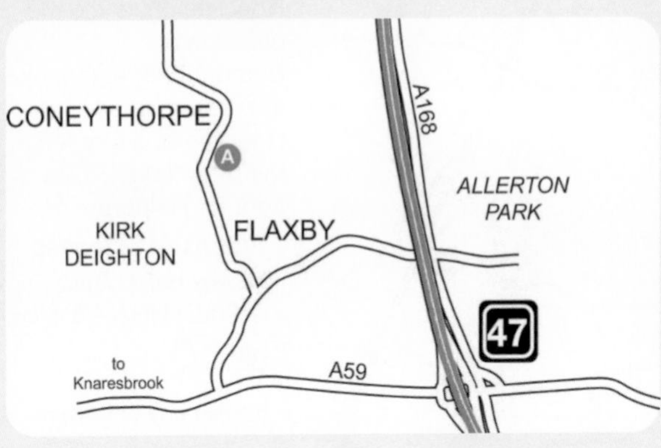


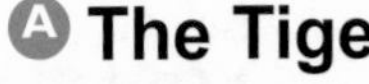

## The Tiger

Satnav
**HG5 0RY**

Shortshill Lane, Coneythorpe, N.Yorks
01423 863 632
www.tiger-inn.co.uk

**Orders for food**: Noon to 9.00pm. Sundays: Noon to 8.00pm.

££

A deservedly popular place as it is family owned and Victoria will make sure that you are given a cheerful Yorkshire welcome. The dining room at the rear is decorated with stags' heads, violins, fishing rods and walking sticks. My mussels, washed down with a glass of Pinot Grigio, were excellent and sensibly priced.

Boroughbridge is a market town and was a coaching stop on the Great North Road. Ferrensby is on the A6055 to Knaresborough. For Roecliffe drive into the outskirts of Boroughbridge and take the road marked Roecliffe and turn left at the roundabout. Turn right for Helperby.

**Places of interest**

Newby Hall (17thC &18thC) HHA – 8 miles.

Roman city of Isurium.

## The Crown Inn

High Street, Roecliffe, N.Yorks.
01423 322 300
www.crowninnroecliffe.com
info@crowninnroecliffe.com

Satnav
**YO51 9LY**

**Orders for food:** Noon to 2.15pm and 6.00pm to 9.00pm. Sundays: Noon to 7.00pm.

Originally a 16th-century inn, it was bought recently by the previous owner of the Bay Horse at Kirk Deighton and he has made it into a friendly, comfortable and relaxed place to have a good meal. A restaurant to the left and a large bar area to the right of the front door. It was even more cheerful when I was there as there was a wedding party who seemed to be enjoying themselves.

## Ⓑ General Tarleton

Satnav
**HG5 0PZ**

Boroughbridge Road, Ferrensby, N.Yorks.
01423 340 284
www.generaltarleton.co.uk
gti@generaltarleton.co.uk

**Orders for food:** Mondays to Thurs: Noon to 2.00pm and 5.30pm to 9.00pm. Fridays and Saturdays: Noon to 2.00pm and 5.30pm to 9.15pm. Sundays: Noon to 2.00pm and 5.30pm to 8.30pm.

££

A privately owned restaurant and hotel with contemporary furnished bedrooms. It is reputed to have the best cuisine in Yorkshire and gives a warm welcome from a young professional staff in a relaxed atmosphere. Children welcome.

## Ⓒ Ye Olde Punch Bowl

Satnav
**YO51 9QY**

Main Road, Marton-cum-Grafton, Yorks
01423 322 519
www.thepunchbowlmartoncumgrafton.com
enquiries@thepunchbowlmartoncumgrafton.com

**Orders for food:** Daily: 12 Noon to 2.30pm and 5.30pm to 9.30pm. Sundays: Noon to 3.00pm and 5.30pm to 8.30pm.

£££

An old 17th Century ale house which has recently been stylishly modernised. It still has low beams and flagstone floors, polished tables and terracotta floors. In the winter there is a log fire and outside there is comfortable seating under the largest parasol/umbrella in Yorkshire. For racing car enthusiasts there is a designated room to Eddie Shine, who, in the 1950's and 60's, was a famous racing driver.

The junction is not directly affected by the upgrading to motorway standard of the A1 to Leeming due to be finished in 2012. Turn off the road marked Asenby.

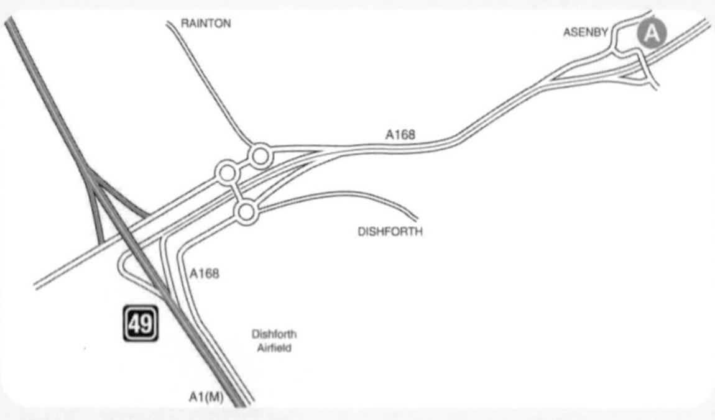


## A The Crab and Lobster

Satnav **YO7 3QL**

Main Street, Asenby, Thirsk, N. Yorks.
01845 577 286
www.crabandlobster.co.uk
reservations@crabandlobster.co.uk

**Orders for food:** Weekdays and Sundays: Noon to 2.00pm and 7.00pm to 9.00pm. Saturdays: Noon to 2.00pm and 6.30pm to 9.00pm.

A quirky restaurant with a bar. One of the more unusual places for a stop-over on a motorway! The décor has been done with imagination and the set menu (which obviously specialises in fish) is value for money. The Crab Manor Hotel next door is in the same ownership.

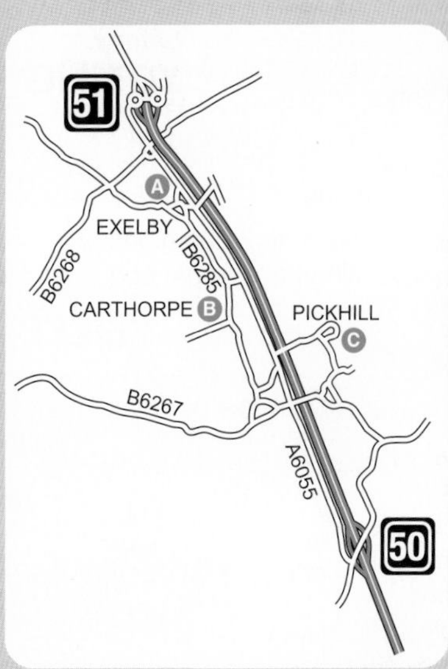


The Fox and Hounds, Nags Head and Green Dragon are between Junction 50 and 51 so take the B6285 or A6065 (the old A1) from either end depending on direction of travel.

## A Fox and Hounds

Satnav **DL8 2LG**

Main Street, Carthorpe, N.Yorks.
01845 567 433
www.foxandhoundscarthorpe.co.uk
info@foxandhoundscarthorpe.co.uk

**Orders for food:** Daily: Noon to 2.00pm and 7.00pm to 9.30pm. Sunday: Noon to 2.00pm and 7.00pm to 9.00pm. Closed Mondays.

££

Vince (who is an ex-Marine) and Helen Taylor run a cheerful pub-cum-restaurant serving high quality traditional fare in what was once the village smithy. The bellows and blacksmith's fire are still in evidence in the dining room.

## B Nags Head

Satnav **YO7 4JG**

Main Street, Pickhill, N.Yorks.
01845 567 391
www.nagsheadpickhill.co.uk
enquiries@nagsheadpickhill.co.uk

**Orders for food:** Weekdays: Noon to 2.00pm and 6.00pm to 9.30pm. Sundays: Noon to 3.00pm and 5.30pm to 8.00pm.

££/£££

14

It is really a restaurant in an agricultural village, with a separate dining room. However excellent bar meals are also available for those in a hurry. Good service and food. Breakfast available.

## C The Green Dragon

Satnav **DL8 2HA**

Main Road, Exelby. N.Yorks.
01677 422 233
www.greendragonexelby.com
greendragonexelby@hotmail.co.uk

**Orders for food:** Noon to 2.30pm and 6.00pm to 9.00pm. Sundays: Noon to 9.00pm.

4

A Free House owned by Mr and Mrs Barraclough who strongly recomm-ended to me the home made soup which was good. It featured in earlier editions but due to the road works taking place then it was difficult to find. It is an old building with a friendly welcome and open fires in the winter. You can have meals either in the restaurant or in the bar depending on the urgency of your journey.

For the Black Horse, follow the turning to Kirkby Fleetham. The Greyhound is signed off the A1 as Hackforth and Hornby.

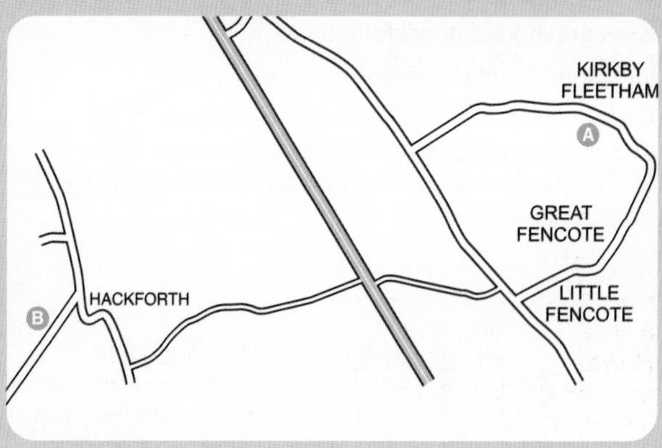


## A Black Horse Inn

Satnav
**DL7 0SH**

Lumley Lane, Kirkby Fleetham, N.Yorks.
01609 749 010
www.blackhorsekirkbyfleetham.com
gm@blackhorsekirkbyfleetham.com

**Orders for food:** Monday to Thursday: Noon to 2.30pm and 5.00pm to 9.00pm. Friday and Saturday: Noon to 2.30pm and 5.00pm to 9.30pm.
Sunday: Noon to 7.00pm.

£££

A village pub which has recently been well renovated with a restaurant and a stone- flagged bar area. Classic dishes with hand-pulled ales and good wines. Friendly staff who have worked hard to make it a success.

## B The Greyhound

Satnav
**DL8 1PB**

Main Street, Hackforth. N.Yorks
01748 813 360

www.greyhoundathackforth.co.uk

info@greyhoundathackforth.co.uk

**Orders for food:** Wednesday to Saturdays: Noon to 2.30pm and 5.30pm to 9.00pm. Sundays: Noon to 3.00pm. Mondays: no food served and no lunch on Tuesdays.

£

The Greyhound has had a chequered history over the past ten years. It is privately owned and Mike Miles has now taken it over. He gave me a friendly welcome even after it had officially closed for food. There is a separate dining room for those wanting more privacy Theakstons and Black Sheep would appear to be the favourite brews.

# SCOTCH CORNER TO NEWCASTLE

## JUNCTIONS 56 TO 65

Not the most inspiring countryside but Durham Cathedral, to the west, is a World Heritage Site and is one of the most remarkable buildings in the country, known as "the loveliest building on Planet Earth".

The Angel of the North will greet you at the other end.

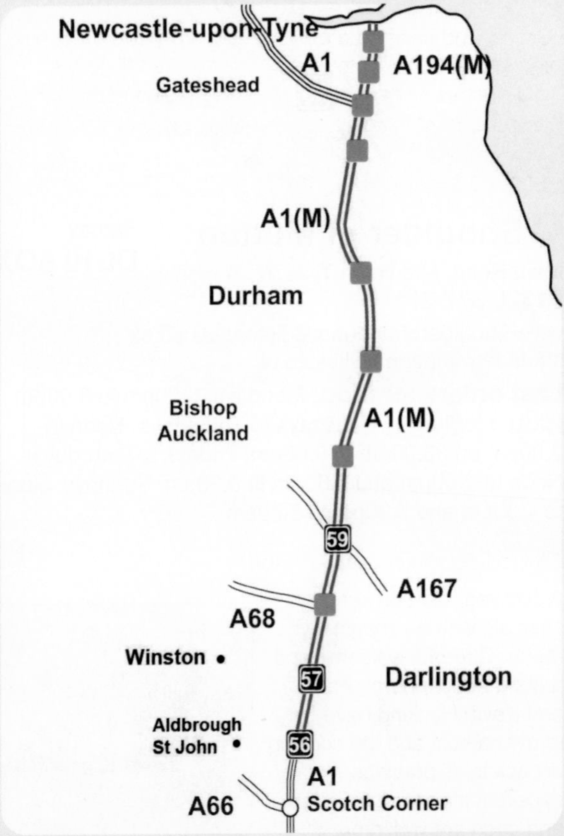

Newcastle-upon-Tyne
A1
A194(M)
Gateshead
A1(M)
Durham
Bishop Auckland
A1(M)
59
A167
A68
Winston
57
Darlington
Aldbrough St John
56
A1
A66
Scotch Corner

The building of the new motorway has been deferred so Junction 56 remains the same. Middleton Tyas is a minute from the motorway.

## Ⓐ Shoulder of Mutton

Satnav **DL10 6QX**

Main Road, Middleton Tyas, N. Yorkshire
01325 377 271
www.shoulderofmuttonmiddletontyas.co.uk
shoulderofmutton1@live.co.uk

**Last orders for food:** Mondays: 6.00pm to 9.00pm (closed for lunch). Tuesdays to Thursdays: Noon to 2.00pm and 6.00pm to 9.00pm. Fridays & Saturdays: Noon to 2.00pm and 6.00pm to 9.30pm. Sundays: Noon to 4.30pm and 5.30pm to 8.30pm.

££

A 300 year old pub serving cask ale with an imaginative menu. Cheerful welcome and a good atmosphere. Fran and Kevin Hacking have rejuvenated it and the cooking is back to its previous excellent standard. Children and dogs are welcome.

## B The Stanwick

Satnav
**DL11 7SZ**

High Green, Aldbrough St. John, N.Yorkshire
01325 374 258
www.thestanwickinn.co.uk
enquiries@thestanwick.co.uk

**Orders for food:** Mondays to Fridays: Noon to 2.00pm and 5.30pm to 9.30pm. Saturdays and Sundays: Noon to 2.00pm and 6.30pm to 9.30pm.

££

Since Neil and Helen Maddison-Potts took it over it has been going from strength to strength as the food is excellent. It is situated on the village green so there is ample scope for exercising the dogs (or children) For the non drivers there is a range of ales including Black Sheep, Old Legover and Freddie Trueman.

## C Bridgewater Arms

Satnav
**DL2 3RN**

Main Street, Winston, Co. Durham
01325 730 302
www.thebridgewaterarms.com

**Orders for food:** Tuesdays to Saturdays: Noon to 2.00pm. 6.00pm to 9.00pm. Closed: Sundays and Mondays.

££

Paul Grundy was at the Black Bull in Moulton before he took over the tenancy so the food is excellent and at a reasonable price. It is a converted school house - hence the alphabet decoration - but is well furnished, comfortable and friendly. Well worth the additional mileage.

Do not bear left on the first roundabout but look out for the Aycliffe sign. At the traffic lights turn right. After some 30 yards turn right at the corner and The County is 100 yards down on the left facing onto the green.

## Ⓐ The County

Satnav
**DL5 6LX**

13 The Green, Aycliffe Village, Co. Durham
01325 312 273
www.thecountyaycliffevillage.com
info@thecountyaycliffevillage.com

**Orders for food:** Weekdays: Noon to 2.00pm and 5.30pm to 9.00pm. Sundays: Noon to 9.00pm.

££

A modernised country-style pub on the village green. It has changed hands and is now carpeted throughout so is less noisy. Tony Blair brought President Chirac of France to have dinner here. Some outside eating. French not essential.

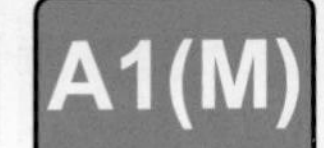


After Washington bear to the left on the A1, as opposed to the motorway continuation. Come off at the first exit signed Birtley and Gateshead. At the roundabout go under the A1 and take the road marked Wreckington. The Angel View Hotel is almost immediately to your left.

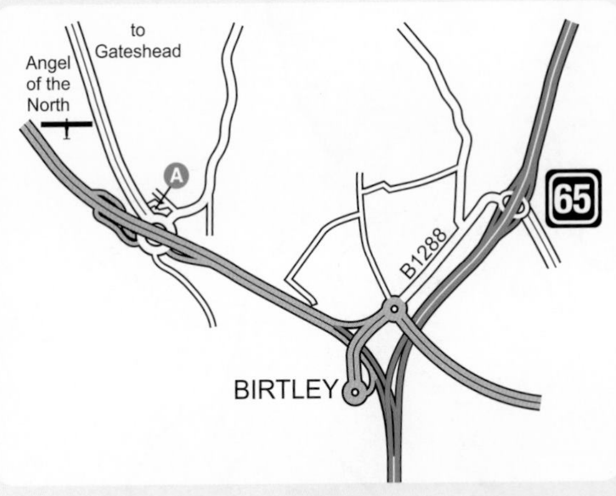


## Ⓐ Angel View Inn

Satnav
**NE9 7UB**

Eighton Bank, Low Fell, Gateshead
0191 410 3219
reception@angelviewinn.co.uk
**Orders for food:** Monday to Saturday: Noon to 9.30pm
Sunday: Noon to 9.00pm

£££

Converted from a 19th Century stable, it is now a comfortable bar cum restaurant with bedrooms. There is a long bar with dining areas surrounding an open courtyard which was previously the farm yard. Friendly service and the Angel of the North is only 200 yards away.

# A3(M)

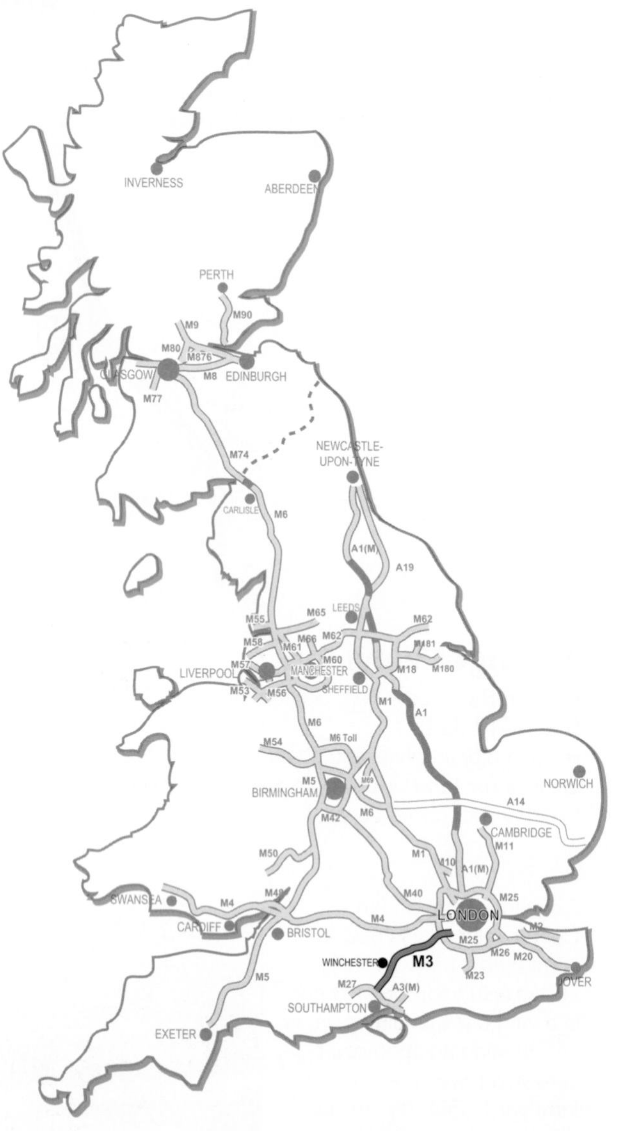
INVERNESS
ABERDEEN
PERTH
M90
M9
M80
M876
GLASGOW
M8
EDINBURGH
M77
M74
NEWCASTLE-UPON-TYNE
CARLISLE
M6
A1(M)
A19
M55
M65
LEEDS
M62
M58
M66
M62
M181
M61
M60
M57
LIVERPOOL
MANCHESTER
M18
M180
M53
M56
SHEFFIELD
M1
A1
M6
M54
M6 Toll
M5
M69
NORWICH
BIRMINGHAM
A14
M42
M6
CAMBRIDGE
M11
M50
M1
M10
A1(M)
M48
M40
M25
SWANSEA
M4
LONDON
CARDIFF
M4
M2
BRISTOL
M25
WINCHESTER
M3
M26
M20
M23
M5
DOVER
M27
A3(M)
SOUTHAMPTON
EXETER

## JUNCTIONS  TO 5



A short stretch of motorway, which was completed in 1979 to ease the traffic flow at the junction of the A3 to the M27.

South of Petersfield, the motorway climbs up to the high ground overlooking Portsmouth Harbour and the naval dockyards. HMS Victory is dry-docked there and the home of the Submarine Museum is over the harbour entrance at Gosport. Along the escarpment are a range of forts built by Palmerston in the 1860s to protect the coast against a possible invasion by the French.

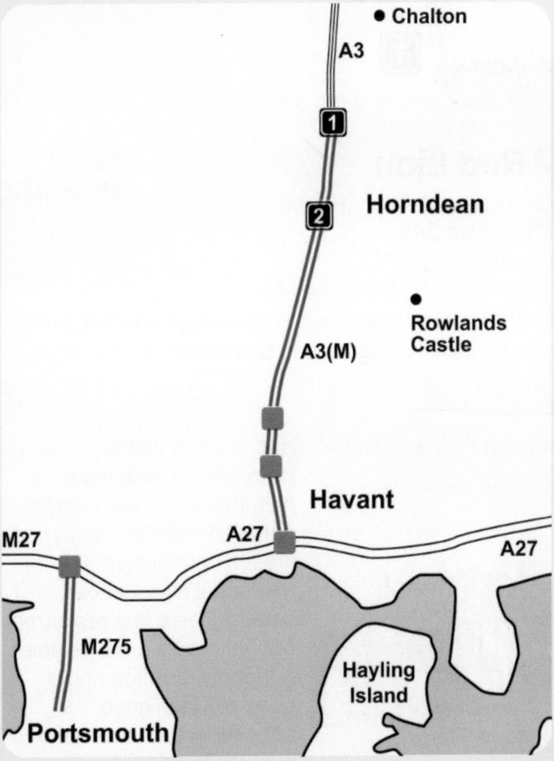

Chalton
A3
1
2
Horndean
Rowlands Castle
A3(M)
Havant
M27
A27
A27
M275
Hayling Island
Portsmouth

Driving south, the turnoff for Chalton is 2 miles from the start of the motorway section. Going north it is more complicated as you will have to take a left turning signed Clanfield, follow along the dual carriageway for half a mile and then cross over. To continue your journey, go over the A3 and drive on north for about a mile.

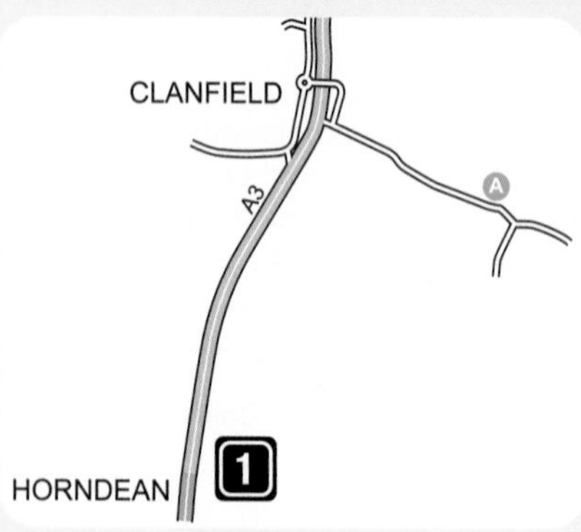


##  Red Lion

Satnav
**PO8 0BG**

South Lane, Chalton, Hants.
02392 592 246
www.fullers.co.uk
redlion.chalton@fullers.co.uk

**Orders for food:** Mondays to Thursdays and Sundays: Noon to 9.00pm. Fridays and Saturdays: Noon to 9.30pm.

Apparently it was first licensed in 1503 and is Hampshire's oldest pub. It has, therefore, low beams, panelled walls and inglenook fires. It is furnished with traditional high-backed settles. There is a restaurant but bar meals are available. A friendly greeting and a good old-fashioned atmosphere. It is under new management.

Come off at Junction 2. Carry on down the B2149 signed Westbourne. After the roundabout go through the woods and left to Rowlands Castle. There is another chance further on if you miss it.

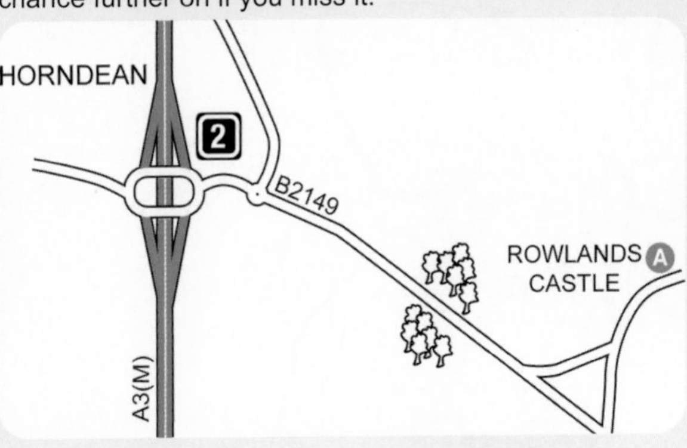


**Places of interest**

Stansted Park (1688-1903) HHA – 5 miles 

## Ⓐ The Robin Hood Inn

Satnav
**PO9 6AB**

The Green, Rowlands Castle, Hants.
02392 412 268
www.rowlandscastle.co.uk
robinhoodinn@hotmail.co.uk

**Orders for food:** Noon to 2.30pm and 6.00pm to 9.00pm.Sundays: Noon to 4.00pm

A restaurant with a bar, it is just within five minutes from the junction. A friendly atmosphere, light and airy, looking out over the village green. It has changed hands.

# A14

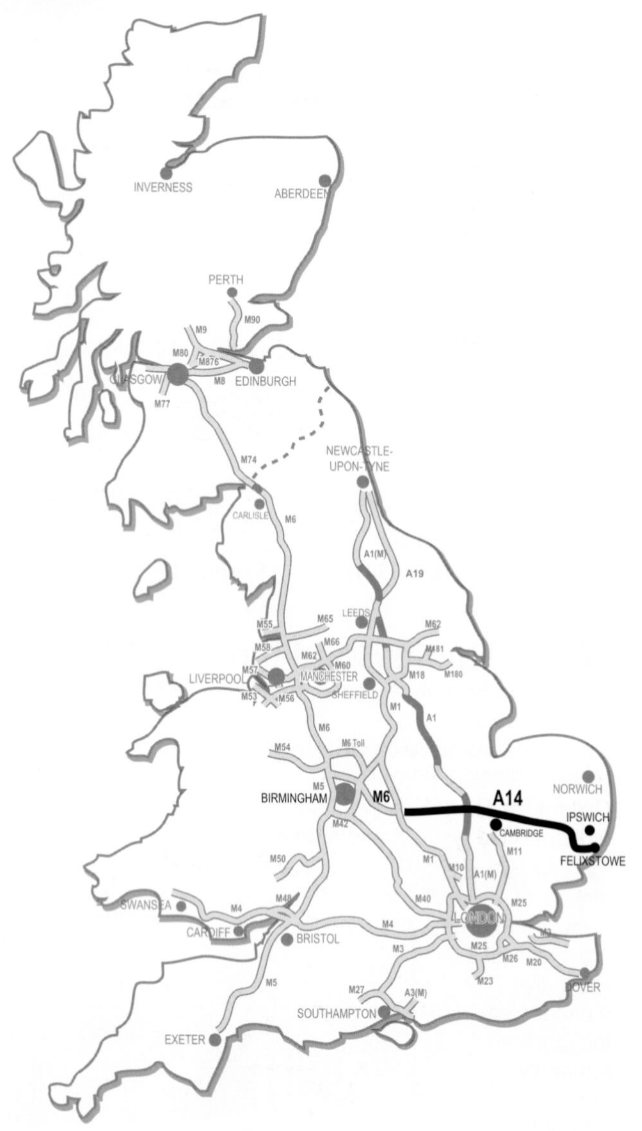

INVERNESS
ABERDEEN
PERTH
M90
M9
M80
M876
GLASGOW
M8
EDINBURGH
M77
M74
NEWCASTLE-UPON-TYNE
CARLISLE
M6
A1(M)
A19
LEEDS
M65
M55
M62
M66
M58
M62
M481
M57
M60
LIVERPOOL
MANCHESTER
M18
M180
M53
M56
SHEFFIELD
M1
A1
M6
M54
M6 Toll
M5
BIRMINGHAM
M6
A14
NORWICH
IPSWICH
M42
CAMBRIDGE
M11
FELIXSTOWE
M50
M1
M10
A1(M)
M48
M40
M25
SWANSEA
M4
LONDON
CARDIFF
M4
BRISTOL
M3
M25
M26
M20
M23
M5
M27
A3(M)
DOVER
SOUTHAMPTON
EXETER

## JUNCTIONS  TO 60

This is a dual carriageway rather than a motorway but each of the junction signs are now numbered for easy recognition. It has become the main link between the Midlands to the port of Felixstowe and is therefore busy.

# M1 TO HUNTINGDON

## JUNCTIONS  TO 

This section, which connects the M1 to the A1, passes through the attractive rolling countryside of the Shires.

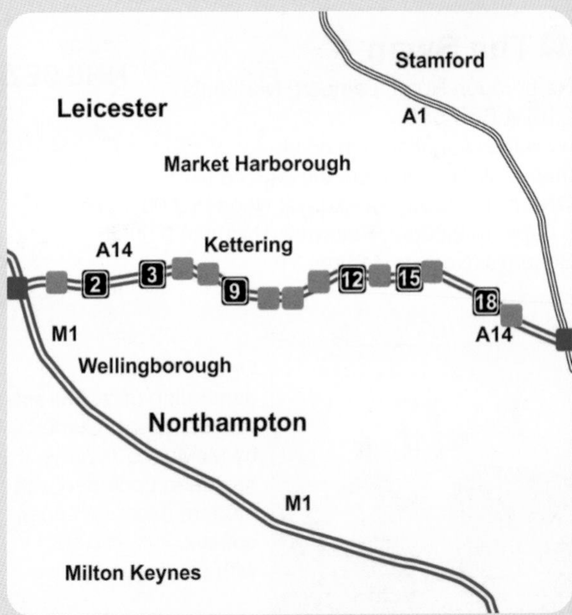

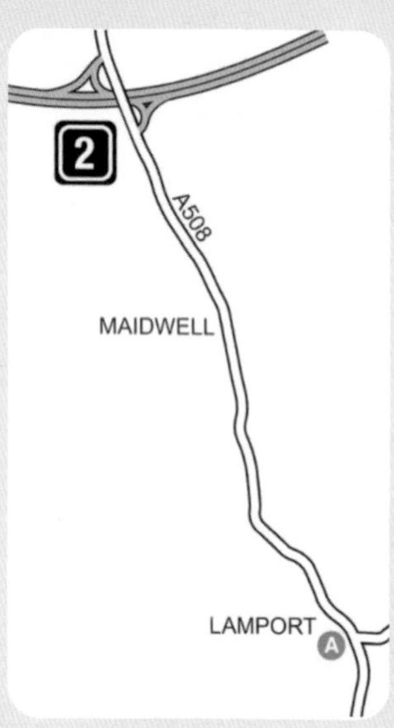


Take the A508 south through Maidwell and Lamport is about 2.5 miles further on.

**Places of interest**
Lamport Hall (17th-18thC) HHA – 1mile
Kelmarsh Hall (1732) HHA – 4 miles
Cottesbrooke Hall and Gardens (1702) HHA – 6 miles

## Ⓐ The Swan

Satnav
**NN6 9EZ**

Harborough Road, Lamport, Northants.
01604 686 555
www.theswanatlamport.co.uk
theswanlamport@mcmanuspub.co.uk
**Orders for food:** Weekdays: Noon to 3.00pm and 6.00pm to 9.00pm. Saturdays: Noon to 9.00pm. Sundays: Noon to 4.00pm.

££

One of the new generation of restaurants with bar areas. Owned by McManus Taverns, it has been upgraded with modern décor and open spaces. It is efficient, with courteous service.

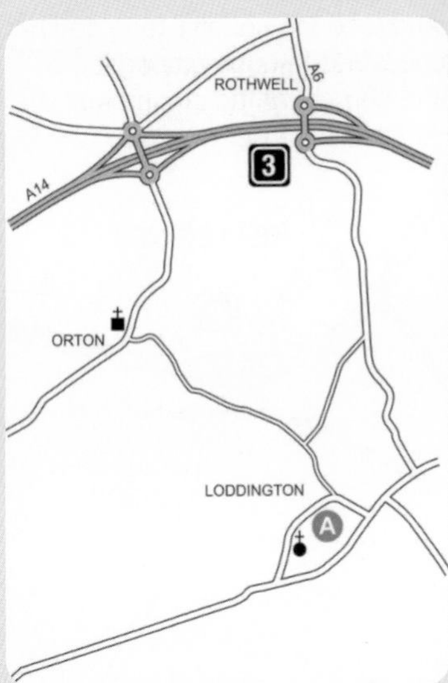


Take the road marked Orton Village Only. Turn left as you get into Orton. In Loddington head for the church spire and the inn is just to the north of it.

## Ⓐ The Hare

Satnav
**NN14 1LA**

Main Street, Loddington, Northants.
01536 710 337

**Orders for food:** Daily: Noon to 2.30pm and 6.00pm to 9.30pm. Saturdays: Noon to 9.30pm. Sundays: Noon to 8.00pm.

££

A privately owned inn which has changed hands but has a reputation for good food. For those in a hurry, there are bar meals and sandwiches. Outside seating in a garden. It is advisable to book in advance.

Come off at Junction 9 and take the country road south-west to Pytchley – a name world-famous amongst the hunting fraternity. After the church, at the crossroads, the overstone is on the left behind a high hedge.

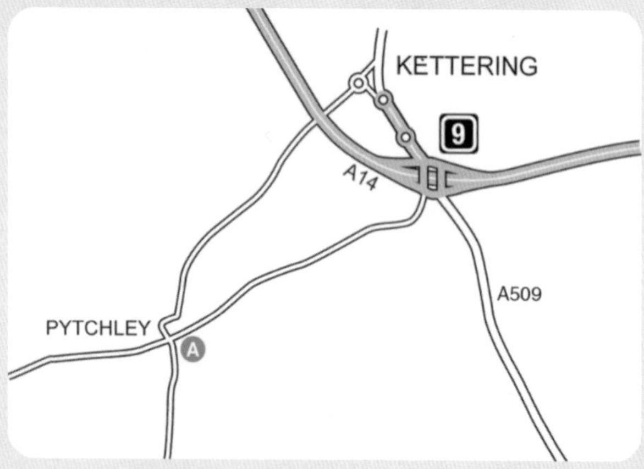


## Ⓐ Overstone Arms

Stringers Hill, Pytchley, Northants.
01536 790 215
www.theoverstonesarms.com
bookings@theoverstonesarms.com

Satnav
**NN14 1EU**

**Orders for food:** Daily: Noon to 2.00pm and 6.00pm to 9.00pm. Sundays: Noon to 2.30pm.

££

A friendly traditional 18th-century pub with good home-cooked food in the centre of a picturesque village, which was once a coaching inn. A large restaurant but bar meals are served. The speciality is the chestnut and stilton pate.

No problems with the motorway-signed junction. Go straight on at the first roundabout going north. After the second road to the right keep a lookout for the road into Lowick – which is sharper than that shown on the plan.

**Places of interest**

Lyveden New Bield (1595) NT – 7 miles

## Ⓐ The Snooty Fox

Satnav
**NN14 3BH**

Main Street, Lowick, Northants.
01832 733 434
www.thesnootyfoxlowick.com
info@thesnootyfoxlowick.com

**Orders for food:** Weekdays: Noon to 2.30pm and 6.00pm to 9.00pm. Saturdays: Noon to 9.30pm. Sundays: Noon to 3.00pm. Mondays: Closed.

££

An upmarket pub-cum-restaurant in a range of old vill-age houses, one being the old Manor House. It has been converted into a comfortable and well-furnished hostelry with original carved beams and a dining area near the bar, which is frequented by the natives. It is noted for its cooking. A garden in front for summer days.

For Keyston head south on the B663 towards Raunds. Zigzag through Keyston with the church on your right. At the end of the village turn right and The Pheasant is 100 yards on the left.

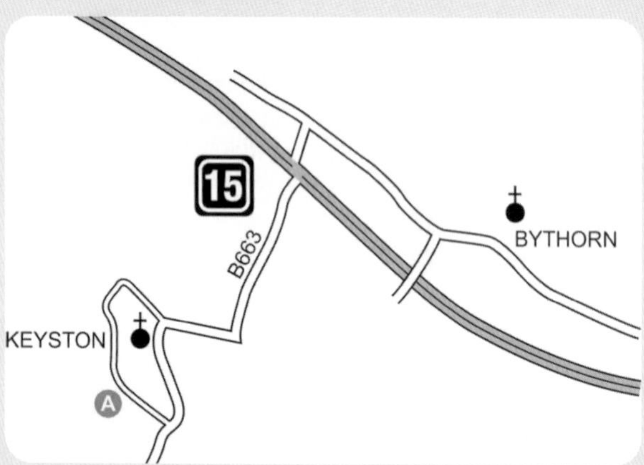


## Ⓐ The Pheasant

Satnav
**PE28 0RE**

Loop Road, Keyston, Cambs.
01832 710 241
www.thepheasant-lowick.co.uk
info@thepheasant-lowick.co.uk

**Orders for food:** Daily: Noon to 2.00pm and 6.30pm to 9.30pm. Sundays: Noon to 3.30pm. Mondays: Closed.

£££

A restaurant with a bar area, which is now privately owned. Converted from a group of thatched cottages in this peaceful hamlet, it has been comfortably furnished with a lounge bar and three dining areas. A car park on the other side of the road. Outside seating in front as well as a garden.

Drive to the village and the George Inn is on the left opposite the village green.

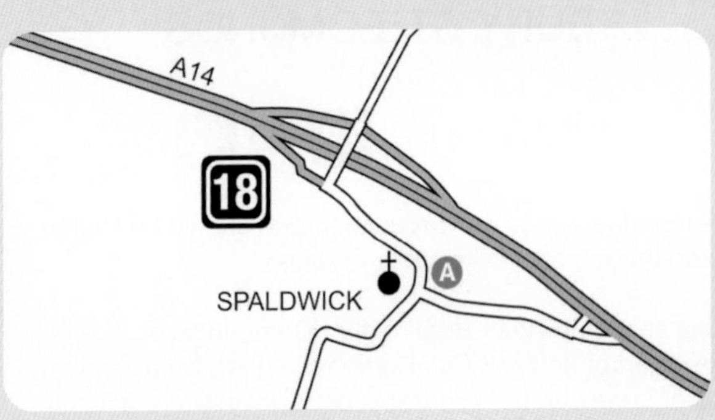


## A The George Inn

Satnav
**PE28 0TD**

High Street, Spaldwick, Cambs.
01480 890 293
www.thegeorgespaldwick.co.uk
info@thegeorgespaldwick.co.uk

**Orders for food:** Weekdays and Saturdays: Noon to 2.30pm and 6.00pm to 9.00pm. Sundays: Noon to 7.00pm.

££

This 16th-century inn has been extensively refurbished and is under the new ownership. However, there are still log fires and beams with a restaurant in the barn conversion. Well known for its black pudding. All produce is fresh and local. Decked outside seating at the rear.

# HUNTINGDON TO BURY ST. EDMUNDS

## JUNCTIONS 22 TO 42

Cambridge needs no introduction and should be visited even though car parking is a problem.

This section passes Huntingdon, Cambridge, Newmarket and Bury St. Edmunds. It is a busy section, full of lorries and speed traps, especially where it joins the M11.

Newmarket is famous the world over for horse racing and the whole area is still renowned for this purpose. There is a certain air of wealth and wellbeing. Going further east, the countryside changes to a more rural atmosphere with small villages and an air of timelessness.

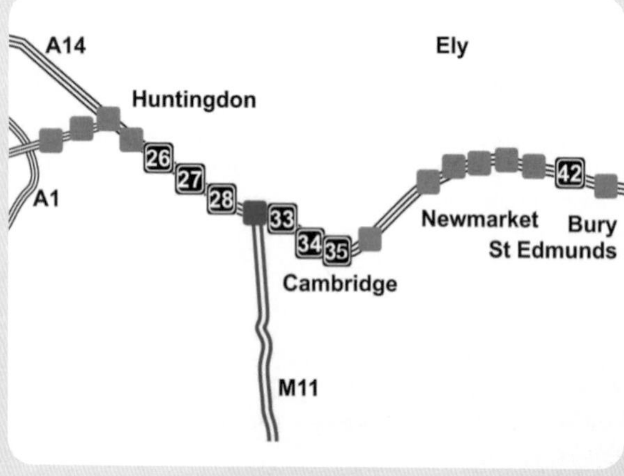

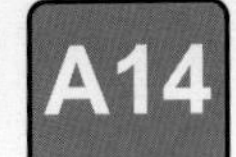


Junctions 25 and 26 have restricted access to the A14. You could use junction 27 but it is a long way. Switch on your Satnav!

## Ⓐ The Cock

Satnav
**PE28 9BJ**

High Street, Hemingford Grey, Cambs.
01480 463 609
www.cambscuisine.com
info@cambscuisine.com

**Orders for food:** Monday to Thursday: Noon to 2.30pm and 6.30pm to 9.00pm. Fridays and Saturdays: Noon to 2.30pm and 6.00pm to 9.30pm. Sundays: Noon to 2.30pm and 6.30pm to 8.30pm.

££

A traditional locals' pub which has been stripped of more recent décor and given a new lease of life. The bar has a range of beer but an excellent meal or a light lunch can be had in the restaurant area with wooden floors and comfy chairs. The owners specialise in my favourite food - bangers and mash. It has been awarded as The Pub of The Year by The Good Food Guide.

You can get to the King William IV by using either junction.

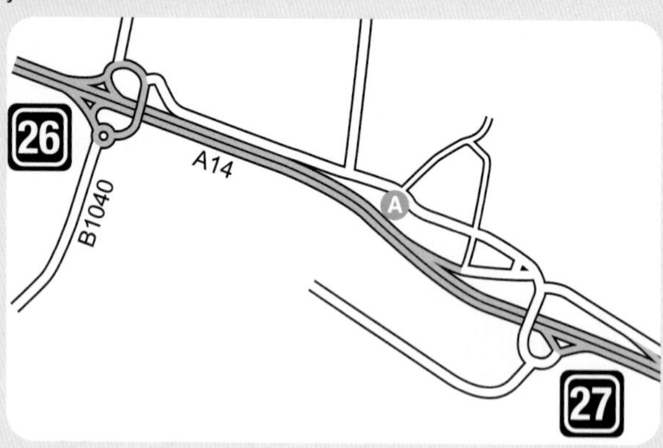


**Places of interest**

Capability Brown's home in Fenstanton.

## Ⓐ King William IV

Satnav
**PE28 9JF**

High Street, Fenstanton, Cambs.
01480 462 467
www.samuelpepys.co.uk
kingwilliamfenstanton@btconnect.com

**Orders for food:** Monday to Thursday: Noon to 2.30pm and 6.00pm to 9.00pm. Fridays & Saturdays: Noon to 2.30pm and 5.30pm to 9.30pm. Sundays: Noon to 3.30pm and 6.00pm to 8.00pm..

£

A cheerful 17th-century pub in a picturesque village with a friendly atmosphere, and beams and inglenook fires. Extensive menu comprising of home made food sourced from local suppliers. I was given a helpful welcome when I could not find Capability Brown's house in the village.

It is a long way from junction 28 but you will get into a muddle if you try coming off at J27 or 27A. Best switch on your satnav!

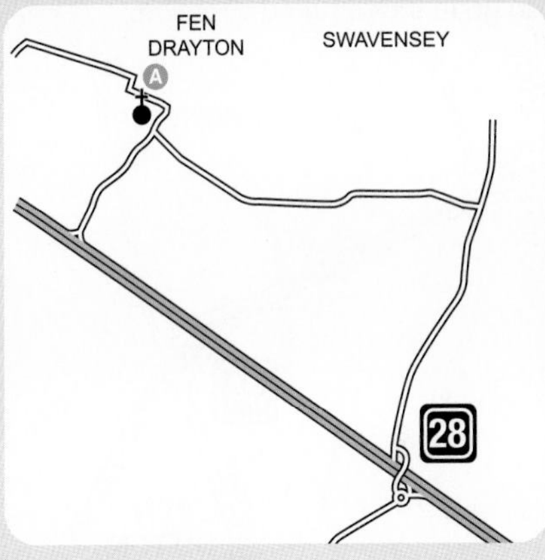


## Ⓐ The Three Tuns

Satnav
**CB24 4SJ**

High Street, Fen Drayton, Cambs.
01954 230 242
www.the3tuns.co.uk
info@the3tuns.co.uk

**Orders for food:** Monday to Friday: Noon to 2.00pm and 6.00pm to 9.00pm. Saturdays: Noon to 2.00pm and 6.00pm to 9.30pm. Sundays: Noon to 2.00pm.

££

A charming family-run pub, which was once the medieval Guildhall of the village. It still retains its traditional atmosphere with low beams and open fires. The menu is wide-ranging and cooked to order if so required but baguettes and lighter fare can be had for those in a hurry. A large covered seating area outside for those brave enough to face the elements.

Junction 34 for Horningsea is for the benefit of those driving east and then deciding to return westwards. However, help is at hand with Junction 33 as you can use that to go in the required direction.

## Ⓐ Crown & Punchbowl

Satnav
**CB25 9JG**

High Street, Horningsea, Cambs.
01223 860 643
www.thecrownandpunchbowl.com
info@thecrownandpunchbowl.com
**Orders for food:** Monday to Saturday: Noon to 3.00pm and 6.30pm to 9.00pm.
Sundays: Noon to 3.00pm.

££

An old pub which has been given a modern makeover of wooden floors, farmhouse tables and chairs, and soft lighting. The low beams and inglenook fire remain as does the friendly service by the helpful staff. There is no bar as such but the food is excellent, specialising in a variety of steak and fish. The bedrooms are clean and modern.

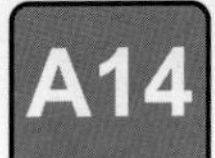


Take the A1303 towards Newmarket. After a mile turn right where signed Little Wilbraham and continue through the village.The Hole in the Wall is after a farm on the right.

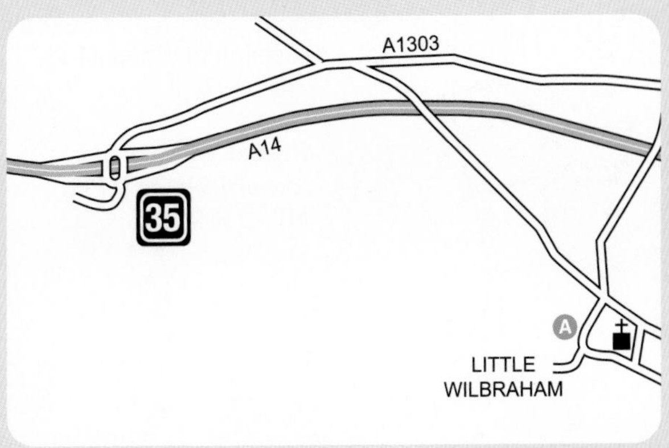


## A The Hole in the Wall

Satnav
**CB21 5JY**

2 High Street, Little Wilbraham, Cambs.
01223 812 282
enquiries@holeinthewallcambridge.co.uk

**Orders for food:** Monday to Saturdays: Noon to 2.00pm (except Tuesdays) and 7.00pm to 9.00pm.
Sundays: Noon to 2.00pm. Closed Mondays.

££

A Free House in an old cottage which has been an Ale House since the 16th century.

It is now a comfortable, low-beamed hostelry with two separate dining rooms serving delicious food (to quote from one of our readers). The kitchen and one of the dining rooms is in a more modern extension and there is an annex forming an L shaped area for outside seating.

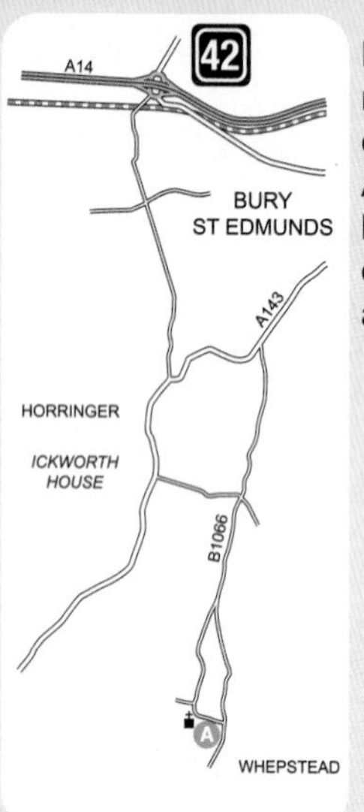


Head south from the junction marked Westley. At the first crossroads continue to Horringer. At the end of this village take a left and then first right at a crossroads. After a mile bear left at a Y junction to Whepstead.

**Places of interest**

Ickworth House (1795) NT - 3 miles.

## A White Horse

Rede Road, Whepstead, Suffolk
01284 735 760
www.whitehorsewhepstead.co.uk
d.i@whitehorsewhepstead.co.uk

Satnav
**IP29 4SS**

**Orders for food:** Weekdays: Noon to 2.00pm and 7.00pm to 9.30pm. Sundays: Noon to 2.00pm.

£££

Garry and Di Kingshott have moved from the Beehive in Horringer, and this old building has been renovated to make a traditional old inn with comfort and good service. The home-made sausages are a speciality. Well-behaved children are welcome and dog owners will be glad to hear that Di has received an award from the local vet.

# BURY ST EDMUNDS TO FELIXSTOWE

## JUNCTIONS 43 TO 60

Bury St Edmunds was once the capital of East Anglia. The martyred King St Edmund is buried in St Edmundsbury Cathedral which still dominates the old town. Apparently he had been the patron saint of England until St George took over in more militant times. It is said that in 1214 various barons met at St Edmund's Altar and swore an oath that they would force King John to sign the Magna Carta.

The independent brewers Greene King, who run a string of good hostelries, have been brewing there since 1799.

East of Bury St Edmunds the countryside becomes increasingly more rural with thatched and plastered houses in a style known as pargetting.

Ipswich is a traditional county town with a small port and some interesting houses.

From there the A14 follows the line of the River Orwell to the busy international port of Felixstowe and the reason for so many lorries.

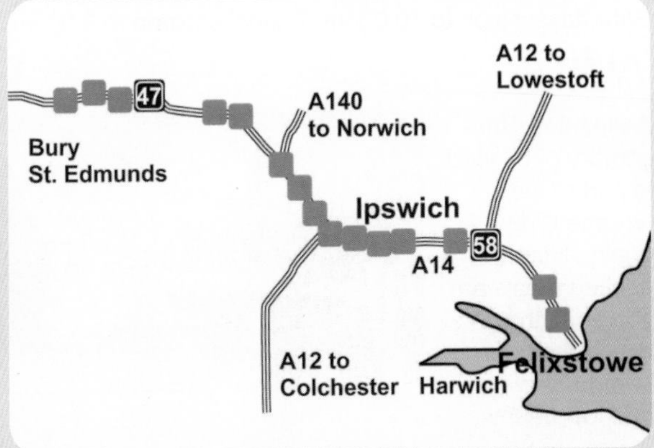

Take the A1088 to Norton and the Dog is on the right as you come into the village.

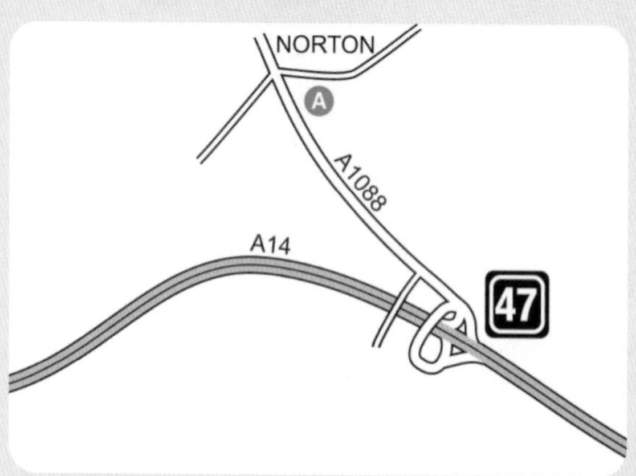


## Ⓐ The Norton Dog

Satnav
**IP31 3LP**

Ixworth Road, Norton, Suffolk
01359 230 440
www.thenortondog.com
info@thenortondog.com

**Orders for food:** Monday to Friday: Noon to 9.30pm. Saturdays: Noon to 10.00pm. Sundays: Noon to 9.00pm.

£

A tenanted 16th-century pub, which is part of the Greene King chain. Home-cooked meals are served in the dining areas of bare brick walls and low beams.

The Ship is signposted from the main road. At Levington bear left and pass the church.

## A The Ship

Satnav
**IP10 0LQ**

Church Lane, Levington, Suffolk
01473 659 573
www.theshipinnlevington.co.uk
susansearing@theshipinnlevington.co.uk

**Orders for food:** Monday to Saturday: Noon to 2.30pm and 6.30pm to 9.00pm. Sundays: Noon to 3.00pm and 6.30pm to 9.00pm in summer.

££

An old inn with a smugglers room upstairs which has changed ownership.
They specialise in fish, which is served in the dining areas featuring nautical memorabilia. In the last hundred years, it has only changed hands four times. A garden where children and dogs must remain.

# A19

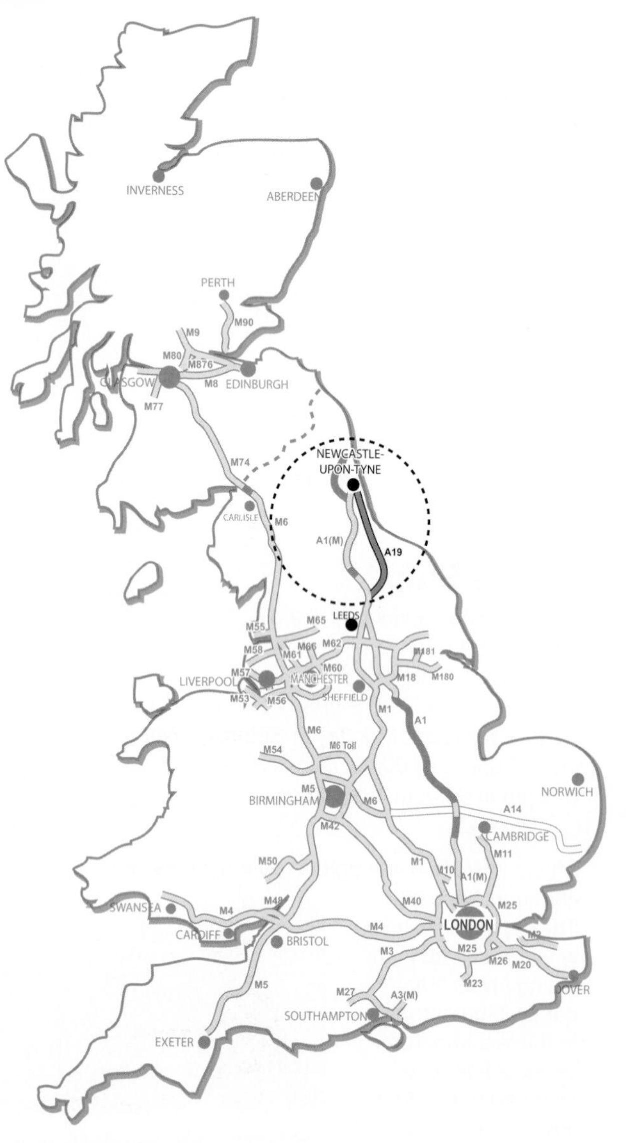

INVERNESS
ABERDEEN
PERTH
M90
M9
M80
M876
EDINBURGH
M8
M77
M74
NEWCASTLE-
UPON-TYNE
CARLISLE
M6
A1(M)
A19
LEEDS
M65
M55
M58
M61
M66
M62
M181
M57
M60
LIVERPOOL
MANCHESTER
M18
M180
M53
M56
SHEFFIELD
M1
A1
M6
M54
M6 Toll
M5
BIRMINGHAM
M6
NORWICH
A14
M42
CAMBRIDGE
M11
M50
M1
M10
A1(M)
M48
M40
M25
SWANSEA
M4
M4
LONDON
CARDIFF
BRISTOL
M3
M25
M26
M20
M5
M23
M27
A3(M)
DOVER
SOUTHAMPTON
EXETER

The upgrading to motorway standard of the A1 between Dishforth and Leeming will mean traffic delays until the summer of 2012. I therefore decided to include the A19 in the guide which will hopefully bypass the problem. Although the exits are not numbered, it is a dual carriageway throughout and I always use it when travelling to or from Northumberland.

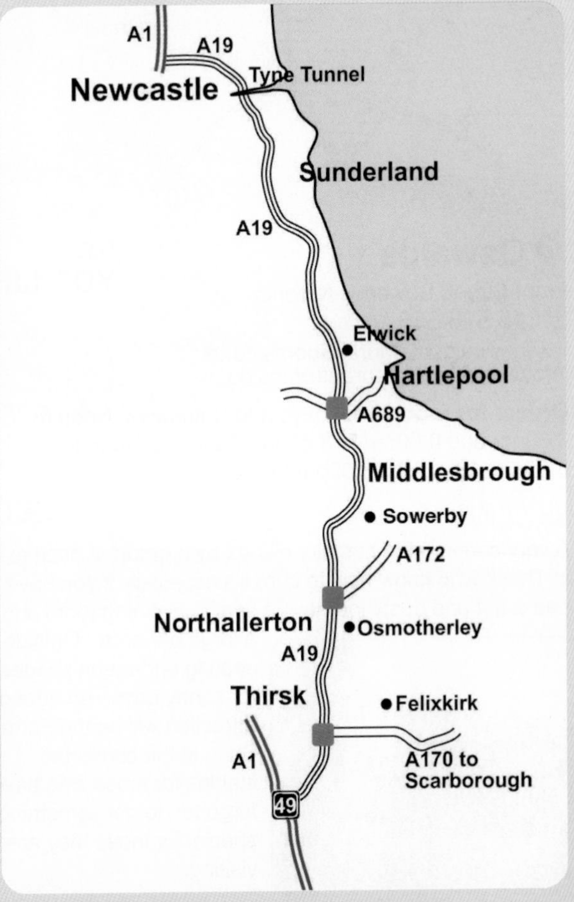

Come off the dual carriageway and take the road to York but after a few hundred yards by a filling station turn right and return under the dual carriageway. Go over a bridge on the River Swale and, at the junction opposite the Crown and Anchor, turn right down Flood Street.

Oswalds is 200 yards down the street up an alley on the left. If in doubt switch on your Satnav!

## Ⓐ Oswalds

Satnav
**YO7 1JF**

Front Street, Sowerby, N.Yorks
01845 523 655
www.oswaldsrestaurantrooms.co.uk
info@oswaldsrestaurantrooms.co.uk

**Orders for food:** Weekdays and Saturdays: Noon to 2.30pm and 6.00pm to 8.45pm. Sundays: Noon to 3.00pm. Mondays: 6.00pm to 8.45pm..

£££

A very comfortable hostelry owned by a group of doctors in Thirsk who know how to cure ills especially if you have had a hot and dusty journey. A spacious dining room and a large bar area. Outside seating under sun shades for sunny days. An added attraction will be the Farm Shop in the converted stables for those who have forgotten to get something special for those they are visiting.

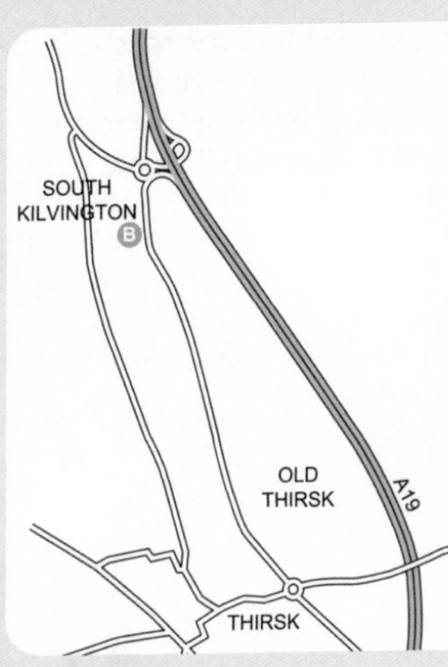


Come off the A19 where South Kilvington is marked. At the roundabout turn left to Thirsk and the village is less than 400 yards down the road. The Old Oak Tree is on the right as you come into the village.

## A The Old Oak Tree

Satnav
**YO7 2NL**

Main Road, South Kilvington, N.Yorks
01845 523 276
www.oldoaktreethirsk.co.uk
info@oldoaktreethirsk.co.uk

**Orders for food:** Daily: Noon to 2.00pm and 5.30pm to 9.00pm.

££

This has recently been taken over by Laurette and Nick who have made it into a friendly and cheerful locals' place with dining areas and outside seating for clement weather. Nick is the chef and when I was there the mussels were just right.

The A684 from Northallerton joins the A19 here. Osmotherley is on a minor road continuation of it. The village is attractive and is the starting point for many of the walkers trekking over the North York Moors.

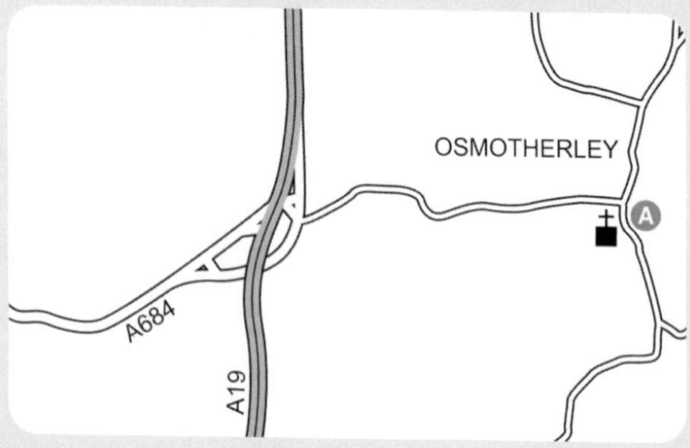


## Ⓐ The Three Tuns

Satnav
**DL6 3BD**

South End, Osmotherley, N.Yorks.
01609 883 301
www.threetunsrestaurant.co.uk
enquiries@threetunsrestaurant.co.uk

**Orders for food:** Weekdays: Noon to 2.30pm and 5.30pm to 9.30pm. Sundays: Noon to 6.00pm.

££

A family-owned and run restaurant in this picturesque village in the North Yorkshire Moors. A well deserved reputation for high quality food in the Rennie Mackintosh inspired dining room. On warm days which we are told will be more often you can relax in the colourful garden. The bedrooms are comfortable for those wanting to spend longer in this part of the country.

An easy junction even though you may have to cross over the dual carriageway. Elwick is attractive with a large green like many northern villages. The Mcorville Inn is next door as an alternative.

## Ⓐ Spotted Cow Inn

Satnav
**TS27 3EF**

31 The Green, Elwick, Cleveland
01429 266 373
sandokev@yahoo.co.uk
**Orders for food**: Tuesday to Saturday: Noon to 9.00pm. Sundays: Noon to 4.00pm. Mondays: 4.00pm to 9.00pm.

£

A locals' pub owned by Enterprise Inns in this attractive village. Dining areas dominated by a large bar but with a cheerful atmosphere. No dogs in the eating areas but children welcome.

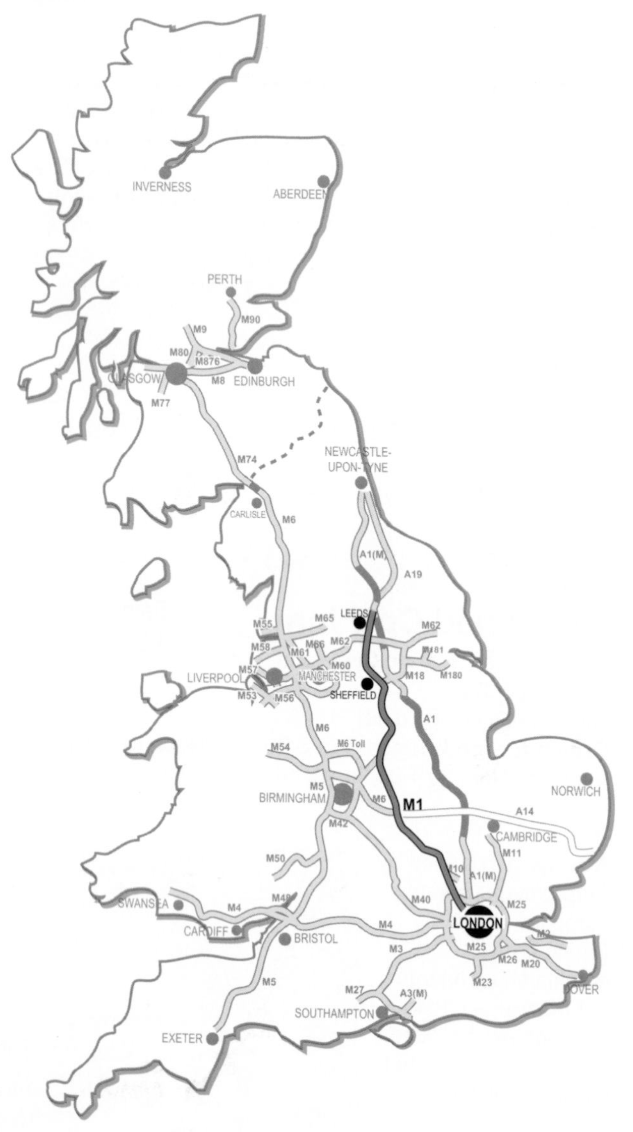
INVERNESS
ABERDEEN
PERTH
M90
M9
M80
M876
GLASGOW
M8
EDINBURGH
M77
M74
NEWCASTLE-UPON-TYNE
CARLISLE
M6
A1(M)
A19
LEEDS
M65
M55
M62
M58
M66
M61
M181
M60
M57
LIVERPOOL
MANCHESTER
M18
M180
SHEFFIELD
M53
M56
A1
M6
M54
M6 Toll
M5
BIRMINGHAM
M6
M1
NORWICH
A14
M42
CAMBRIDGE
M11
M50
M10
A1(M)
SWANSEA
M48
M40
M25
M4
LONDON
CARDIFF
BRISTOL
M4
M2
M3
M25
M26
M20
M23
M5
M27
A3(M)
DOVER
SOUTHAMPTON
EXETER

## JUNCTIONS 8 TO 48

The M1 was the first major motorway to be built in the U.K. The first section of 72 miles was built by Messrs. Laing & Son at a cost of £50 million and was completed in 19 months. It was opened in November 1959 by the then Minister of Transport, Ernest Marples, who in real life was a director of a building contracting firm. In 1965 a 70mph speed limit was imposed after it was being used as a test track by an AC Cobra Le Mans car doing 183mph at 4am one wintry morning. The final link of the M1, from Leeds to the A1(M), of about 9 miles, was completed in 1999 at a cost of £140 million.

# HEMEL HEMPSTEAD TO CRICK

## JUNCTIONS  8 TO 18

A congested section of the motorway until past the junction with the M6.

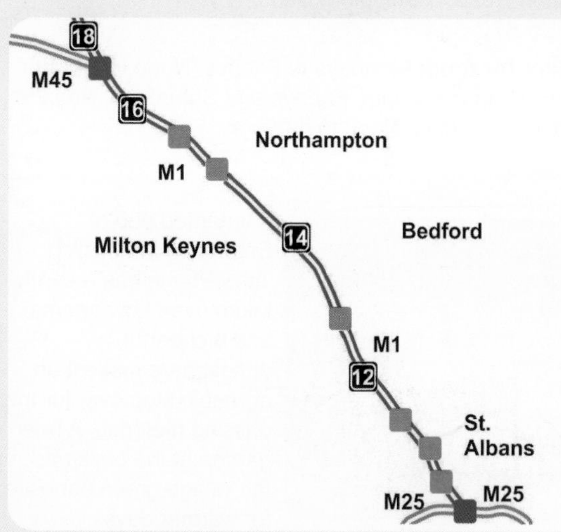

The junction has now been upgraded and rebuilt so is therefore more confusing. However Harlington is still clearly signed. In the village turn right at the T junction by the green.

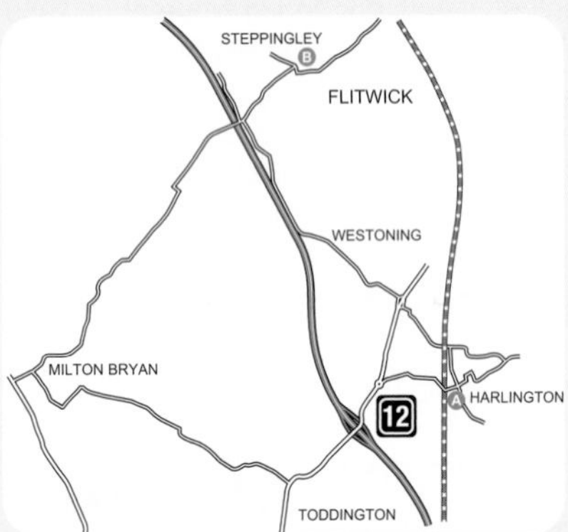


## Ⓐ The Carpenters Arms

Satnav **LU5 6LS**

Sundon Road, Harlington, Beds.
01525 872 384

**Orders for food:** Mondays to Fridays: Noon to 2.00pm and 6.00pm to 9.00pm. Fridays and Saturdays: Noon to 9.00pm. Sundays: Noon to 4.00pm

££

A tenanted pub of Enterprise Inns which Terry Payne has recently taken over. Low beams and a cheerful atmosphere make it an agreable stop over for the passing motorist. A beer garden at the back and the village green opposite for warmer days.

## B The French Horn

Satnav
**MK45 5AU**

Church End, Steppingley, Beds.
01525 720 122
www.thefrenchhornpub.com
info@thefrenchhornpub.com

**Orders for food:** Weekdays: Noon to 3.00pm and 6.00pm to 10.00pm. Saturdays: Noon to 10.00pm. Sundays: Noon to 9.00pm.

Originally a late 18th-century farmhouse it has been converted to give a warm welcome by the owners, into an old-world atmosphere of flagstoned floors, leather chairs and wooden tables. There is a spacious dining room but it can get busy at peak periods, so it is advisable to book.

Nothing much to explain, as it is very straightforward.

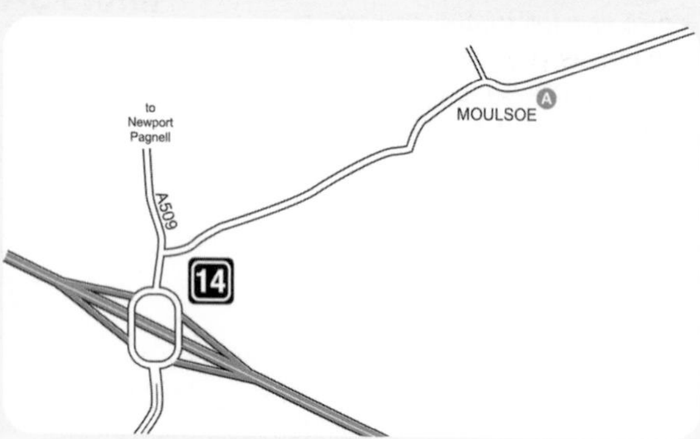


**Places of interest**
Bletchley Park (Pte) – 6 miles

## Ⓐ Carrington Arms

Satnav
**MK16 0HB**

Cranfield Road, Moulsoe, Bucks.
01908 218 050
www.thecarringtonarms.co.uk
enquries@thecarringtonarms.co.uk

**Orders for food:** Daily: Noon to 10.00pm.

8

£££

A family run traditional English Inn. Guests choose from a selection of local Bedfordshire beef prime cuts cooked to thier instruction on the charcoal grill and served by attentive staff. An à la carte is also available. The Bar Menu offers lighter options and pub favourites.

From the junction take the A45 to Flore. After less than a mile turn left to Nether Heyford. For the Bliss Tearoom turn left, as you enter Flore, down a narrow residential road - but it is signed. The White Hart is on the left in the village.

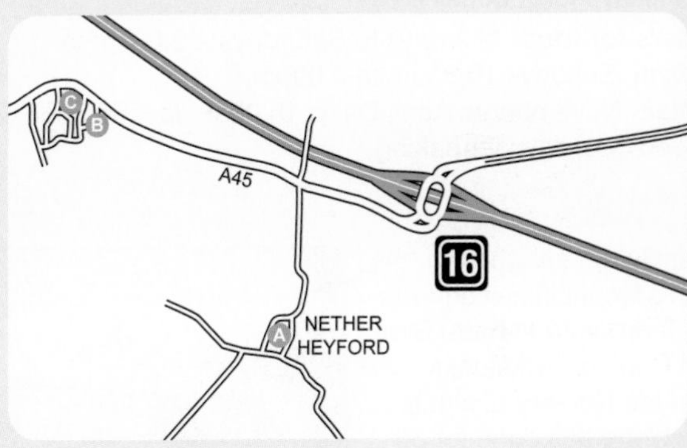


## Ⓐ Olde Sun

Satnav
**NN7 3LL**

Middle Street, Nether Heyford, Northants.
01327 340 164

**Orders for food:** Monday to Thursday: Noon to 2.00pm and 6.30pm to 9.00pm. Fridays & Saturdays: Noon to 2.30pm and 6.30pm to 9.00pm.
Sundays: Noon to 4.00pm.

£

A traditional old 18th-century pub with a warm welcome. An eclectic mix of brass bric-a-brac to keep visitors occupied. Bar meals from two bar areas available for lunch, but the restaurant is open in the evenings.

## B The Bliss Tearoom

Satnav **NN7 4LJ**

34 Bliss Lane, Flore, Northants.
01327 342 283
www.blisslanenursery.co.uk/tearoom
geoflittlewood@hotmail.com

**Orders for food:** Mondays to Saturdays: 10.00am to 5.00pm. Sundays:10.00am to 4.00pm.
Winter: November to April: Daily: 10.00am to 4.00pm
Closed Tuesdays for baking.

£

A family run enterprise where Geof Littlewood runs the Tearoom and Farm Shop and Chris his wife looks after the Nursery of plants which she has done for 35 years. The Tearoom serves breakfasts, light lunches and cream teas, all freshly prepared on the premises.

## C The White Hart

Satnav **DL8 2HA**

54 High Street, Flore, Northants.
01327 341 748
www.whitehartflore.co.uk
info@whitehartflore.co.uk

**Orders for food:** Tuesday to Friday: Noon to 2.30pm and 6.00pm to 9.00pm. Saturdays: Noon to 3.00pm and 6.00pm to 9.30pm. Sundays: Noon to 5.00pm. No meals on Mondays.

££

It has recently been refurbished with timber or flagged floors, comfortable chairs and polished tables. As a result it has gained an enviable local reputation as a place to dine and relax.

To get to The Moorings, (which was previously called Edwards), go straight on at the first roundabout and on again at the next one, over the canal and it is on the banks of the canal to the right. For Crick, take the A428 to the east and turn right at the first roundabout and left at the next. In Crick the Red Lion is on the right further on.

## Ⓐ The Moorings

Satnav
**NN6 7SQ**

West Haddon Road, Crick, Northants.
01788 822 517
www.themooringscrick.co.uk
themooringscrick@yahoo.co.uk

**Orders for food:** Daily: 11.00am to 9.30pm (in summer). Noon to 2.30pm and 6.30pm to 9.30pm (in winter). Sundays: 11.00am to 2.30pm. Closed Mondays.

££

A privately owned restaurant by the canal. Simple home cooking with fresh produce and served with the minimum of fuss. Dogs may appreciate a walk along the canal bank.

# B The Red Lion

Satnav
**NN6 7TX**

Main Street, Crick, Northants.
01788 822 342
ptmarks180@tiscali.co.uk

**Orders for food:** Daily: Noon to 2.00pm and 6.30pm to 9.00pm. Sundays: Noon to 2.00pm.

It has been a coaching inn since the early 1700s and is still family-run with a dining area. It has low beams, as tall visitors will discover. Some outside seating and a car park at the rear. A congenial place where they pride themselves on their homemade steak pie with real ales.

# RUGBY TO CHESTERFIELD

## JUNCTIONS 19 TO 29

This seems to be a culinary desert, but there are some places worthy of a stopover.

There are however, some interesting places to see off the motorway, such as Stanford Hall and the Civil War battlefield of Naseby off Junction 19.

At Junction 27 is Lord Byron's old home of Newstead Abbey, which he sold in 1816 when he went abroad. Lastly, there are those stupendous buildings of Hardwick Hall, Bolsover Castle, Sutton Scarsdale and further afield, Haddon Hall and Chatsworth.

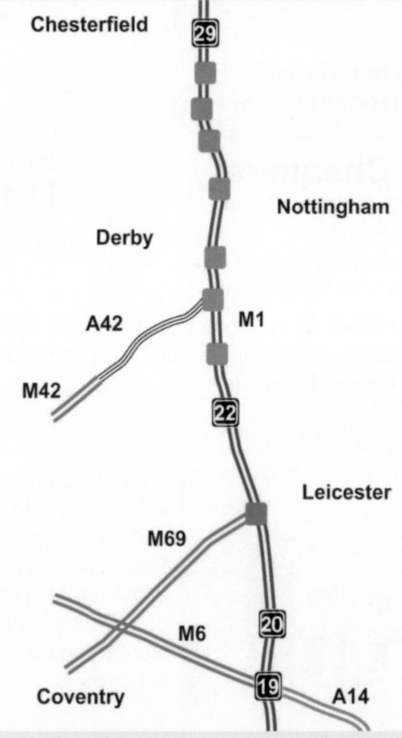

For those driving south follow the signs marked A14 Felixstowe. Turn left at the first roundabout for Swinford, or continue round for the Manor Farm Shop. You then have to work out how to continue South. The same applies for these driving North!. You can either go to Junction 20 and head back – or else take the M6 to Junction 1 and do the same or else drive on.

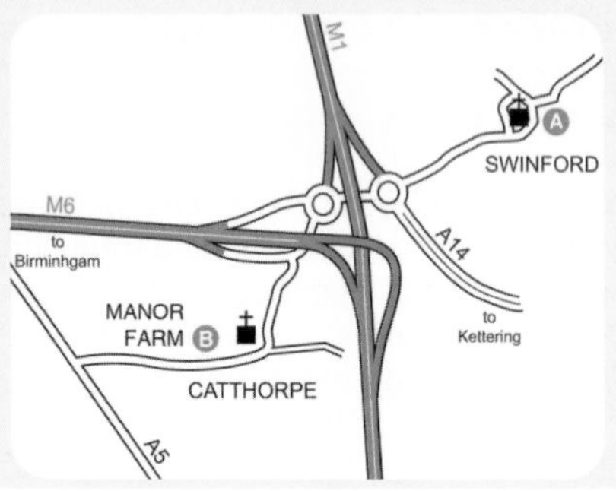


**Places of interest**

Stanford Hall HHA – 2 miles 

## Ⓐ The Chequers

High Street, Swinford, Leics.
01788 860 318
www.chequersswinford.co.uk
chequersswinford@aol.com

Satnav
**LE17 6BL**

**Orders for food:** Daily: Noon to 2.00pm and 6.00pm to 9.00pm. Sundays: Noon to 3.00pm. No evening meals. Mondays: Closed for meals

A traditional friendly village pub with pub games and gas log fires. Meals are served in the bar with real ales or in the dining area. Garden and a playground.

## B Manor Farm Shop

Satnav
**LE17 6DB**

Main Street, Catthorpe, Leics.
01788 869 002
www.manorfarmcatthorpe.co.uk
enquiries@manorfarmcatthorpe.co.uk

**Orders for food:** Monday to Saturday: 9.00am to 4.00pm. Sundays: 10.00am to 4.00pm.

£

A genuine working farm which has diversified. In a converted barn there is a Farm Shop selling a wide range of local produce; a gift shop for kitchen accessories, books, toys and cards and the Tea Room which serves morning coffee, light lunches and afternoon teas. There is outside seating and a car park. Dogs on leads and children are welcome.

Lutterworth is a charming old market town and well worth visiting. The Greyhound is on the left but for those in more of a hurry there is The Shambles opposite which is a timbered thatched Marstons pub even older than the Greyhound.

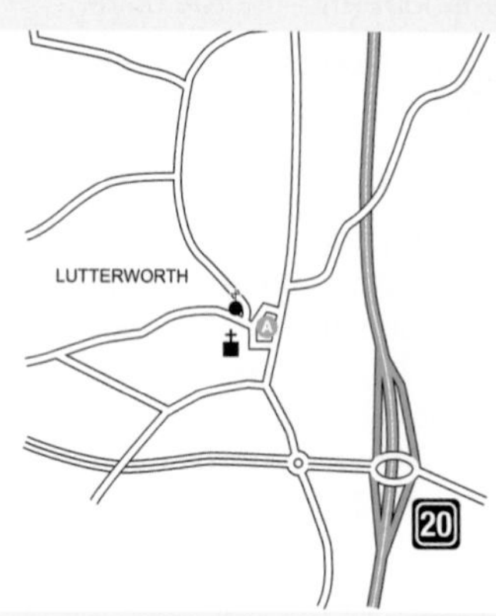


## Ⓐ Greyhound Inn

Market Street, Lutterworth, Leics.
01455 553 307
www.greyhoundinn.co.uk
bookings@greyhoundinn.co.uk

Satnav
**LE17 4BP**

**Orders for food:** Weekdays: Noon to 2.00pm and 7.00pm to 9.30pm. Sunday: 12.30pm to 2.30pm and 7.00pm to 8.45pm.

£££

It was once an important Coaching Inn on the Old Great North Road and it is still an hospitable place redolent of a bygone age with a varied collection of clocks with varied times. Nevertheless it gives a warm welcome and a friendly service. The old yard at the back is now full of topiary and seats where you sit on warm evenings and the bedrooms are located around.

Could not be easier to find. Take the dual carriageway towards Markfield for 1.5 miles and at the first roundabout the Field Head Hotel is facing you.

## Ⓐ Field Head Hotel

Satnav
**LE67 9PS**

Markfield Lane, Markfield, Leics.
01530 245 454
www.thefieldhead.com
9160@greeneking.co.uk

**Orders for food:** Daily: Noon to 10.00pm.

££

A modern hotel but with all the plusses of being near the motorway. Friendly and efficient service. A spacious bar for a quick meal and several restaurant areas. Outside seating in the courtyard.

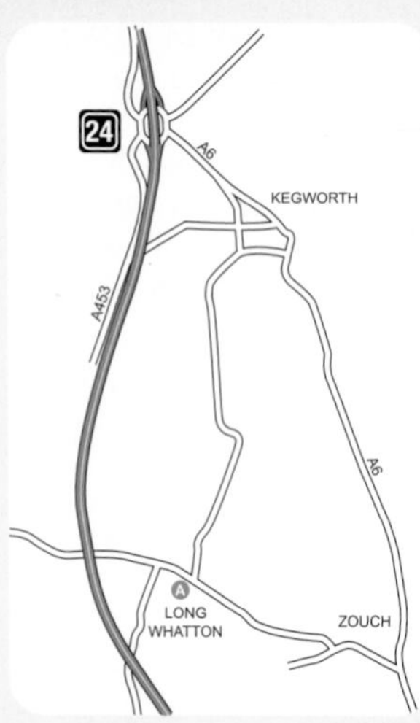


It is brown signed from the motorway. Take the A6 through Kegworth. At the end of the dual carriageway in Zouch look out for the B5324 to Ashby de la Zouch. After half a mile turn right to Long Whatton. The Falcon is on the south side of the road.

## Ⓐ The Falcon Inn

Satnav
**LE12 5DG**

64 Main Street, Long Whatton, Leics. .
01509 842 416
www.thefalconinnlongwhatton.com
enquiries@thefalconinnlongwhatton.com

**Orders for food:** Daily: Noon to 2.00pm and 7.00pm to 9.15pm. Sundays: Noon to 5.00pm.

£££

A privately owned hotel cum pub. There is a garden at the rear equipped with patio heaters or umbrellas depending on the vagaries of the weather. The bedrooms are in a courtyard annex so easy for wheelchair users. It has an imaginative menu with an overtone of the Lebanon.

The junction is studded with the brown signs of the Tourist Board to all the great houses in the vicinity. The sign to Heath off the A6175 to the right is not easy to see. For the other two, take the small road to the left and continue until you go under the motorway. Hardstoft is to the right and bear left for the Hardwick Inn and Hardwick Hall.

**Places of interest**

Hardwick Hall (c 1597) NT – 2 miles
Bolsover Castle (c1620) EH – 1 mile
Chatsworth (c1552-1820) – 18 miles
Sutton Scarsdale (c1720) – 1 mile
Haddon Hall (c1380 to 17thC) – 17 miles

## Ⓐ Elm Tree

Satnav
**S44 5SE**

Mansfield Road, Heath, Derbys.
01246 850 490
www.theelmtreeheath.co.uk
info@theelmtreeheath.co.uk

**Orders for food:** Weekdays: Noon to 2.00pm and 6.00pm to 9.00pm. Fridays & Saturdays: Noon to 9.00pm. Sundays: Noon to 8.00pm.

££

A restaurant with a bar that featured in a previous edition. It is now refurbished with more space. The soup, served with home made bread and vegetables from their own garden, was particularly good.

## B The Hardwick Inn

Satnav
**S44 5QJ**

Hardwick Park, Derbys.
01246 850 245
www.hardwickinn.co.uk
batty@hardwickinn.co.uk

**Orders for food:** Monday to Saturday: 11.30 to 9.30pm. Sundays: Noon to 9.00pm.

££

Built in the 16th century it has been converted into a popular family owned Inn with several dining rooms, friendly service and a busy but comfortable ambiance. There is plenty of outside seating. It could become crowded during the summer. Dogs outside please.

# CHESTERFIELD TO A1(M)

## JUNCTIONS 30 TO 48

Here again there seem to be few, if any, worthwhile places to stop and rest. This is a pity as at this stage of the journey you will be looking for just such a stop.

There are places to see on the way, however. These include the Cannon Hall Museum off Junction 37. Near Junction 46 there is Harewood House and also Temple Newsam House which is known as the Hampton Court of the North.

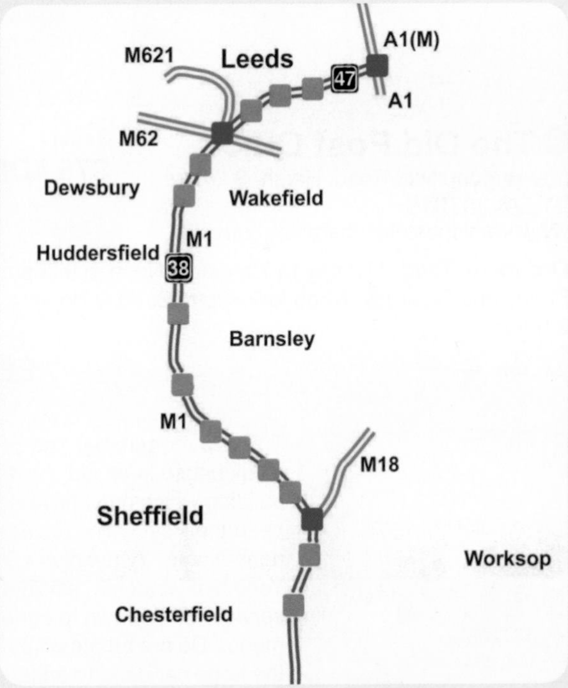

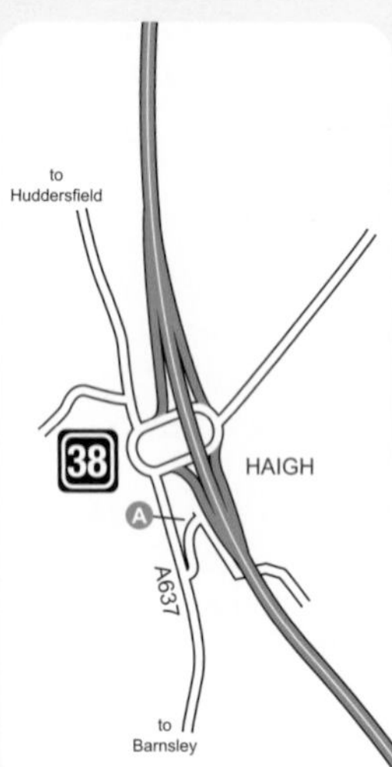


This must be one of the closest pubs to a motorway junction as you can see it as soon as you come off. It must have been an industrial site, judging by the expanse of made up ground with only the early Victorian building still standing.

## Ⓐ The Old Post Office

600 Huddersfield Road, Haigh, S. Yorks
01226 387619
www.theoldpostofficebarnsley.com.uk

Satnav
**S75 4DE**

**Orders for food:** Monday to Thursday: Noon to 9.00pm Friday and Saturday: Noon to 9.30pm. Sunday Noon to 6.00pm

££

This is a modern bar and steak house in an old building which must have been the Post Office once upon a time. A friendly Yorkshire welcome, efficient service with a down to earth menu. Do not be put off by the large car parking area.

The last junction on the M1 before it merges with the A1. Aberford is an attractive village on the old Great North Road. The Swan Hotel is in the centre of the village.

**Places of interest**
Lotherton Hall (Pte) – 2 miles

## A The Swan Hotel

Satnav
**LS25 3AA**

Great North Road, Aberford, North Yorks.
0113 281 3205
info@grantswanaberford.co.uk
**Orders for food:** Weekdays: Noon to 2.00pm and 5.30pm to 9.00pm. Saturdays: Noon to 2.30pm and 5.30pm to 10.00pm. Sundays: Noon to 9.00pm.

£

It started life in the 16th Century and continued as a Georgian Coaching Inn. A rusting sign outside states that J.Heaton is licensed to let Post Horses. Inside there is a busy cheerful welcome. Outside there is seating for those wanting some fresh air, either *en pleinair* or under a glass roof.

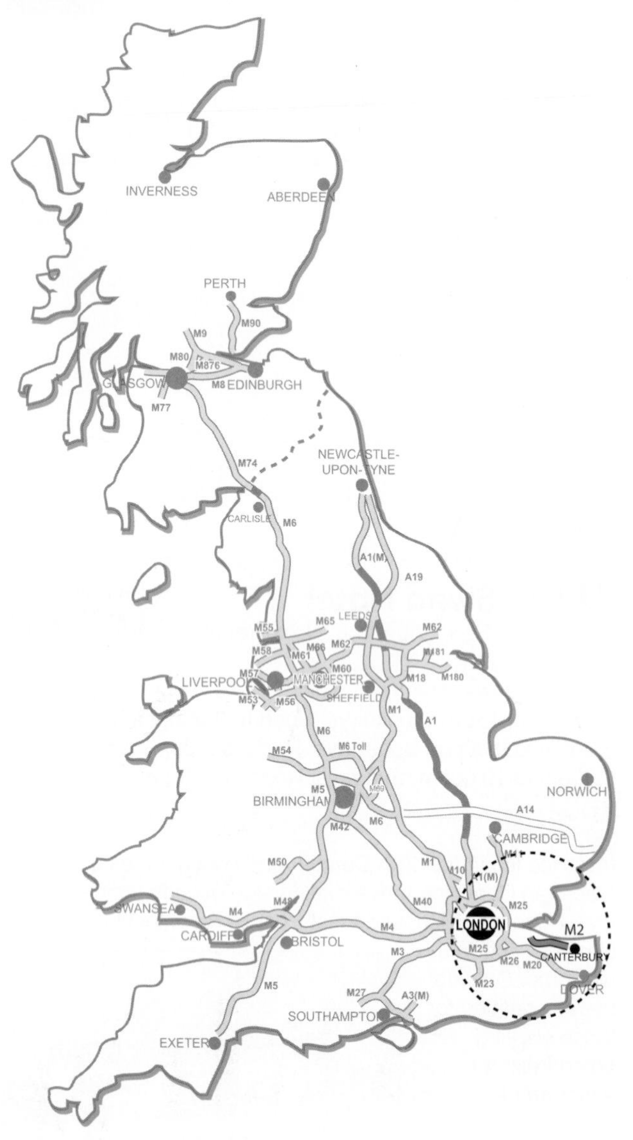
INVERNESS
ABERDEEN
PERTH
M90
M9
M80
M876
GLASGOW
M8 EDINBURGH
M77
M74
NEWCASTLE-UPON-TYNE
CARLISLE
M6
A1(M)
A19
M65
LEEDS
M62
M55
M58
M66
M62
M61
M181
M60
M57
LIVERPOOL
MANCHESTER
M18
M180
M53
M56
SHEFFIELD
M1
A1
M6
M54
M6 Toll
M5
M69
NORWICH
BIRMINGHAM
A14
M6
M42
CAMBRIDGE
M11
M50
M1
M10
A1(M)
M48
M40
M25
SWANSEA
M4
LONDON
M2
CARDIFF
M4
BRISTOL
M25
CANTERBURY
M3
M26
M20
M5
M23
DOVER
M27
A3(M)
SOUTHAMPTON
EXETER

## JUNCTIONS 1 TO 7

One of the shorter motorways being only 25 miles in length but one of the first to be built in 1963.

It was designed to create a faster journey between London and the Channel Ports linking up with existing roads. The approach to London however remained abysmal. The connecting road from the Blackwall Tunnel and Greenwich and the link with the M25 has been much improved.

The traffic density was reduced after the construction of the M20 to the south and you can interchange easily between the two should the conditions become unbearable.

The motorway passes some historic towns such as Rochester, the setting for *Pickwick Papers* by Charles Dickens; the old Naval Dockyards at Chatham which was burnt by the Dutch in 1667; the ancient city of Canterbury, settled by the Romans and where Saint Augustine introduced Christianity to the country in AD 597 and where Thomas a Becket was murdered in the cathedral in 1173.

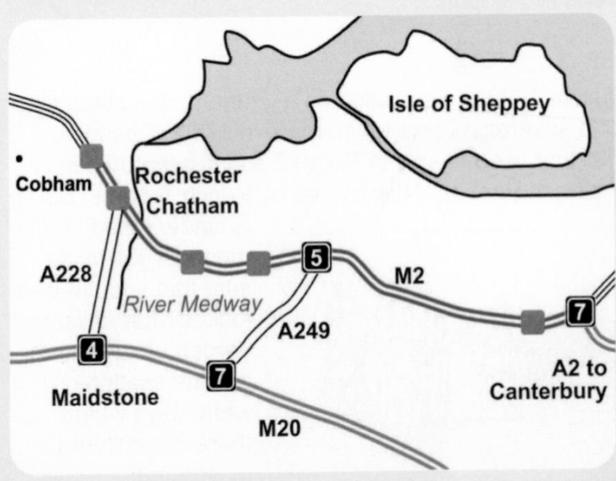

Cobham is on the London side of Junction 1 and the turnings are directly off the dual carriageway. The Leather Bottle is on the bend in the middle of the village.

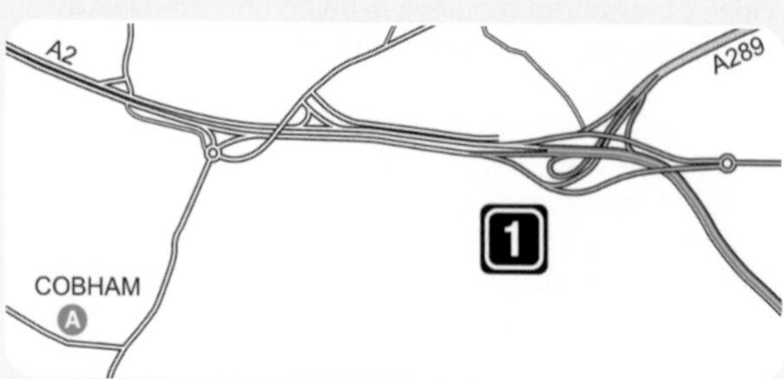


**Places of interest**
Cobham Hall

## Ⓐ The Leather Bottle

Satnav
**DA12 3BZ**

54-56 The Street, Cobham, Kent
01474 814 327
www.theleatherbottle.co.uk
info@theleatherbottle.co.uk

**Orders for food:** Daily: Noon to 9.00pm. Sundays: Noon to 7.00pm.

££

Built in 1629 it is so called as a leather bottle containing gold sovereigns was found there in 1720. Charles Dickens used to stay in Room 6 and it is featured in Pickwick Papers. Now owned by Punch Taverns, Sarah Saunders the friendly manager will make sure that you are well looked after. A large garden at the rear for outside seating on warm days where there is a children's playground.

Easy enough to get to Stockbury, as there is a gap in the dual carriageway opposite the turning off. The Oad Street Centre is up on a hill via some fairly narrow roads.

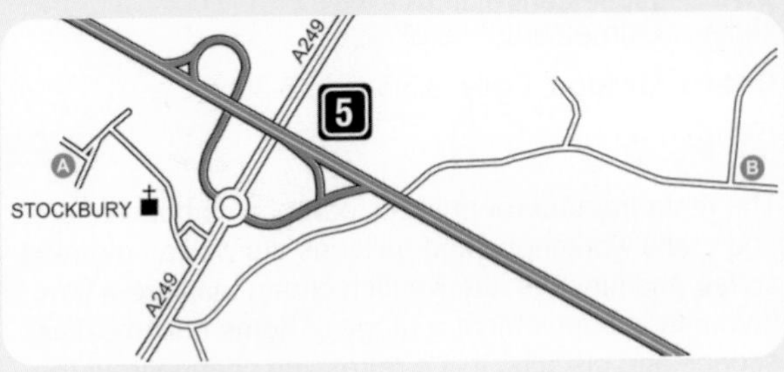


### Places of interest

Stockbury features in the Domesday Book in 1086 as Stochinberge.

## A The Harrow Inn

Satnav
**ME9 7UH**

The Street, Stockbury, Kent
01795 842 546
theharrowstockbury@btconnect.com

**Orders for food:** Daily: Noon to 3.00pm and 6.00pm to 9.00pm. Sundays: Noon to 3.00pm. Mondays: No meals served.

££

A typical 200-year-old country pub opposite the village green. A small dining area and a snack menu at the bar. Seating in the garden. In the past Morris Dancing has taken place on the green in summer and it is hoped that it will continue.

## B Oad Street Centre

Satnav
**ME9 8LB**

Oad Street, Nr Borden, Kent
01795 842 244
www.oadstreetcentre.co.uk
info@oadstreetcentre.co.uk

**Orders for food**: Daily: 9.30am to 5.30pm.

££

The restaurant/tearoom forms part of a complex of arts and crafts workshops and galleries. As well as morning coffee and lunches, the Kentish cream teas are a firm favourite to supplement a range of home baked cakes, scones and biscuits. It is a refreshing change from the norm for a quiet meal or a light snack.

Continue on the A299 towards Whitstable. After some two miles turn off on a minor road signed Fostall and Hernhill. Right at the T-junction and then left after 400 yards to Hernhill. The Red Lion is on the crossroads in the centre of the village.

## A Red Lion

The Green, Hernhill, Kent
01227 751 207
www.theredlion.org
enqurmoney@theredlion.org

Satnav
**ME13 9JR**

**Orders for food:** Monday to Saturday: Noon to 2.30pm and 6.00pm to 9.00pm. Sundays: Noon to 8.00pm.

££

A privately owned half-timbered 14th-century pub with a restaurant upstairs. A garden for summer seating and a sundial dating from 1364 to speed you on your way. It has changed hands.

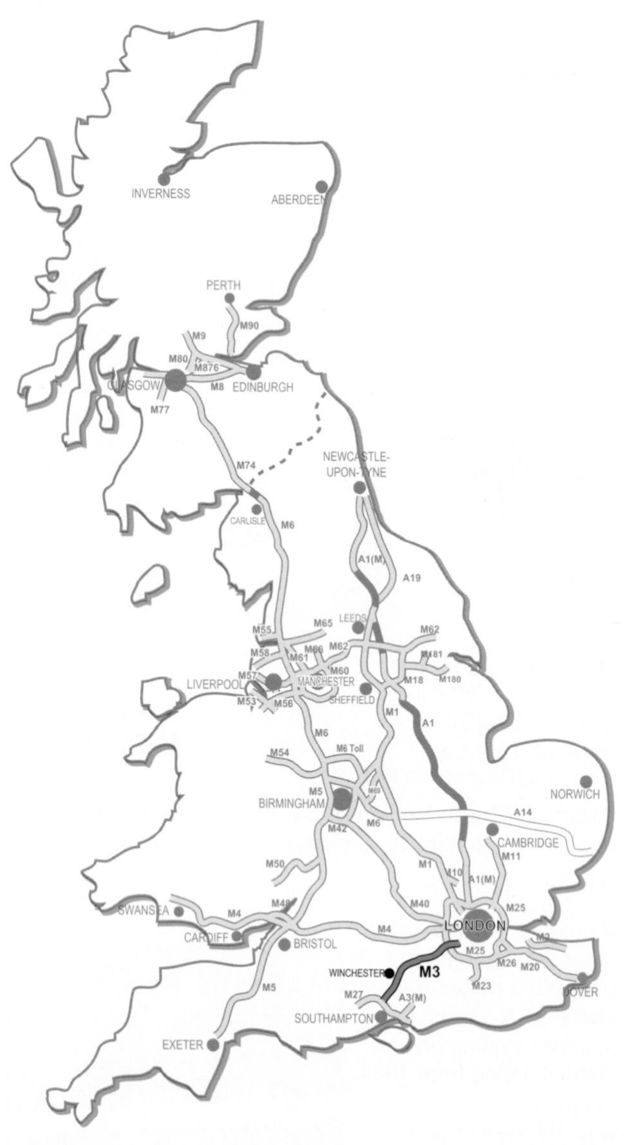

INVERNESS
ABERDEEN
PERTH
M90
M9
M80
M876
GLASGOW
M8
EDINBURGH
M77
M74
NEWCASTLE-UPON-TYNE
CARLISLE
M6
A1(M)
A19
M55
M65
LEEDS
M62
M58
M66
M61
M62
M181
M57
M60
LIVERPOOL
MANCHESTER
M18
M180
M53
M56
SHEFFIELD
M1
A1
M6
M54
M6 Toll
NORWICH
M5
M69
BIRMINGHAM
A14
M6
M42
CAMBRIDGE
M11
M50
M1
M10
A1(M)
M48
M40
M25
SWANSEA
M4
LONDON
CARDIFF
BRISTOL
M4
M2
M25
WINCHESTER
M3
M26
M20
M23
M5
M27
A3(M)
DOVER
SOUTHAMPTON
EXETER

## JUNCTIONS 1 TO 12

This motorway connects London with the port at Southampton and with the south west of England by way of the A303.

The building of the continuation of the motorway past Winchester in 1994 meant the cutting of a trench at Twyford Down. This caused massive unrest by protestors and increased subsequent cost. It might have been cheaper to build a tunnel. The motorway passes Basingstoke, a new town which has managed to destroy any vestige of what had once been a pleasant market town. Winchester retains its historic atmosphere and is therefore full of visitors.

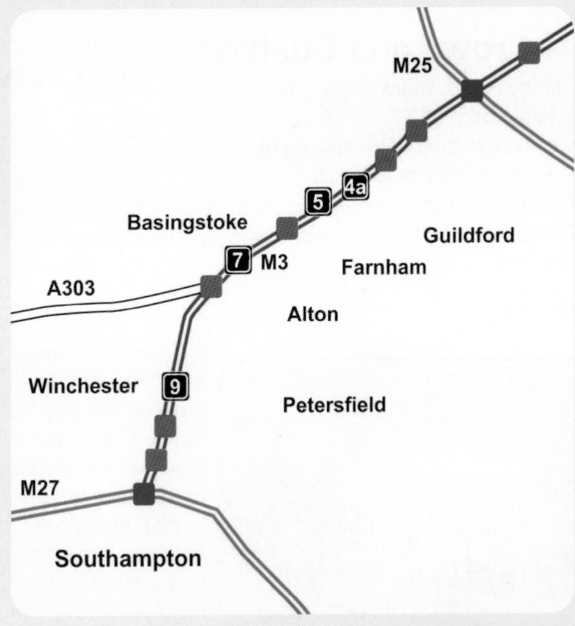

A simple junction and the pub is easy to find.

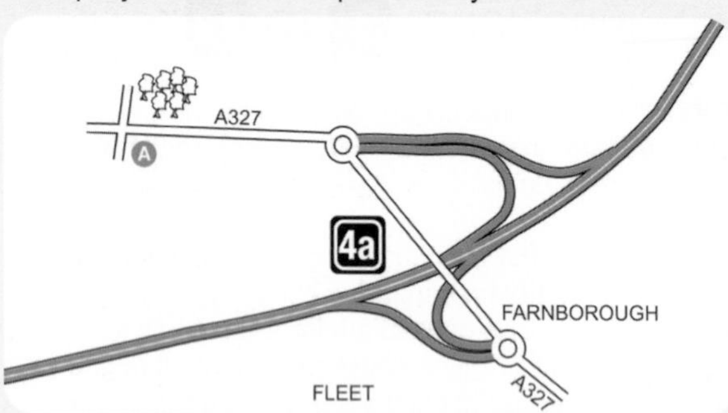


**Places of interest**

Napoleon III's Mausoleum, Farnborough – 3 miles
Airborne Forces Museum, Aldershot – 4 miles

## A Crown and Cushion

Satnav **GU17 9UA**

Minley Road, Blackwater, Surrey.
01252 545 253
www.crowncushionminley.co.uk
willupton65@yahoo.co.uk

**Orders for food:** Weekdays: Noon to 3.00pm and 6.00pm to 9.00pm. Saturdays and Sundays: Noon to 9.00pm.

££

An attractive rural pub in a wooded area on the way to Yateley Common. It serves traditional meals from the bar or else in the beer garden. It is said to be haunted by the mistress of Captain Blood who tried to steal the Crown Jewels in 1671.

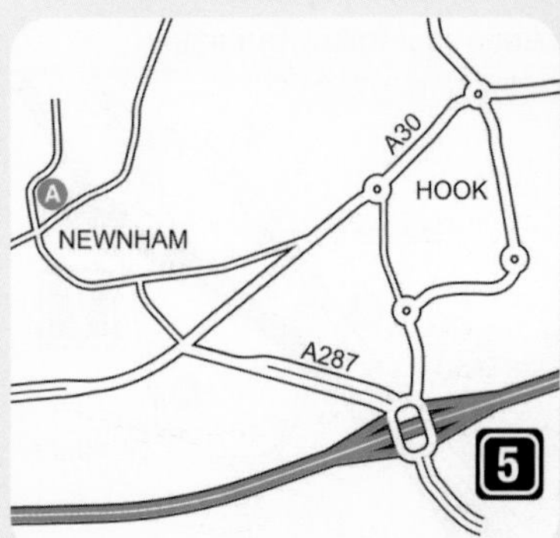


From the junction take the A287 to the A30 and cross over to the road to Newham. The Old House is on the far side of the green. There is the Hogget and the Star of India on the crossroads for those who do not want to drive further.

**Places of interest**

Old Basing House,
Hants C.C. - 5 miles

## Ⓐ Old House at Home

Satnav
**RG27 9AH**

The Green, Newham, Hants.
01256 762 222
www.oldhousenewnham.co.uk
sukicblofeld@aol.com

**Orders for food:** Monday to Friday: Noon to 2.30pm and 6.00pm to 9.00pm. Saturdays: Noon to 3.00pm and 6.00pm to 9.00pm. Sundays: Noon to 3.00pm.

££

A country pub-cum-restaurant on the edge of the green. Outside seating in front and more sheltered seating in the garden behind.

Wooden floors, a separate dining room and an imaginative menu. Suki and Olli Williams have been the owners for the past 8 years and run it with style and panache. Dogs outside and well-behaved children inside.

Not that difficult a junction - just follow the signs.

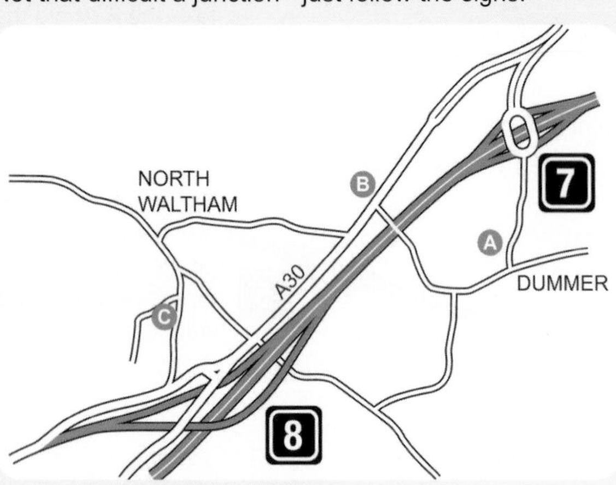


**Places of interest**

The Grange (18thC) EH – 8 miles

## Ⓐ Queen Inn

Satnav
**RG25 2AD**

Down Street, Dummer, Hants.
01256 397 367
www.thequeendummer.com
richardmoore49@btinternet.com

**Orders for food:** Daily: Noon to 2.30pm and 6.30pm to 9.30pm. Sundays: Noon to 2.30pm and 7.00pm to 9.00pm.

££

A popular and well-known family-owned pub. It gets its name from the fourth wife of Henry VIII who was Anne of Cleves, the Mare of Flanders. There is a garden at the back where dogs are welcome.

## B The Sun Inn

Satnav
**RG25 2DJ**

Winchester Road, Dummer, Hants.
01256 397 234
www.suninndummer.com
suninndummer@hotmail.co.uk

**Orders for food:** Monday to Saturday: Noon to 2.30pm and 6.30pm to 9.00pm. Sundays: Noon to 2.30pm.

£

Once a coaching inn on the old A30, it was closed in June 2010, but was then revived and is now a cheerful, busy place, where children and dogs are welcome.

## C The Fox Inn

Satnav
**RG25 2BE**

Popham Lane, North Waltham, Hants.
01256 397 288
www.thefox.org
info@thefox.org

**Orders for food:** Weekdays: Noon to 2.30pm and 6.30pm to 9.30pm. Sundays: Noon to 3.00pm and 6.30pm to 8.30pm.

££

An old vernacular Hampshire flint-stone house overlooking quiet farming countryside. It is privately owned and has built up a reputation for home-sourced food, and has made special provision for children. A heated patio for inclement weather and log fires when in extremis.

For the Chestnut Horse, take the A34 towards Sutton Scotney and then take slip road on the A53 towards Basingstoke. At the end of the dual carriageway bear right on the A3047 towards New Alresford. After two miles, before Martyr Worthy, turn right to Easton. For The Bush take the A31 and for the Flower Pots the A272.

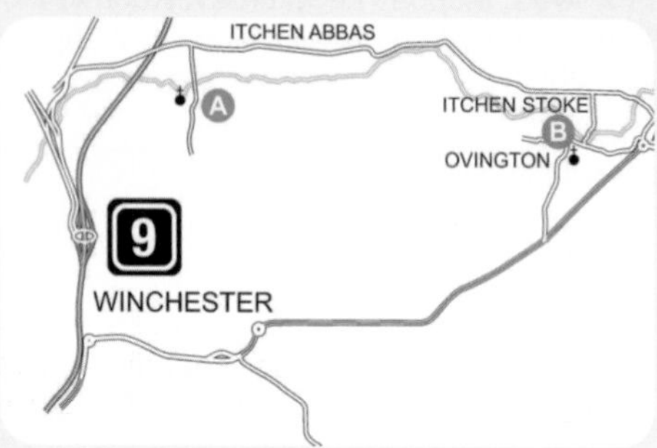


**Places of interest**

The Grange (18thC) EH – 8 miles

## Ⓐ Chestnut Horse

Satnav
**SO21 1EG**

Main Road, Easton, Hants.
01962 779 257
www.thechestnuthorse.com
info@thechestnuthorse.com

**Orders for food:** Daily: Noon to 2.30pm and 6.00pm to 9.30pm. Sundays: Noon to 8.00pm.

££

A tenanted pub of Hall & Woodhouse, so a good range of beers. An old 16th-century building with low beams, log fires and a cheerful atmosphere. Traditional cooking and friendly service. Outside seating on a terrace at the rear for summer days.

Satnav
**SO24 0RE**

## Bush Inn

East Lane, Ovington, Hants.
01962 732 764
www.thebushinn.co.uk
bushinn@wadworth.co.uk

**Orders for food:** Monday to Saturday: Noon to 2.00pm and 6.30pm to 9.00pm. Sundays: Noon to 2.30pm and 6.30pm to 8.30pm.

A four-roomed country pub at the end of a quite lane on the banks of the River Itchen (hence the sign 'Please remove muddy boots') and a large garden for summer days. Bar meals are also available in the dining areas. A cheerful and cosy atmosphere with friendly service.

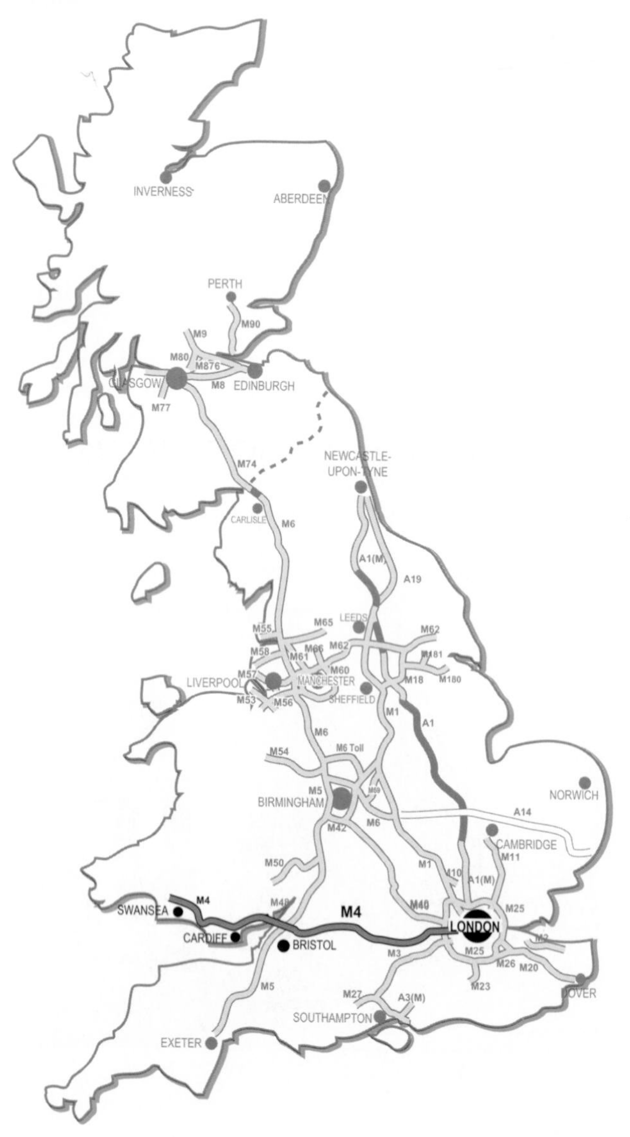
INVERNESS
ABERDEEN
PERTH
M90
M9
M80
M876
GLASGOW
M8
EDINBURGH
M77
NEWCASTLE-UPON-TYNE
M74
CARLISLE
M6
A1(M)
A19
LEEDS
M65
M55
M62
M58
M66
M62
M61
M181
M60
LIVERPOOL
M57
MANCHESTER
M18
M180
M53
M56
SHEFFIELD
M1
A1
M6
M6 Toll
M54
M5
BIRMINGHAM
M69
NORWICH
A14
M42
M6
CAMBRIDGE
M11
M50
M1
M10
A1(M)
M4
M48
M4
M40
M25
SWANSEA
LONDON
CARDIFF
BRISTOL
M2
M3
M25
M26
M20
M23
M5
M27
A3(M)
DOVER
SOUTHAMPTON
EXETER

## JUNCTIONS 8/9 TO 49

The M4, which is 121 miles long, is the fourth longest motorway in the UK. It is a direct link from London to South Wales and interconnects with the M5 north of Bristol. The first part, the Chiswick Flyover, was opened in 1959 by a blonde starlet called Jayne Mansfield. The last part was completed in 1973. It may be continued to Fishguard at some future date, instead of terminating in a rather bleak part of South Wales. It passes through some of the most varied scenery in southern England. It has been divided into three sections.

# WINDSOR TO HUNGERFORD

## JUNCTIONS 8/9 TO 14

This section of the motorway follows the Thames to Reading and from there the River Kennet to Newbury before rising up to the open expanses of the Marlborough Downs.

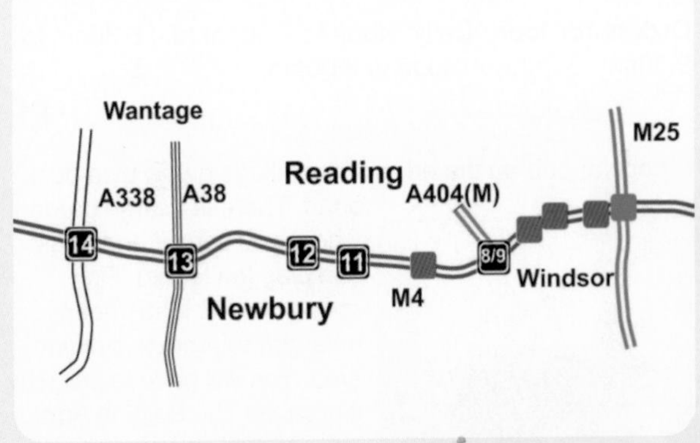

Take the spur road A308(M) to the roundabout. Take the A330 for Ascot and Bracknell and left again at the village green. The Belgian Arms is 200 yards on the left.

**Places of interest**

Dorney Court HHA – 5 miles 

## Ⓐ The Belgian Arms

Satnav **SL6 2JR**

Holyport Street, Holyport, Berks.
01628 634 468
www.thebelgian.co.uk
thebelgianarms@live.co.uk

**Orders for food:** Daily: Noon to 2.30pm and 6.30pm to 9.30pm. Sundays: Noon to 3.00pm.

££

A popular pub on the edge of the village green by a duck pond. There is a large garden where you can sit and dogs can play (on leads). Fish specials daily. It has been enlarged to provide a dining area. You will have to ask why it is called The Belgian Arms.

At the roundabout turn left to Three Mile Cross, but avoid getting onto the dual carriageway. This junction has been recently upgraded and is therefore more complicated.

**Places of interest**

Silchester (Calleva Atrebartum) – 7 miles

Stratfield Saye HHA – 5 miles

## A The Swan

Satnav **RG7 1AT**

Basingstoke Road, Three Mile Cross, Berks.

01189 883 674

www.theswan-3mx.co.uk

jenny.dove@hotmail.co.uk

**Orders for food:** Weekdays: Noon to 2.30pm and 7.00pm to 9.30pm. Saturdays: Noon to 2.00pm and 7.00pm to 9.30pm. Sundays: Noon to 3.00pm.

££

Traditional Free House with dining areas, and bar meals, all washed down with real ales. There is outside seating and a garden beyond the car park. The resident Irish Wolfhound, Mr Niall, is the mascot of London Irish RFC. A recent addition is a large covered patio with its own bar almost hidden by bushes planted by Vic Harrison, the owner 30 years ago.

At the first roundabout turn right to Theale, which is a surprisingly attractive little town. It is so named as it was the second night's stop out of London for wagoners and was called The Ale. It certainly seems to have more than its fair share of pubs and hotels, so if the one mentioned below is full, there are alternatives.

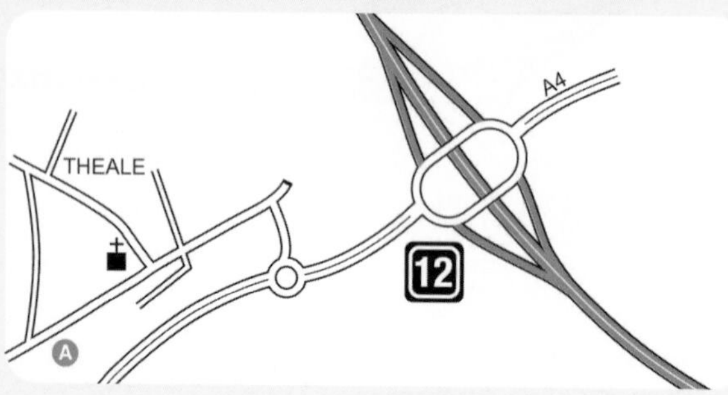


**Places of interest**

Engelfield House Garden HHA – 3 miles
Basildon Park (1776-1783) NT – 7 miles 

## Ⓐ The Volunteer

Satnav
**RG7 5BX**

Church Street, Theale, Berks.
01189 302 489
thevolunteer@btinternet.com

**Orders for food:** Daily: Noon to 2.30pm and 6.00pm to 9.00pm. Sundays: Noon to 4.00pm, no evening meals.

£

A Fuller's pub which has changed hands. It serves traditional meals with home cooking. There is outside seating with part of it under a verandah. An interesting collection of military and sporting prints.

For Chieveley bear first left off the A34 to Oxford. The Olde Red Lion is on the left as you come into the village. The Langley Hall is to the north alongside the A34. The Red House is off the old A4 from Newbury to Hungerford.

## Ⓐ Ye Olde Red Lion

Satnav
**RG20 8XB**

Green Lane, Chieveley, Berks.
01635 248 379
www.yeolderedlion.com
redlion@toucansurf.com

**Orders for food**: Weekdays: Noon to 2.30pm. 6.30pm to 9.30pm. Sundays: Noon to 3.00pm. 6.30pm to 9.00pm.

££

An old country pub with dining areas around a central bar. A friendly atmosphere enhanced by prints and pictures. A constant feature in the guide owing to its value for money.

## B Langley Hall Inn

Satnav
**RG20 8SA**

Old Oxford Road, Beedon, Berkshire.
01635 248 332
www.langley-hall-inn.co.uk
landlord@langley-hall-inn.co.uk

**Orders for food:** Weekdays: Noon to 2.00pm and 6.00pm to 9.00pm. Saturdays and Sundays: Noon to 3.00pm and 6.00pm to 9.00pm. Mondays: 6.00pm to 9.00pm.

££

A locals' pub which has been revived by Mark and Lorraine who were new to the business. Low beamed traditional atmosphere and a cheerful welcome. Dogs and children are welcome as there is a large garden as well as outside seating.

## C The Red House

Satnav
**G20 8LY**

Main Road, Marsh Benham, Berks
01635 582 017
www.redhousepub.com

**Orders for food:** Daily: Noon to 3.00pm and 7.00pm to 9.30pm. Sundays: Noon to 4.00pm and 7.00pm to 9.30pm.

£££

A privately owned elegant restaurant cum pub in a thatched house with a dining room overlooking a garden near the River Kennet. English and Continental menu using local produce either a la carte or with a Bistro menu at the bar.

Follow the B400 towards Lambourn for the Pheasant Inn and the Hare Restaurant. The Tally Ho is on the Hungerford Road.

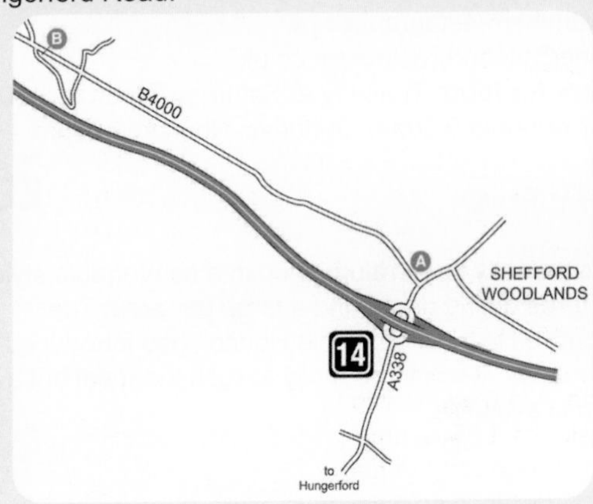


**Places of interest**

Ashdown House (c1690) NT – 9 miles

## Ⓐ The Pheasant Inn

Satnav
**RG17 7AA**

Ermin Street, Shefford Woodlands, Berks.
01488 648 284
www.thepheasant-inn.co.uk
enquiries@thepheasant-inn.co.uk

**Orders for food:** Daily: Noon to 2.30pm and 7.00pm to 9.00pm.

££

It has always been a popular rendezvous and now has eleven modern, comfortable and quiet bedrooms. There is a restaurant with an excellent chef and a convivial bar where members of the racing fraternity meet. It is a pleasant and congenial place.

## B The Hare Restaurant

Satnav
**RG17 7SD**

Lambourn Woodlands, Berks.
01488 713 86
www.theharerestaurant.co.uk
cuisine@theharerestaurant.co.uk

**Orders for food:** Tuesday to Saturday: Noon to 2.30pm and 7.00pm to 9.30pm. Sundays: Noon to 3.00pm.

£££

It has recently been refurbished in a comfortable style with three dining areas and a large bar area. The Executive Head Chef, Jamie Hodson has introduced new menus. It would be a pity to rush the meal but a bar menu is available.

# HUNGERFORD TO SEVERN BRIDGE

## JUNCTIONS 15 TO 22

From Junction 15 to Junction 18, the motorway passes through the south of the Cotswolds. From there, it descends down the escarpment towards the River Severn.

Swindon was the centre of the locomotive workshops for the Great Western Railway and is now a modern commercial town with a railway museum. Chippenham, once a picturesque market town, has now been modernised out of all recognition. Bath, south of Junction 18, is famous for its Georgian architecture.

In 1996 the second Severn Bridge was completed to cope with the increased traffic. The old bridge crossing was then renamed the M48 and the new section became the M4. The M49 link to Avonmouth is best avoided if seeking a meal.

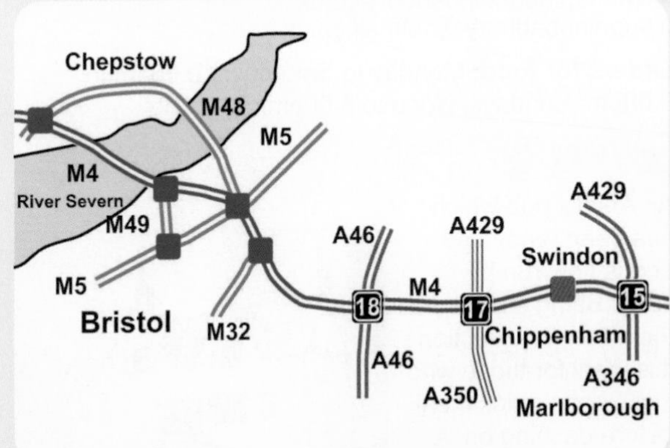

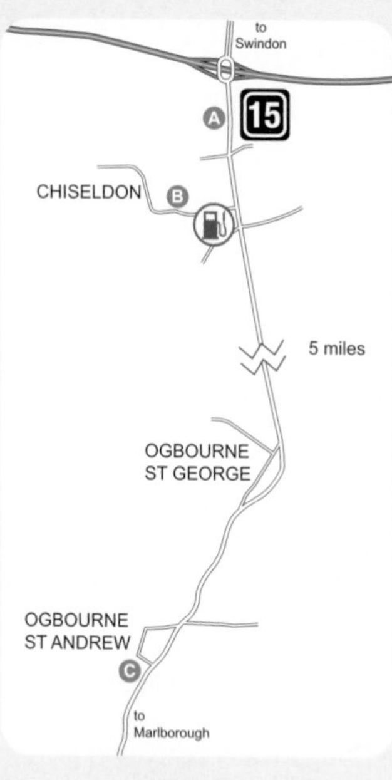


The Plough Inn is 200 yards from the junction on the A346 to Marlborough. The Patriots Arms is in Chiseldon but easy to find. The Silks on the Downs is 5 miles from the junction on the Marlborough road and is on the right hand side.

## A Plough Inn

Satnav **SN4 0EP**

Marlborough Road, Badbury, Wilts.
01793 740 342
www.theploughinnbadbury.co.uk
ploughinnbadbury@hotmail.co.uk

**Orders for food:** Monday to Saturday: 10.00am to 9.00pm. Sundays: Noon to 8.00pm.

£

An Arkells pub which has been renovated and is now run by Terry. Being so close to the motorway junction it is ideal for those who just want a quick meal before dashing on. A patio for those wanting fresh air.

## B Chiseldon House Hotel

Satnav
**SN4 0NE**

New Road, Chiseldon, Wilts.
01793 741 010
www.chiseldonhouse.com
welcome@chiseldonhouse.com

**Orders for food:** Daily: Noon to 2.00pm and 7.00pm to 9.00pm. Sundays: Noon to 2.00pm and light evening meals.

£££

A late Georgian manor house with a friendly and relaxed atmosphere set in three acres of gardens. Comfortable restaurant, bar and lounge.

## C Silks on the Downs

Satnav
**SN8 1RZ**

Main Road, Ogbourne St Andrews, Wilts.
01672 841 229
www.silksonthedowns.co.uk
info@silksonthedowns.co.uk

**Orders for food:** Monday to Tuesday: Noon to 2.00pm and 7.00pm to 9.00pm. Wednesday to Saturday: Noon to 2.30pm and 7.00pm to 9.30pm. Sundays: Noon to 2.00pm.

£££

Those in the racing fraternity will know why it is called Silks. For the others you will have to go there and see. It is a comfortable and roomy restaurant with a garden at the rear. My crab cakes were especially good. The menu gives an amusing rundown on all the staff.

The Hit or Miss in Kington Langley could be missed, which would be a pity but take the narrow road after the roundabout by the Junction, The Jolly Huntsman is in Kington St. Michael on the left. The New Inn is harder to find, but follow the signs. The same could be said for Grittleton, before regaining the motorway at Junction 18.

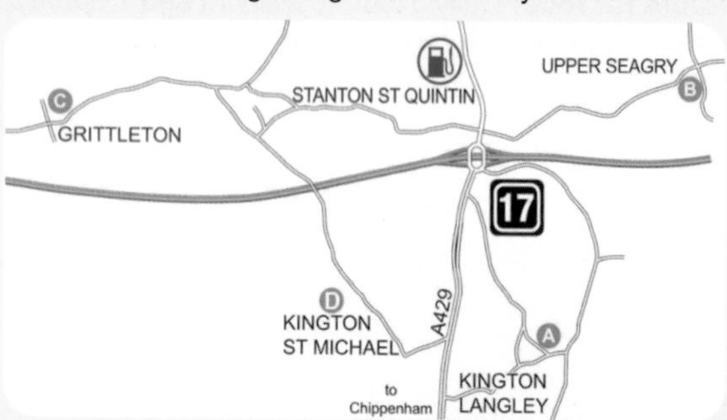


**Places of interest**
Bowood House (c1720-1760) HHA – 6 miles
Lacock Abbey (1232-1540) NT – 7 miles
Corsham Court (1582) HHA – 9 miles

# Ⓐ The Hit or Miss

Satnav
**SN15 5NS**

Days Lane, Kington Langley, Wilts.
01249 758 830
natsgough@aol.com

**Orders for food:** Weekdays: Noon to 2.30pm and 6.30pm to 9.30pm. Sundays: Noon to 7.30pm.

££

A popular village pub and restaurant dating from the 18thC and thus with low beams in this scattered hamlet. There is a friendly welcome to all, including dogs and it has an imaginative menu. A good ambiance as it is privately owned.

## B New Inn

Satnav
**SN15 5HA**

32 Hen Lane, Upper Seagry, Wiltshire
01249 721 083
www.thenewinnseagry.co.uk
thenewinnseagry@hotmail.co.uk

**Orders for food:** Weekdays: Noon to 2.00pm and 6.00pm to 9.00pm. Sundays: Noon to 2.00pm. Closed on Mondays.

£

A locals' pub in the village, with beams, red carpets and wooden tables. The outside seating is enclosed with lattice fencing as the houses are close by. Pleasant, helpful and cheerful atmosphere. Yes to children. Dogs on leads.

## C Neeld Arms

Satnav
**SN14 6AP**

The Street, Grittleton, Wilts.
01249 782 470
www.neeldarms.co.uk
info@neeldarms.co.uk

**Orders for food:** Monday to Saturday: Noon to 2.00pm and 6.30pm to 9.30pm. Sunday Noon to 2.30pm and 7.00pm to 9.00pm.

££

A Free House owned by Charlie & Boo West. It is still a locals' village pub, but now has a restaurant with traditional meals. A cheerful and friendly place and ideal for those coming to Mary Howard's Gift Fair at Hullavington.

# The Jolly Huntsman

Satnav
**SN14 6JB**

High Street, Kington St Michael, Wilts
01249 750 305
www.jollyhuntsman.com
thejollyhuntsman@aol.com

**Orders for food:**
Daily: 11.30am to 2.00pm and 6.30pm to 9.30pm.
Sundays: Noon to 2.00pm and 7.00pm to 9.00pm.

A popular locals' pub in this attractive village. It is well known for its Real Ales of which there are six different varieties as well as a range of ciders. An extensive menu is available and meals can be taken in the bar or restaurant areas. Well behaved children and dogs are welcome.

The Bull seems further than it is. The Tollgate is down the road from The Crown if tea or a light lunch beckons.

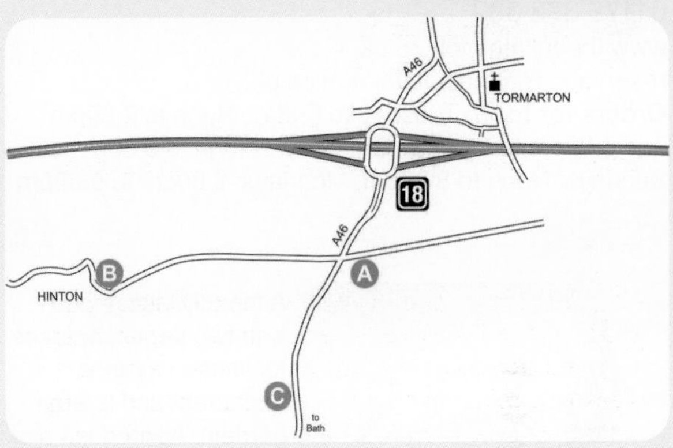


**Places of interest**

Dyrham Park (1691) NT – 1 mile

Horton Court (c1690) NT – 7 miles

## A The Crown

Satnav **SN14 8HZ**

Dyrham, Glos.
01225 891166
www.ohhcompany.co.uk
thecrown@ohhcompany.co.uk

**Orders for food:** Weekdays and Sundays: Noon to 9.30pm. Fridays and Saturdays: Noon to 10.00pm.

££

A country pub-cum-restaurant just two minutes from Junction 18. Once a coaching stop in the 1700s, it still gives a friendly welcome and serves home-cooked meals all day. A children's playground and garden where dogs are allowed.

## B Bull Inn

Satnav
**SN14 8HG**

Main Road, Hinton, Glos.
01179 372 332
www.thebullathinton.co.uk
reservations@thebullathinton.co.uk

**Orders for food:** Tuesday to Friday: Noon to 2.00pm and 6.00pm to 9.00pm. Saturdays: Noon to 9.30pm. Sundays: Noon to 8.30pm. Mondays: 6.00pm to 9.00pm.

££

A friendly village pub with two large fireplaces for winter nights, a restaurant and a large garden. All food is cooked on the premises. It is highly rated by other motorists.

## C Tollgate Teashop

Satnav
**SN14 8LF**

Oldfield Gatehouse, Dyrham, Glos.
01225 891 585
www.tollgateteashop.com

**Orders for food:** Daily: 9.30am to 5.00pm. Summer weekends: 9.30am to 6.00pm. Closed on Mondays.

£

A small privately owned teashop for the past 23 years, which was once a Toll House. Good breakfasts, light lunches and old fashioned teas with clotted cream. Outside seating in the garden at the rear with views over to the Welsh hills and the bridges over the Severn.

# MAGOR TO PONTARDDULAIS

## JUNCTIONS 23 TO 49

As the map suggests there are few places where it is worth leaving the motorway to eat, which may account for the large number of service stations. There are however, plenty of places of interest to see.

Caerleon off Junction 24 is the site of Isca, the Roman base of the II (Augusta) Legion raised in Spain. Nearby is Caerwent, the old Roman capital the of Silures. In Cardiff, the Castle is built on the walls of the Roman fort, whilst to the north there is the medieval Castell Coch, both restored by the 3rd Marquess of Bute in the 19th century with the help of the architect William Burges. Some six miles beyond Castell Coch to the east are the imposing ruins of Caerphilly Castle, mute evidence of the occupation of Wales by Edward I.

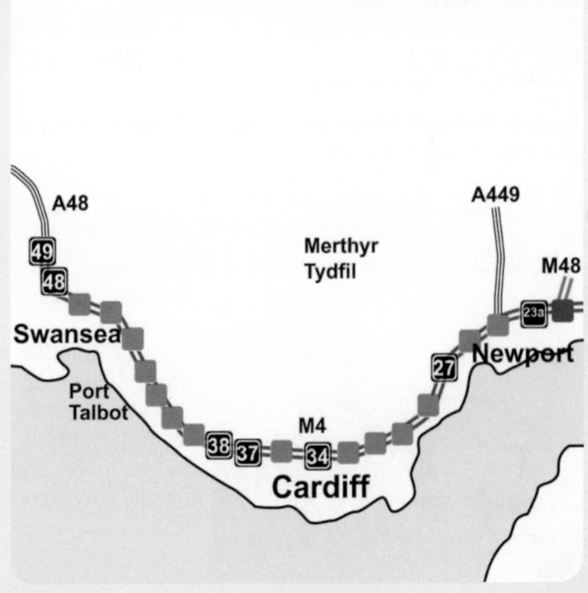

Fairly simple. Either bear right at the traffic lights or straight on and turn right. To get back to the motorway, you will have to go left and go round the roundabout.

## Ⓐ Wheatsheaf

The Square, Magor, S.Wales.
01633 880 608
wheatsheafinn@msn.com

Satnav
**NP26 3HN**

**Orders for food:** Monday to Saturday: Noon to 9.30pm.
Sundays: Noon to 3.00pm.

££

A leasehold from Enterprise Inns. It is some two hundred years old with large modernised open-plan dining areas and a restaurant beyond. Home cooked meals and friendly service.

Take the B4591 road north to Risca and Abertilley. After about 1 mile The Rising Sun will be on your left behind a red telephone box.

**Places of interest**

The 14 canal locks

## A The Rising Sun

Satnav
**NP10 9AQ**

1 Cefn Road, Rogerstone, S.Wales
01633 895 126
www.therisingsunnewport.co.uk
russel@therisingsunnewport.co.uk

**Orders for food:** Daily: Noon to 2.15pm and 5.30pm to 9.30pm. Sundays: Noon to 7.00pm.

££

A family-run pub with a good reputation. It has a two-storey conservatory at the rear of the restaurant, with two large bars elsewhere. The menu is imaginative with self-service at lunch. A surprise to find a deservedly popular place which looks unassuming at first sight.

At Junction 37 take the short dual carriageway south. At the roundabout turn left. After the next roundabout, turn right onto a very narrow road signed Kenfig where the pub is on your right. Alternatively, turn right at the first round-about, through North Connelly, and first left.

**Places of interest**

Margam Abbey(1147). Margam Orangery (1790), the longest in the UK.

## Ⓐ Prince of Wales

Satnav
**CF33 4PR**

Ton Kenfig, Nr Porthcawl, Mid Glam.
01656 740 356
www.princekenfig.com
prince_of_wales@btconnect.com

**Orders for food:** Weekdays: Noon to 2.30pm and 6.00pm to 8.30pm. Sundays: Noon to 2.15pm. Mondays: No meals.

£

A plain-looking building but with a fascinating past. It is a 16th-century family-owned pub which has been a mortuary for shipwrecked bodies. It was also the old Parliament and Court House for the now lost port of Kenfig which was swept away by a tsunami in 1550. It is reputed to be the most haunted pub in Wales but it is, however, a very friendly place with a warm welcome.

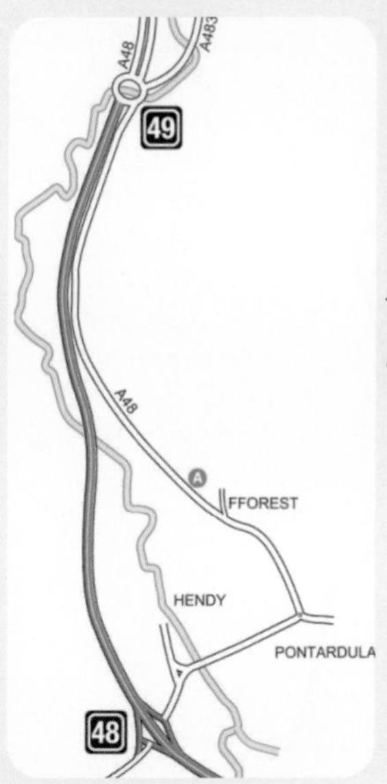


Exit at Junction 49 and take the A48 south towards Pontarddulais. The Bird in Hand will be on your left before Fforest. You can get back onto the motorway at junction 48 via Pontarddulais but easier to return to junction 49.

## Ⓐ Bird In Hand

Satnav
**SA4 0TU**

24 Camarthen Road, Fforest
01792 886 651
www.sizzlingpubs.co.uk
info@sizzlingpubs.co.uk

**Orders for food:** Daily: Noon to 9.00pm.

£

It is now a managed house of Sizzling Pubs - an offshoot of Mitchell & Butler. It is on the main road facing onto the hills with a row of terraced houses to the rear. A long dining room has been added so room for all as well as the bar area. A community pub with a cheerful atmosphere and the natives are friendly.

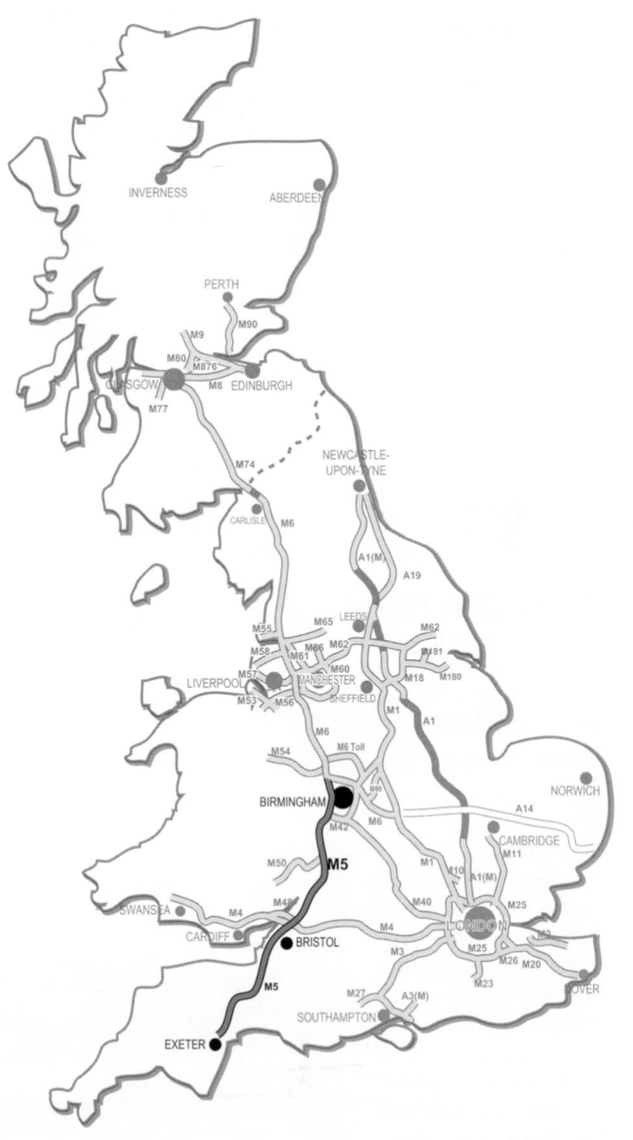
INVERNESS
ABERDEEN
PERTH
M90
M9
M80
M876
GLASGOW
M8
EDINBURGH
M77
M74
NEWCASTLE-UPON-TYNE
CARLISLE
M6
A1(M)
A19
LEEDS
M65
M55
M62
M66
M58
M61
M60
M57
LIVERPOOL
MANCHESTER
M18
M180
SHEFFIELD
M53
M56
M1
A1
M6
M54
M6 Toll
BIRMINGHAM
NORWICH
A14
M42
M6
CAMBRIDGE
M11
M50
M5
M1
A1(M)
M40
M25
SWANSEA
M4
M48
LONDON
CARDIFF
BRISTOL
M4
M3
M25
M26
M20
M23
M5
M27
A3(M)
DOVER
SOUTHAMPTON
EXETER

## JUNCTIONS 1 TO 31

The M5 is 168 miles in length and was built in stages, the first part being completed in 1969 and the last in 1976. It was designed to link the Midlands with the South West via Bristol. It is one of the few motorways which has no connection with London. Considering that it passes through some of the prettiest of the English countryside, the needs of motorists are poorly served.

It is divided into three sections.

## DROITWICH TO TEWKESBURY

### JUNCTIONS 1 TO 10

A boring stretch of motorway until you get to the south of Worcester.

The roundabouts tend to confuse, but look out for the signs to Droitwich

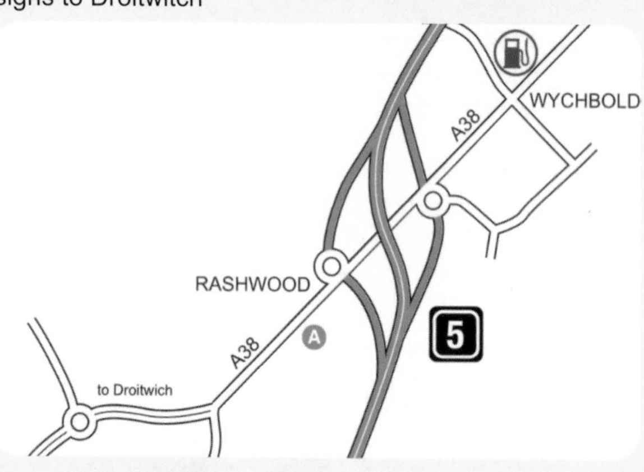


**Places of interest**
Hanbury Hall NT – 4 miles

## Ⓐ Robin Hood

Satnav
**WR9 0BS**

Rashwood Bank, Rashwood, Worcs.
01527 869 302
www.vintageinn.co.uk/therobinhooddroitwich

**Orders for food:** Daily: 8.00am to 10.00pm.
Sundays: 8.00am to 9.30pm.

££

A Mitchell & Butler-owned pub with tiled and wooden flooring and a well-laid-out dining area. It is deservedly well known to the passing motorist. Outside seating and a beer garden at the rear, where dogs are allowed. It has recently changed management.

From the junction take the A 4538. Left at the roundabout and after a mile, at a sharp left-hand bend, turn right at a badly-signed junction to Crowle Green.

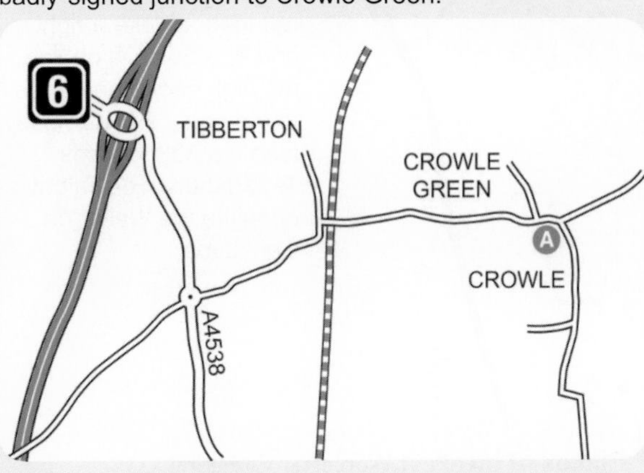


## Ⓐ Old Chequers

Satnav
**WR7 4AA**

Crowle Green, Crowle, Worcs.
01905 381 275
www.oldchequersinn.co.uk
oldchequersinn@btinternet.com

**Orders for food:** Monday to Saturday: Noon to 2.30pm and 6.00pm to 9.00pm.
Sundays: Noon to 3.00pm.

££

A 400 year-old old village free house pub which David and Lesley Newbrook have taken over. Spacious dining room and a large bar area. Friendly service with an imaginative menu and Real Ales. A large garden for warm days where you can also play *boules*.

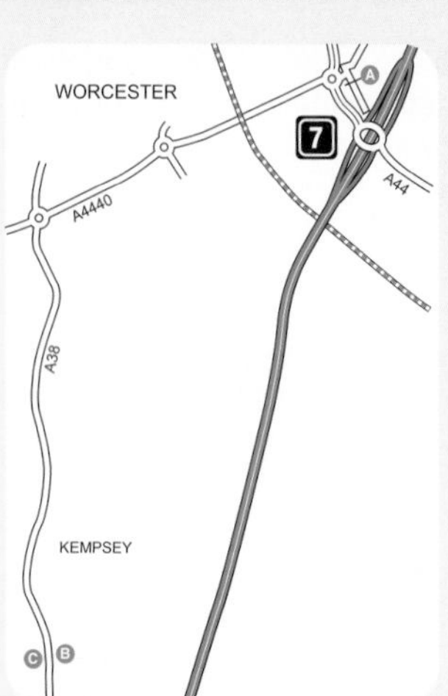


You can practically see The Swan from the junction. At the first roundabout take a right and The Swan is behind the high hedge and trees to the right. For Kempsey take the A38 towards Tewkesbury. The Talbot is opposite the Walter de Cantalupe.

**Places of interest** Worcester Cathedral.

## Ⓐ The Swan

Satnav
**WR5 2RL**

Main Road, Whittington, Worcs
01905 351361
www.swanatwhittington.com
info@swanatwhittington.com

**Orders for food:** Monday to Friday: 9.00am to 9.30pm
Saturday and Sunday: 10.00am to 9.30pm

££

The Swan is part of a group of three other places in the neighbourhood. Airy open plan seating surrounds a central bar. There is a beer garden at the rear and a children's playground. Deservedly popular, as it is within a few hundred yards of the junction. The staff are friendly and efficient, who will provide a newspaper to read if asked.

## B The Walter de Cantelupe Inn

Satnav
**WR5 3NA**

Main Road, Kempsey, Worcs.
01905 820 572
www.walterdecantelupe.co.uk
info@walterdecantelupe.co.uk

**Orders for food:** Tuesday to Saturday: Noon to 2.30pm and 5.30pm to 9.30pm. Sundays: Noon to 3.00pm. Closed Mondays, except bank holidays.

££

Named after a 13th-century Bishop of Worcester, this old merchant's house, under the aegis of the proprietor who was trained in France, offers everything to the weary traveller, including supper after the official closing hour. In summer they have a paella party in the walled garden with home-produced food and even a local wine.

## C The Talbot

Satnav
**WR5 3JA**

87 Main Road, Kempsey, Worcs.
01905 828 473

**Orders for food:** Daily: Noon to 9.00pm. Sundays: Noon to 5.00pm

£

A tenanted locals' pub in the village. It is well known for its Real Ales and different varieties of cider. There is ample seating in the dining areas around a bar where homemade English food is available. Well behaved dogs are welcome as indeed are children.

The Hobnails is about 4 miles from the junction. Take the A46 towards Evesham. At the roundabout go straight on towards Stow-on-the-Wold on the B4077. The inn is on the left after about 2 miles.

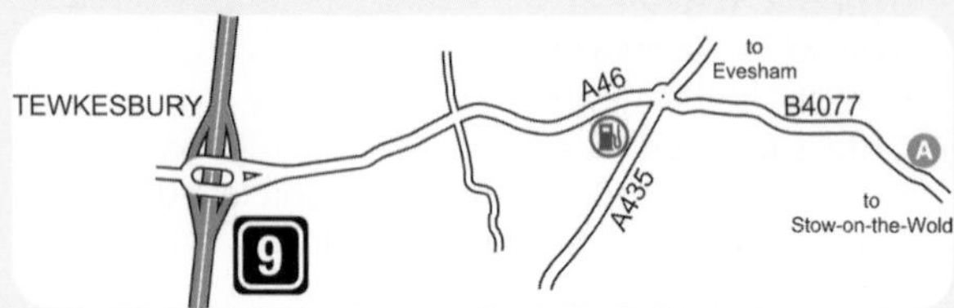


**Places of interest**
Tewkesbury Abbey (1089)

## A Hobnails Inn

Satnav
**GL20 8NQ**

Main Road, Little Washbourne, Glos.
01242 620 237
www.hobnailsinn.co.uk
enquiries@thehobnailsinn.co.uk

**Orders for food:** Monday to Saturday: Noon to 2.30pm and 5.30pm to 9.00pm. Sundays: Noon to 9.00pm.

££

A wayside inn dating back to 1493. It has been refurbished in a more modern style with several small dining areas. The cooking is traditional using local produce and the carvery is popular. The service is efficient and friendly and there is a good ambience. A large patio and garden area.

# TEWKESBURY TO WELLS

## JUNCTIONS 11A TO 21

This stretch takes you from Gloucester, with its historic cathedral where Edward II is buried, to the south of Bristol.

The motorway passes through pleasant countryside and there are interesting houses and places to visit along the River Severn. Near Junction 18, Kings Weston House, designed by Sir John Vanbrugh, can be seen on the hills to the east. You can divert along the Avon Gorge into Bristol with its restored dockside and where the SS Great Britain is dry-docked, after being brought back from the Falklands in 1970.

During the summer the stretch south from the M4 intersection to the bridge over the Avon can get gridlocked.

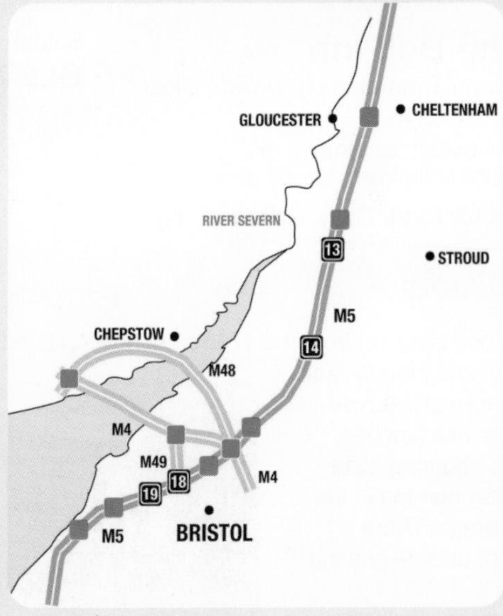

For the Bell take the A38 towards Bristol. After 1 mile turn right to Frampton on Severn. The inn is on the edge of the village green. The Frombridge Mill is straight on at the roundabout down a private road.

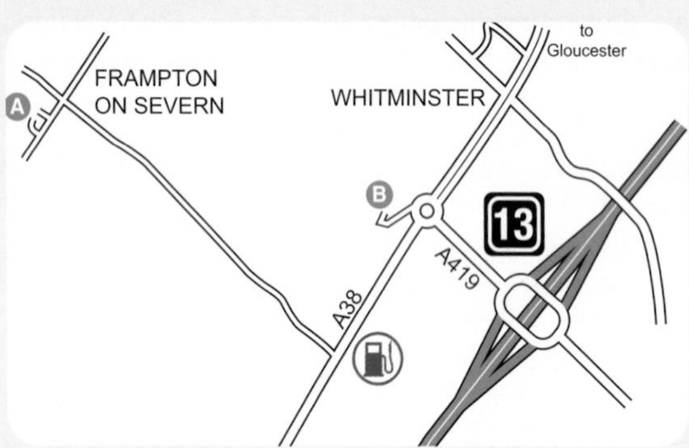


**Places of interest**

Frampton Court Pte – 3 miles 
Wildfowl Centre (Slimbridge) – 5 miles

## A The Bell Inn

Satnav **GL2 7EP**

The Green, Frampton on Severn, Glos.
01452 740 346
www.thebellatframpton.co.uk
relax@thebellatframpton.co.uk

**Orders for food:** Daily: Noon to 9.00pm.

££

An old coaching inn from the 1700's but now updated with cheerful and friendly staff.

Bar snacks are served together with lunches, dinners, morning coffee and afternoon tea in the dining areas. There is plenty of outside seating and
children may look at some rare breed farm animals.

## Ⓑ Frombridge Mill

Satnav
**GL2 7PD**

Frombridge Lane, Whitminster, Glos.
01452 741 796
www.frombridge-mill-whitminster.co.uk
6452@greeneking.co.uk

**Orders for food:** Sundays to Thursdays: Noon to 9.00pm. Fridays and Saturdays: Noon to 10.00pm

££

As the name implies this was a working water mill and indeed the River Frome flows past on either side. The interior is now stripped of machinery so it makes an ideal place to have lunch or dinner, sit outside if the weather permits or even go for a walk. Dogs and well behaved children welcome.

Come off the motorway and drive south through Falfield. After two miles, bear right on the B4061 to Thornbury. Turn right at a crossroads, as you come onto the town signed Oldbury-on-Severn. In the village, turn left to Kington. The Anchor is on left as you go over a stream. This area is steeped in history and atmosphere and is well worth the additional time.

**Places of interest**

Berkeley Castle (12th C) HHA - 5 miles 

## The Anchor Inn

Satnav **BS35 1QA**

Church Road, Oldbury-on-Severn, Glos.
01454 413 331
www.anchorinnoldbury.co.uk
info@anchorinnoldbury.co.uk

**Orders for food:** Weekdays: 11.30 am to 2.00pm and 6.00pm to 9.00pm. Saturdays: 11.30am to 2.30pm and 6.00pm to 9.00pm. Sundays: Noon to 3.00pm and 6.00pm to 9.00pm.

 £

A locals' pub in this old village by the River Severn. It has a traditional public bar and a comfortable lounge. A dining area at the rear of the house overlooking the garden. Awarded Best Value Pub of the Year.

Take the A38 dual carriageway to Thornbury. Turn left to Almondsbury, opposite the Swan Inn on the right. Bear left down the hill and turn right at memorial cross. Turn right again after the church. If coming from the north, turn right down an unmarked road just before the 30mph sign.

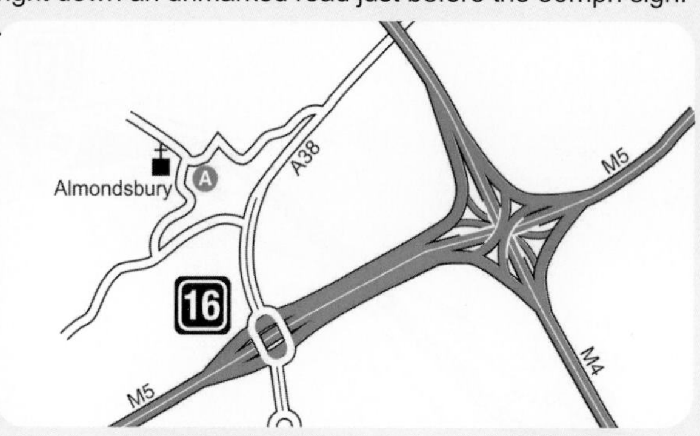


## A The Bowl Inn

Satnav
**BS32 4DT**

Church Road, Lower Almondsbury, S.Glos.
01454 612 757
www.thebowlinn.co.uk
bowlinn@sabrain.com

**Orders for food:** Monday to Thursday: Noon to 2.30pm and 6.00pm to 9.30pm. Fridays and Saturdays: Noon to 9.30pm. Sundays: Noon to 8.00pm.

£££

A village inn now owned by S.A.Brain with a restaurant and recently refurbished bedrooms under the beamed roof. The original cottages were built in 1146 to house the builders of the church and it is now a friendly, efficient hostelry with a good menu and service. Bar meals are available and can be eaten while admiring the view over the River Severn to Wales.

Take the A369 but immediately turn right onto the road signed Portbury. Turn right in the village and follow signs to Clapton in Gordano. Both roads are narrow. In the village, turn sharp left up a lane and the pub is on the right. The Priory in Portbury is easy to find.

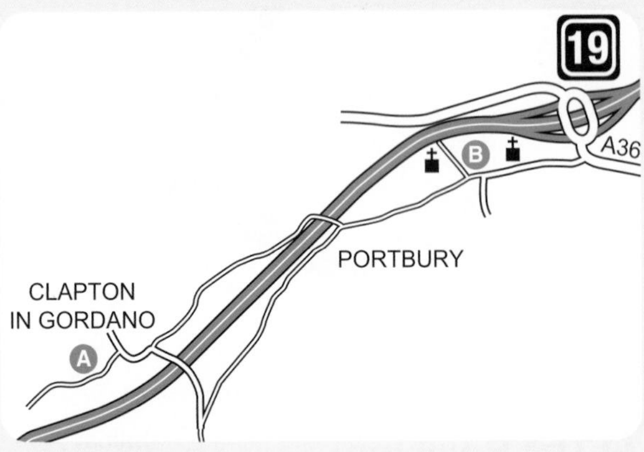


## A The Black Horse

Satnav **BS20 7RH**

Clevedon Lane, Clapton in Gordano, Som.
01275 842 105
www.thekicker.co.uk
theblackhorse@talktalkbusiness.net

**Orders for food:** Monday to Saturday: Noon to 2.00pm. Sundays: No meals served.

£

A charming old-fashioned pub serving bar meals such as bowls of homemade soup, as well as a full-blown meal. A large garden at the rear where children are welcome. Inside low beams and snugs with flagstone floors. A cheerful and bustling atmosphere and frequented by the locals.

## B The Priory

Satnav
**BS20 7TN**

Station Road, Portbury, Bristol.
01275 376 307
www.vintageinn.co.uk/theprioryportbury/
prioryhotelportbury@vintageinn.co.uk

**Orders for food:** Weekdays. Noon to 10.00pm.
Sundays: Noon to 9.30pm

££

So named from the monastery which used to stand across the road. The present building started life in 1822 as a hotel and has been serving food and drink ever since. It has a rustic character and a cheerful atmosphere. Outside seating where children and dogs are welcome. For those who need to stretch their legs there is a footpath to The Mount and Windmill Hill.

# WELLS TO EXETER

## JUNCTIONS 21 TO 31

The motorway winds over the Mendip Hills before crossing the flat levels of Sedgemoor, which is remembered for the defeat of the Duke of Monmouth in 1685 and the Bloody Assizes of "Hanging" Judge Jeffreys who was aged 26 at the time.

Glastonbury, famous for the supposed site of the Holy Grail and also for the annual music festival, is within reach of the motorway.

Taunton is an attractive county town, with a good antique market.

The motorway ends south of Exeter with its fine medieval cathedral. It continues as a dual carriageway to Plymouth and Cornwall.

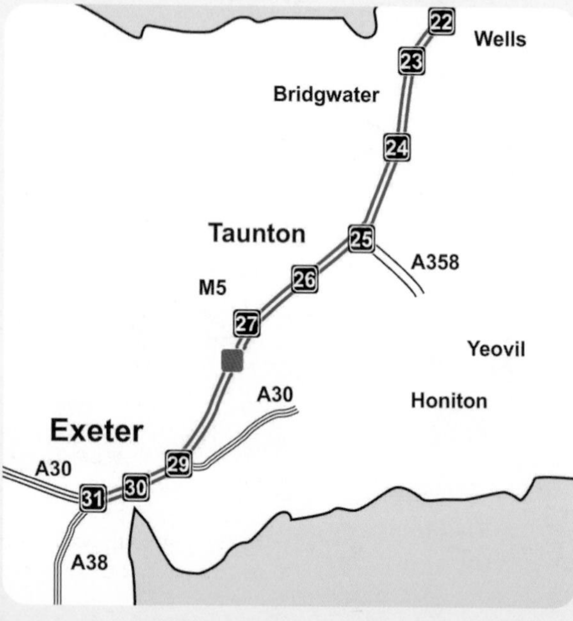

Driving south it is relatively simple. Take the A38, and the White Cottage is on the left at the end of the village of West Huntspill. Get back onto the M4 from junction 23. Going north, come off at junction 23 adn drive up the A38, rejoining the motorway at junction 22.

## A The White Cottage

Satnav
**TA9 3RQ**

Old Pawlett Road, West Huntspill, Som.
01278 794 692
colinfrost@aol.com

**Orders for food:** Wednesday to Saturdays: Noon to 1.45pm and 6.30pm to 8.45pm. Sundays: Noon to 1.30pm and 6.30pm to 8.30pm. Closed Mondays and Tuesdays.

A privately owned restaurant as opposed to a pub so no noisy background, but low-beamed with old-fashioned charm and a helpful and friendly staff. They were very busy when I passed by but the soup was good and homemade. A garden but no outside meals.

The Puriton Inn is signed just off the junction on the left.

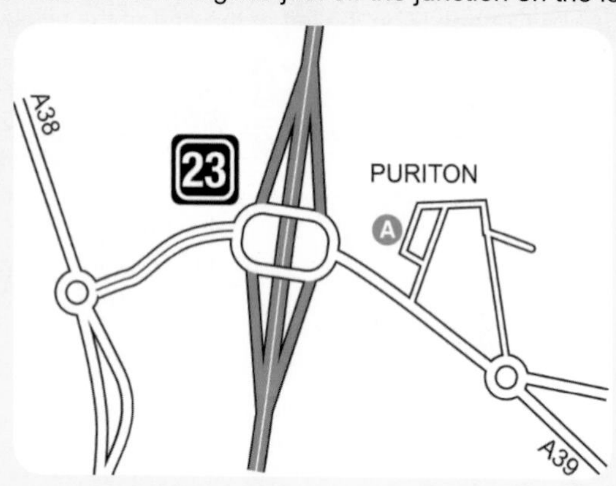


**Places of interest**

Glastonbury Abbey – 13 miles

## Ⓐ Puriton Inn

Satnav
**TA7 8AF**

Puriton Hill, Puriton, Som.
01278 683 464
www.thepuritoninn.co.uk
info@thepuritoninn.co.uk

**Orders for food**: Monday to Thursday: 11.30am to 2.30pm and 6.00pm to 9.00pm. Friday to Saturday: 11.30am to 9.00pm. Sundays: Noon to 9.00pm.

££

A 200 year old village pub just off the motorway. It has a dining area with two bars serving real ales. Outside, there is a children's playground with outdoor seating where dogs are allowed and a shelter for smoking.

This is one of the easiest places to find. From the motorway, go left at the roundabout on the A38 and the Compass Inn is just 100 yards south. There is a Filling Station on the roundabout.

## A The Compass Tavern

Satnav
**TA6 6PR**

Taunton Road, North Petherton, Som.
01278 662 283
www.thecompassinn.co.uk
martgill@btconnect.com

**Orders for food:** Daily: Noon to 2.45pm and 6.00pm to 9.00pm.Sundays: Noon to 9.00pm.

££

A converted 16th-century mock-Tudor building, with large open beamed dining areas, but pay heed to the notices to "Mind your step or mind your head". Friendly atmosphere with home cooked meals and real ales.

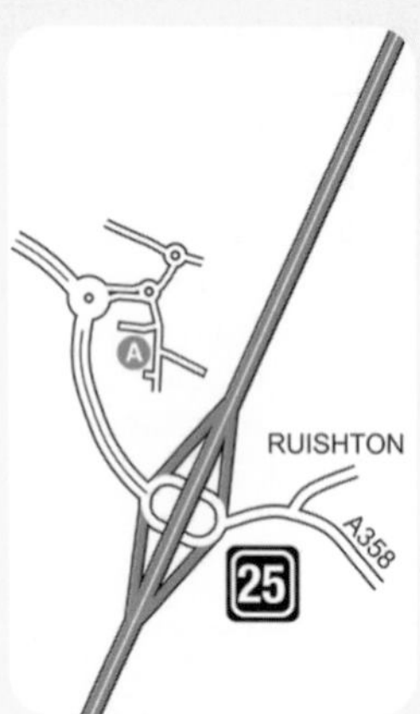


At the junction head towards Taunton. At the first roundabout go right and again right at the next. The Hankridge Arms will be on the right surrounded by supermarkets.

**Places of interest**

Hestercombe Gardens (1750s and Gertrude Jekyll)
HHH – 5 miles

## The Hankridge Arms

Satnav **TA1 2LR**

Hankridge Way, Taunton, Som.
01823 444 405
www.thehankridgearms.com
info@thehankridgearms.com

**Orders for food:** Monday to Saturday: Noon to 2.00pm and 6.00pm to 9.00pm. Sundays: Noon to 2.30pm and 5.30pm to 8.30pm.

£££

Now a restaurant with a bar area, it was once an Elizabethan farmhouse of some importance, rescued from dereliction at some considerable cost. No sooner was it completed than it was surrounded by a shopping precinct. It is, however, a comfortable and friendly place, which offers a two-course lunch at £10 (except on Sundays).

Both the alternative roads to reach the Merry Harriers are single track for the first mile so take the shorter route via Blackmoor. When you reach the top of the Blackdown hills, turn left to Blagdon Hill. The inn is about two miles on the right.

**Places of interest**

Cothay Manor Gardens (1480) HHA – 4 miles 

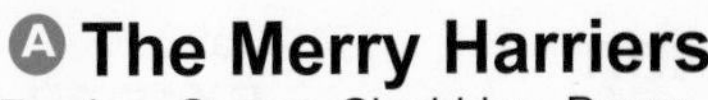

## The Merry Harriers

Satnav
**EX15 3TR**

Forches Corner, Clayhidon, Devon
01823 421 270
www.merryharriers.co.uk
peter.gatling@btinternet.com

**Orders for food:** Tuesday to Saturday: Noon to 2.00pm and 6.30pm to 9.00pm. Sundays: Noon to 3.00pm.

An old coaching inn which stands where highwaymen once held sway. The greeting is much friendlier now with low beams and inglenook fires adding to its character. Fresh fish from Brixham is on the menu and an array of local beers on tap. In summer there is a large shaded garden, with a play area for children. It has been awarded Best Licensee of the Year and in the Top Ten UK Pubs.

Getting there is easy enough, but the return is more difficult with what seems to be a needlessly complicated system of roundabouts.

**Places of interest**

Knightshayes Court (1874) NT – 6 miles 

## A The Globe Inn

Satnav
**EX16 7BJ**

Lower Town, Sampford Peverell, Devon
01884 821 214
www.the-globeinn.co.uk
info@the-globeinn.co.uk

**Orders for food:** Daily: Winters: Noon to 2.30pm and 6.00pm to 9.00pm. Summers: Noon to 9.00pm.

££

A popular locals' pub with a dining area and a long bar as well as six double bedrooms which have been renovated. A smarter dining area has been made at the other end of the bar. A children's playgound and a beer garden at the rear. Dogs are welcome and there are facilities for the disabled. A skittle alley for use on wet days.

## B Old Well Garden Centre

Satnav
**EX15 3ES**

Waterloo Cross, Uffculme, Devon.
01884 840 873
www.theoldwell.co.uk
theoldwellgardencentre@hotmail.co.uk

**Orders for food:** Monday to Saturday: 9.00am to 4.30pm.
Sundays and Bank Holidays: 10.00am to 4.00pm.

£

As the name implies it is a small family owned Garden Centre but there is a coffee shop where the coffee is excellent, the service friendly and an opportunity to buy cakes, scones and pies, all of which are home baked on the premises.

Take the A30 towards Honiton. After 300 yards, turn left onto B3174 and pass Clyst Honiton and Exeter Airport. Keep on this road for about three miles to Jack-in-the Green and the pub will be on the left. They are building a new town alongside the B3174 so it could be slower.

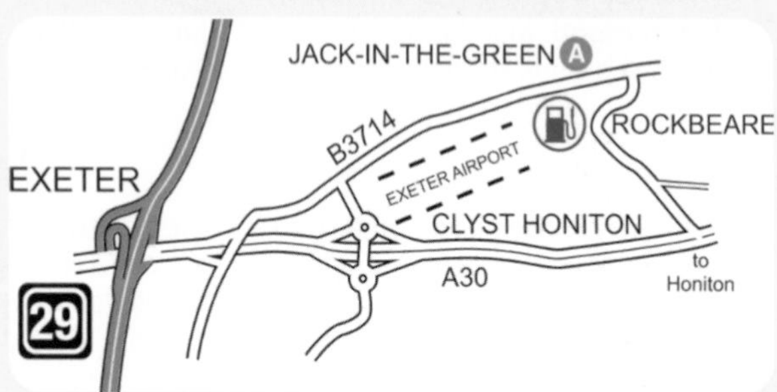


## A Jack in the Green Inn

Satnav
**EX5 2EE**

Main Road, Rockbeare, Devon
01404 822 240
www.jackinthegreen.uk.com
info@jackinthegreen.uk.com

**Orders for food:** Daily: Noon to 2.00pm and 6.00pm to 9.00pm. Sundays: Noon to 9.00pm.

££

A free house which has been there for several centuries. It has been modernised with a lounge bar and a restaurant in the old part. Leather sofas in the sitting areas and outside seating in an enlarged patio for summer days. It is the venue for the local hot air balloon club for those wanting an uplifting experience!

For the Blue Ball – up to the first roundabout and return. Take the first left before the motorway. From the Blue Ball you can continue on the minor road into Topsham. Head for Ebford and the Bridge Inn is on the left before the bridge. For the Digger's Rest go to Clyst St. George – then right on the B3179 towards Woodbury and then take the second left to Woodbury Salterton.

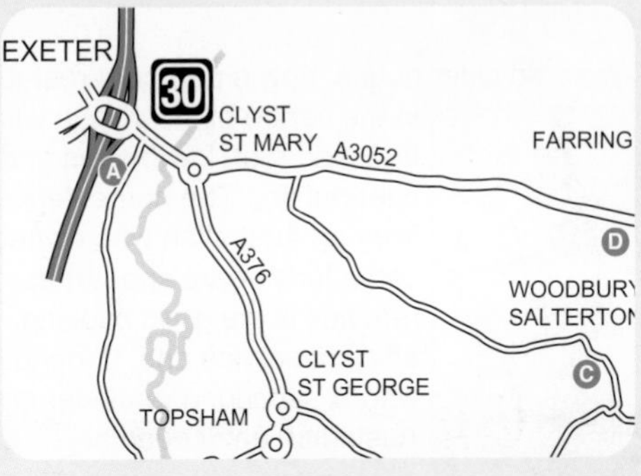


## Ⓐ Blue Ball Inn

Satnav
**EX2 7JL**

Clyst Road, Sandygate, Devon
01392 873 401
www.blueballpub.com
info@blueballpub.com

**Orders for food:** Monday to Thursday: Noon to 2.30pm and 6.00pm to 9.00pm. Friday to Saturday: Noon to 2.30pm and 6.00pm to 9.30pm. Sundays: Noon to 8.00pm.

££

An attractive 18th-century pub-cum-restaurant which has had a makeover. Scrubbed tables, tiled floors, low-beamed ceilings and home cooking give a homely feeling. A carpeted, comfortable dining room has been added. Coffee and teas available. There is a large garden, but dogs are not welcomed.

## B Digger's Rest

Satnav
**EX5 1PQ**

Main Road, Woodbury Salterton, Devon
01395 232 375
www.diggersrest.co.uk
bar@diggersrest.co.uk

**Orders for food:** Daily: Noon to 2.00pm and 6.00pm to 9.00pm.

££

A fifty-year-old cider house, now a pub-cum-restaurant in the centre of the village with a thatched roof, low beams and a cheerful fire. The name derives from an Australian who owned it some forty years ago. What remains is the good cooking, efficient service and, depending on who is serving, a reminder of its Australian antecedents.

## C Greendale Farm Shop

Satnav
**EX5 2JU**

Sidmouth Road, Nr Farringdon, Devon
01395 232 836
www.greendalefarmshop.co.uk
greendalefarmshop@gmail.com

**Orders for food:** Mondays to Saturdays: 8.30am to 5.00pm. Sundays and Bank Holidays: 9.30am to 4.00pm.

Greendale is a family owned farm who sell meat from their farm, vegetables from their fields and fish from their own boats. It also has a range of goodies for those on their way to stay with friends and have forgotten to buy a little something suitable for their stay. There is a small but cosy coffee shop and café to pep you up on your journey.

The Nobody Inn is 4 miles from the A38 and the Exeter Race Course road. Turn left opposite the Haldon Belvedere. The last part is through narrow Devon lanes and avoid the oncoming buses. This could be the lollipop of the M5 towards the end of a long journey. Switch on your Sat Nav to avoid getting lost.

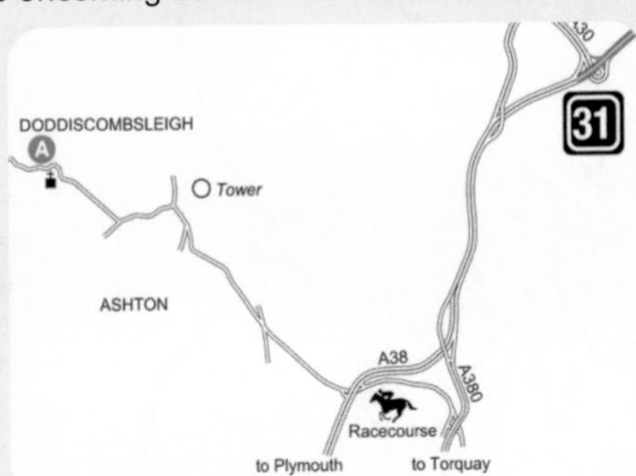


## Ⓐ Nobody Inn

Satnav
**EX6 7PS**

Main Road, Doddiscombsleigh, Devon
01647 252 394
www.nobodyinn.co.uk
info@nobodyinn.co.uk

**Orders for food:** Weekdays: Noon to 2.00pm and 6.30pm to 9.00pm. Fridays and Saturdays: Noon to 2.00pm and 6.30pm to 9.30 pm. Sundays: Noon to 3.00pm and 7.00pm to 9.00pm.

£££

A free house tucked away in deep countryside. It has a large bar for lunches and a restaurant for evening meals with a renowned wine cellar with over 300 wines and whiskies. A good menu and a friendly service. The menu states that there is a wide range of cheeses, most from Devon but some are imported from Cornwall and Somerset.

M6

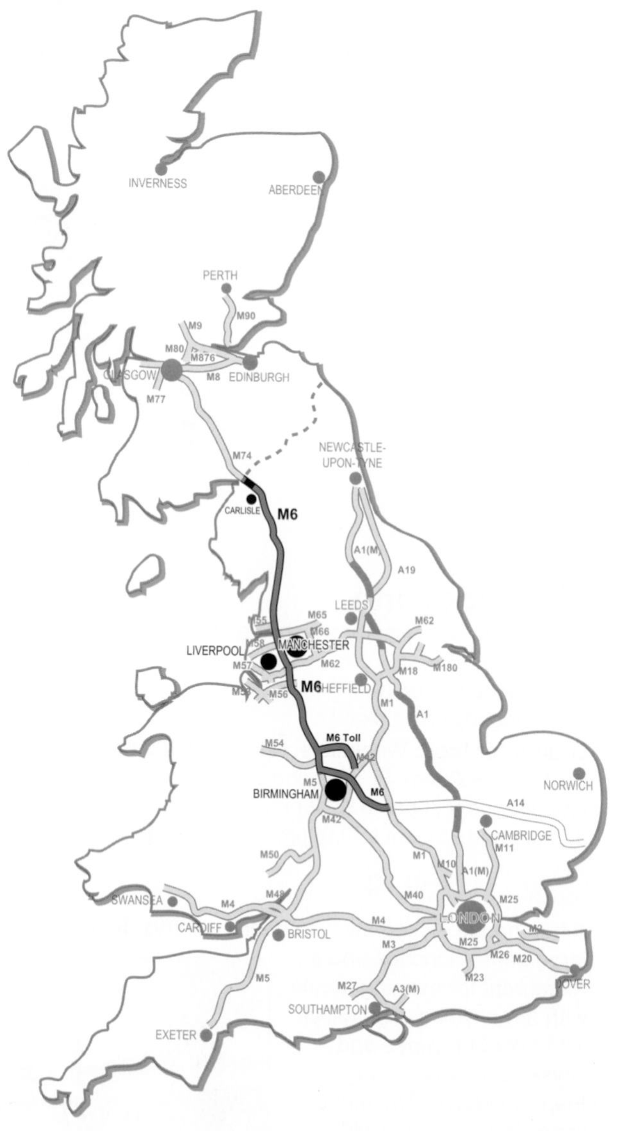
INVERNESS
ABERDEEN
PERTH
M90
M9
M80
M876
GLASGOW
M8
EDINBURGH
M77
M74
NEWCASTLE-UPON-TYNE
CARLISLE
M6
A1(M)
A19
LEEDS
M65
M62
M66
MANCHESTER
LIVERPOOL
M58
M57
M62
M18
M180
M6
M56
SHEFFIELD
M1
A1
M6 Toll
M54
M42
M5
BIRMINGHAM
M6
NORWICH
A14
M42
CAMBRIDGE
M11
M50
M1
M10
A1(M)
SWANSEA
M4
M48
M40
M25
LONDON
CARDIFF
BRISTOL
M4
M3
M25
M26
M20
M23
M5
M27
A3(M)
DOVER
SOUTHAMPTON
EXETER

## JUNCTIONS  TO 

This is the latest addition to the motorway network and was opened in 2004, apparently using pulped old books to strengthen the foundations.

Built by private enterprise under the aegis of the then government, it has certainly improved those endless traffic jams at Spaghetti Junction which added hours to journey times but you must pay for this advantage. You will also have to pay to regain the motorway after having a meal, so I have decided to omit any entries there may be.

# RUGBY TO CARLISLE

## JUNCTIONS  TO 44

The first trial section of a motorway was built as the Preston Bypass in 1958 and then became part of the M6. The M6 is one of the longest motorways, being some 180 miles in length. It was built over a period of years, starting in 1962 and the last stage was finished in 1972. The link over the Scottish Border connecting up with the M74 has been completed to motorway standard.

It is divided into three sections.

# RUGBY TO STAFFORD

## JUNCTIONS  TO 14

This section of the motorway is dull and when combined with the inevitable snarl-up at Spaghetti Junction, it becomes downright tedious. It gets better just south of Stafford. The opening of the new M6(Toll) has improved matters, but I should hurry on as best you can.

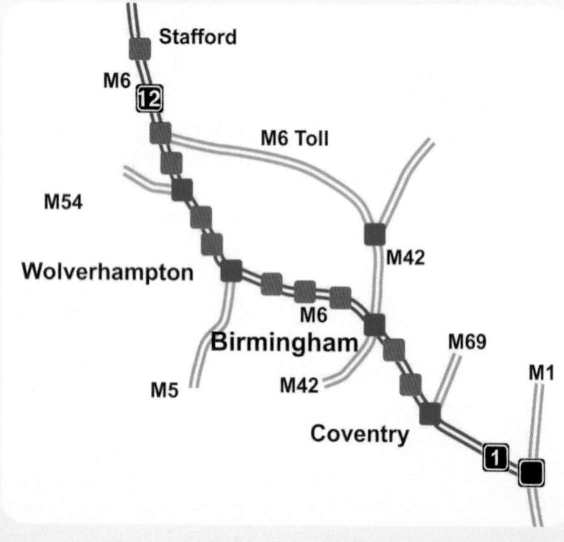

Weston Park is more than 5 miles from the Junction but, as the A5 is the old Roman Watling Street, it is a straight road. Penkridge is to the right at the first roundabout on the A449. The Littleton Arms is on the left as you come into the centre of the town. If you want a quicker stopover, the Dickens of a Tea Shoppe round the corner from the Littleton Arms will give you a freshly made sandwich. Ifdriving from the north come off at Junction 13 which is signed Stafford (S&C) A449.

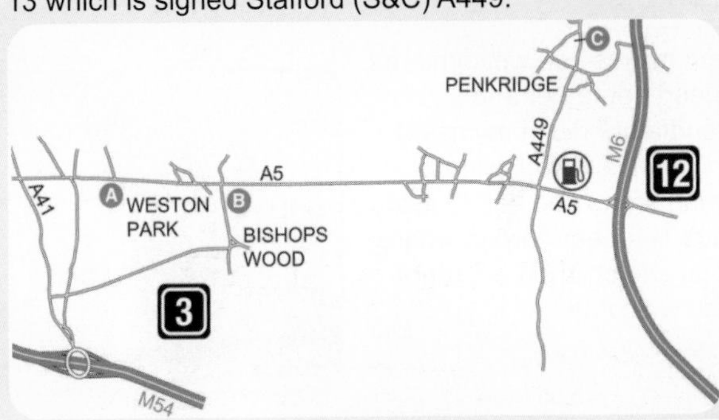


## A Granary Grill Restaurant

Satnav
**TF11 8LE**

Weston Park, Nr Shifnal, Shropshire
01952 852 107
www.weston-park.com
enquiries@weston-park.com

**Orders for food**: Monday and Tuesday: Noon to 2.30pm. Wednesday to Saturday: Noon to 2.30pm and 6.30pm to 9.30pm. Sundays: Noon to 3.30pm.

£££

Something a bit different! It was formed from the granary of Weston Park, a magnificent 17th Century ancestral home that is well worth seeing. The welcome in the Granary (built in 1767) is friendly and efficient. You can see the adjoining art gallery or else stock up in the Farm Shop below. If in more of a hurry the Stables Coffee Bar, which is open from May to September, has snacks and light refreshments.

## B Bell Inn

Satnav **ST19 9LN**

Watling Street, Stretton, Staffs.
01902 850 237
thebellstretton@aol.com

**Orders for food:** Daily: Noon to 2.30pm and 6.30pm to 9.30pm. Sundays: Noon to 2.30pm and 6.30pm to 9.00pm.

££

Sam makes you welcome (as indeed her father and grandfather did in my case). Spacious and well laid-out dining areas and bar. Outside there is a beer garden where dogs and children are more than welcome.

## C The Littleton Arms

Satnav **ST19 5AL**

St Michaels Square, Penkridge, Staffs
01785 716 300
www.thelittletonarms.co.uk
littletonarms@gmail.com

**Orders for food:** Mondays to Fridays: Noon to 2.30pm and 5.00pm to 9.30pm (Fridays 10.00pm). Saturdays: Noon to 10.00pm. Sundays: Noon to 8.00pm.

£££

It started life as the village ale house but was rebuilt in Georgian times as a Coaching Inn. It has since then been updated and is now a cheerful and efficient hostelry. The décor however remains Georgian in that it is not fussy and overdone. It is by the main road so you can watch the world go by if its warm enough to sit outside. Well behaved children welcome and dogs (but not in the dining areas).

# STAFFORD TO PRESTON

## JUNCTIONS 15 TO 32

Stoke-on-Trent is (or was) the home of pottery, most of which is attractive, but the same could not be said for the town itself. Nearby Barlaston Hall was built in 1756 by the architect Sir Robert Taylor for the Wedgwood family as their home and factory. It was shamefully neglected by the firm, until saved at the last moment by SAVE Britain's Heritage in 1978.

The countryside in Cheshire is pleasant enough, but once over the Manchester Ship Canal, the surroundings are crowded with motorways. It is small wonder that the local inhabitants were beginning to complain as more and more of their land was being taken to build yet another motorway.

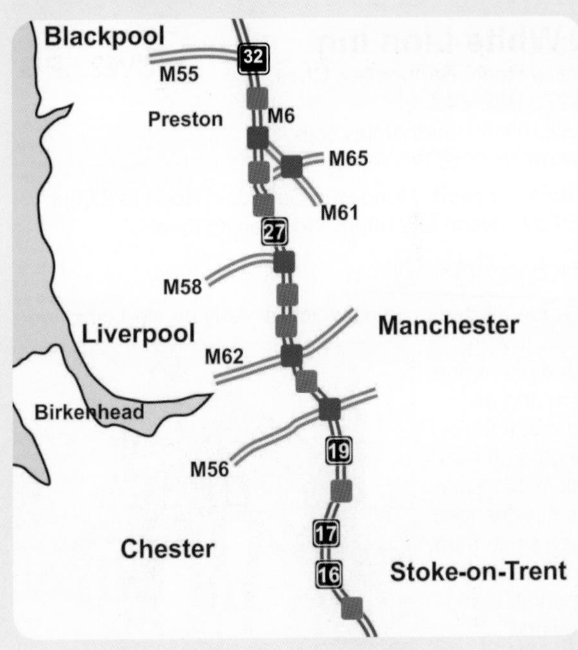

Barthomley is one mile from the junction. Do not take the A500 to Crewe! Follow the signs to Alsager, Barthomley and Radway Green. After ½ mile, Barthomley is signed to the left. The White Lion is to the left of a junction opposite the church. The Hand and Trumpet in Wrinehill will provide an evening meal.

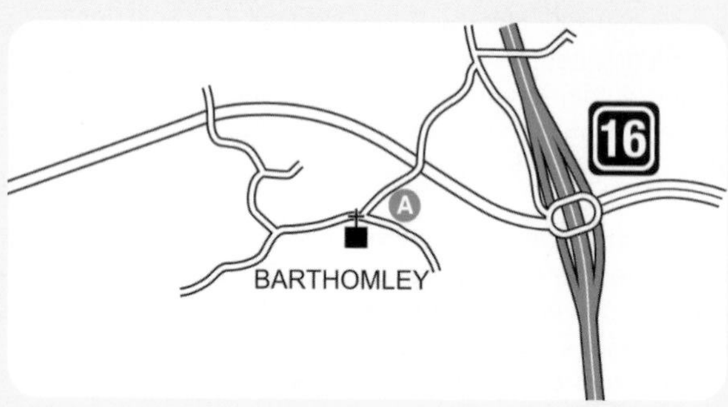


## Ⓐ White Lion Inn

Satnav **CW2 5PG**

Audley Road, Barthomley, Ches.
01270 882 242
www.whitelionbarthomley.com
laurawhitelion@hotmail.co.uk

**Orders for food:** Monday to Saturday: Noon to 2.00pm. Sundays: Noon to 2.30pm. No evening meals.

££

A Grade II listed building which is really an old-fashioned locals' tavern with a bar in one room and an inglenook fire in the other. It was built in 1614 and has not changed much since then. An interesting experience and old-world hospitality.

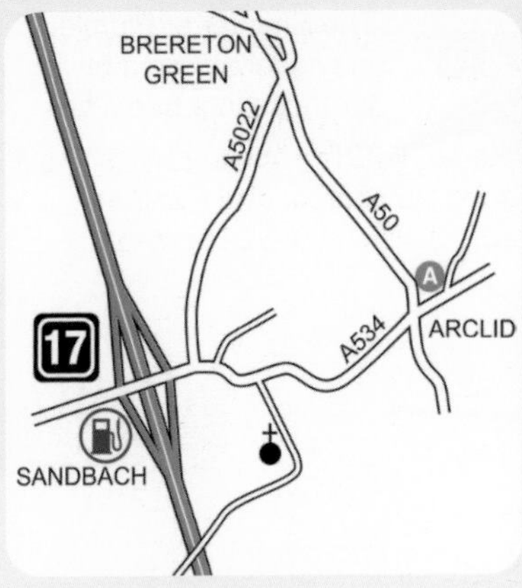


Take the A534 to Congleton. After about a mile there is a cross roads with A50 governed by traffic lights. The Zest is opposite, to the left. If that is full, the Bears Head in Brereton serves as an alternative.

**Places of interest**

Little Moreton Hall (1504-1610) NT – 6 miles 

## Zest Restaurant

Satnav
**CW11 2SN**

Newcastle Road, Arclid, Ches.
01477 500 440
www.visitzest.co.uk
zest.arclid@gmail.com

**Orders for food:** Weekdays: Noon to 2.30pm and 5.00pm to 11.00pm. Saturdays: Noon to midnight. Sundays: Noon to 11.00pm.

££

And now for something to spice up a long car journey. It has had several changes of ownership over the years, but the present owner opened it in April 2011, specialising in a range of Indian, Thai and Chinese food. Clean, spacious and with efficient service, it makes a change from the normal.

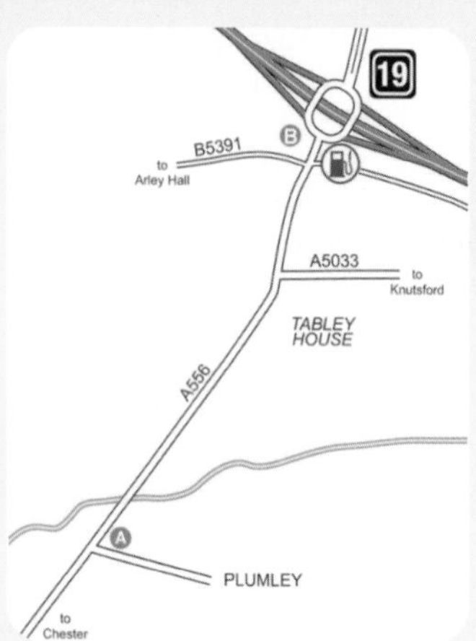


The Smoker at Plumley may seem to be a bit far for those in a hurry, but worth it.

**Places of interest**

Arley Hall & Gardens (19thC) HHA – 5 miles
Tatton Park (18th & 19thC) NT – 3 miles
Tabley House (18thC) University of Manchester – 2 miles

## Ⓐ The Smoker

Satnav **WA16 0TY**

Chester Road, Plumley, Ches.
01565 722 338
www.thesmokerinn.com
info@thesmokerinn.com

**Orders for food:** Monday to Friday: 11.30am to 2.15pm and 6.00pm to 9.15pm. Saturday and Sunday: Noon to 9.00pm.

££

A well-known hostelry which has been modernised into a comfortable restaurant and a bar area with an imaginative menu. For those in a hurry there is a sandwich menu. In addition there is a large garden, open fires and plenty of seating. You will have to ask why it is called The Smoker.

## B The Windmill Inn

Satnav
**WA16 0HW**

Chester Road, Tabley, Knutsford, Cheshire
01565 625 885
windmill@thewindmillattabley.co.uk

**Orders for food:** Monday to Saturday: 8.00am to 10.30am. Noon to 9.00pm. Sunday: 8.00am to 10.30am. 12.30pm to 4.00pm

££

The Windmill has reappeared in the guide as it has been refurbished and the service is efficient. Open-plan seating, facing a long bar. I borrowed a paper to read and the soup was good – though not what I had ordered. A handy stopover, especially for breakfast.

From Junction 27 take the B5250 towards Eccleston. Wrightington Bar is 2.5 miles along this road. The Corner House is at the apex of a fork in the road at the end of the village. On the way The White Lion is on the right.

## Ⓐ The Corner House

Satnav
**WN6 9SE**

9 Wood Lane, Wrightington Bar, Lancs.
01257 451 400
www.cornerhousewrightington.co.uk
info@cornerhousewrightington.co.uk

**Orders for food:** Daily: Noon to 2.30pm and 5.00pm to 9.30pm. Saturday and Sunday: Noon to 9.30pm

££

It has recently been taken over by Ross Lawson who had been the chef when it was called the Mulberry Tree. It has a large open area dining area by the bar but there is a separate restaurant. Traditional British cooking but with a twist. Efficient service and a pleasant change from the motorway. Best to book over a weekend.

## B The White Lion

Satnav **WN6 9RE**

117 Mossy Lea Road, Wrightington, Lancs.
01257 425977
www.thewhitelionlancs.co.uk
info@thewhitelionlancs.co.uk

**Orders for food:** Daily: Noon to 9.00pm
Saturday and Sunday: 10.00am to 9.00pm.

££

A Marstons owned pub with a friendly welcome from Matt and Ellie Furzeman. It is the centre of activity, especially after 5.00pm when the locals are returning from work. It is justly renowned for having eight real ales on offer in keeping with its tradition as an Ale House. A beer garden at the rear for warm summer evenings.

Come off at the motorway interchange. From Junction 1 on the M55, drive into Broughton. At the traffic lights turn right to Longridge on the B5269. The Italian Orchard is brown-signed on the right just before you go under the motorway.

## Ⓐ Italian Orchard

Satnav
**PR3 5DB**

96 Whittingham Lane, Broughton, Lancs.
01772 861 240
www.italianorchard.com
info@italianorchard.com

**Orders for food:** Monday to Saturday: Noon to 2.00pm and 6.00pm to 10.30pm. Sundays: Noon to 10.00pm.

££

A modern open-plan restaurant, partly under a double-height timber roof and a cosy bar area. Comfortably furnished with linen tablecloths and napkins. It is reasonably priced and a two course lunch without wine could be £11 per head. Extensive grounds with a long drive.

# PRESTON TO CARLISLE

## JUNCTIONS 33 TO 45

This section is the most scenic of any of the motorways in the UK. After Lancaster, which is an interesting county town, the motorway climbs up past Kendal with views of the Lake District to the west and the Pennines to the east. Once over Shap, the highest point of the motorway, it descends past Penrith, which is a picturesque market town to the south of Carlisle. From there the motorway crosses over the River Esk into Scotland.

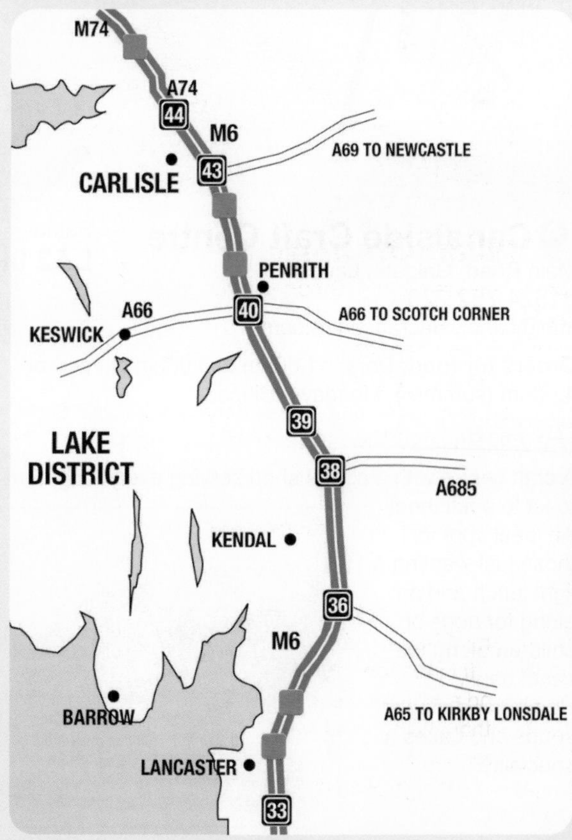

The Canalside Craft Centre is on the left when you come into Galgate.

For the Bay Horse turn left at the roundabout on the A6 towards Garstang. After 400 yards bear left, where it is brown-signed to the Bay Horse for a mile. Coming from the south at Potters Brook bear right as signed.

## Ⓐ Canalside Craft Centre

Satnav
**LA2 0LQ**

Main Road, Galgate, Lancs.
01524 752 223
info@canalsidecraftcentre.com

**Orders for food:** Daily: 11.00am to 3.00pm (winter) or 4.00pm (summer). Mondays: Closed.

£

A craft centre with a coffee shop serving everything from toast to a full meal. An ideal spot for those just wanting a light lunch and an airing for dogs or children along the canal bank. Homemade meals, soups and cakes a speciality.

## B The Bay Horse Inn

Satnav
**LA2 0HR**

Bay Horse Lane, Forton, Lancs.
01524 791 204
www.bayhorseinn.com

**Orders for food:** Tuesday to Saturday: Noon to 2.00pm and 6.30pm to 9.00pm. Sundays: Noon to 3.00pm. Closed on Mondays.

It is a secluded 18th-century pub-cum-restaurant down a quiet country lane. It has a well-deserved reputation for food and a friendly ambiance with a cheerful bar, log fires and a separate dining room.

££

A boring junction with dual carriageways on either side. Look out for the Crooklands Hotel signs.

**Places of interest**

Levens Hall (16thC) Gardens (1614) HHA – 4 miles 

Sizergh Castle (14th & 16thC) NT – 5 miles

## Ⓐ Crooklands Hotel

Satnav **LA7 7NW**

Crooklands, Lancs.
01539 567 432
www.crooklands.com
reception@crooklands.com

**Orders for food:** Daily: Noon to 2.00pm and 6.00pm to 9.00pm.

££/£££

A comfortable privately owned hotel with 30 double rooms in a new extension. It has a restaurant as well as a carvery and bars also serving meals. Morning coffee for the passing motorist. Children, but no dogs.

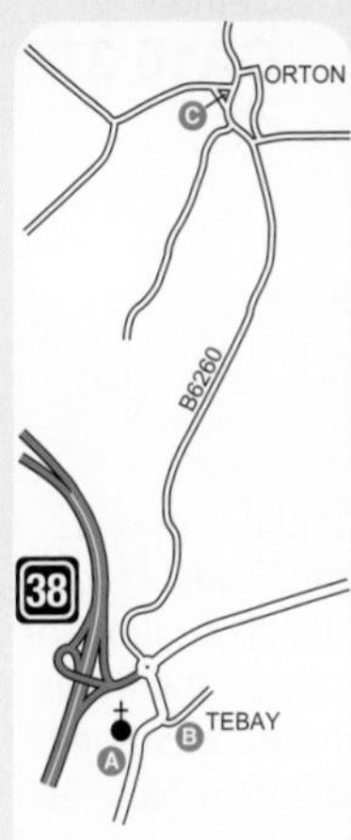


Dual carriageways lead off the motorway on to a roundabout. Take the A685 towards Kendal for The Cross Keys and the Old Barn Tearoom. For Kennedys Chocolates take the B6260 to Orton and Kennedys will be on the left of the road.

**Places of interest**

The Roman fort and road at Low Borrowbridge. (If you can get to them!)

## A The Cross Keys Inn

Satnav
**CA10 3UY**

Tebay, Penrith, Cumbria
01539 624 240
www.crosskeystebay.co.uk
reservations@crosskeystebay.co.uk

**Orders for food:** Monday to Friday: Noon to 3.00pm. 5.00pm to 9.00pm. Saturday and Sunday: Noon to 9.00pm

This was in previous editions, but then changed hands. It is now owned by Enterprise Inns and has become yet again a friendly and well run place with a restaurant, as well as bar meals being available. There is a garden behind for warm days. A good atmosphere and a cheerful welcome by Tony Gerrard.

## B The Old School

Satnav
**CA10 3TP**

Kendal Road, Tebay, Cumbria
01539 624286
www.oldschooltebay.co.uk
dunkinsste@aol.com
**Orders for food:** Daily: 10.30am to 5.00pm.
In Winter: Closed Mondays and Tuesdays.

The Old School is now a Tearoom and Guest House. There is outside seating for warmer weather and offers a choice of predominantly homemade light meals, as well as teas. It is family run and Joanne and Steve will make your journey more comfortable.

## C Kennedys Fine Chocolates

Satnav
**CA10 3RU**

The Old School, Orton, Cumbria
01539 624781
www.kennedys-chocolates.co.uk
kennedys.chocolates@btinternet.com
**Orders for food:** Monday to Saturday 9.00am to 4.30pm
Sundays: 11.00am to 4.30pm

Another old School house, but this one is now Kennedys Chocolate Factory. The chocolates are all hand-made on the premises, with over 80 different varieties of fillings, and make an ideal present should you be on your way to stay with friends. It also has a café for light refreshments, as well as teas.

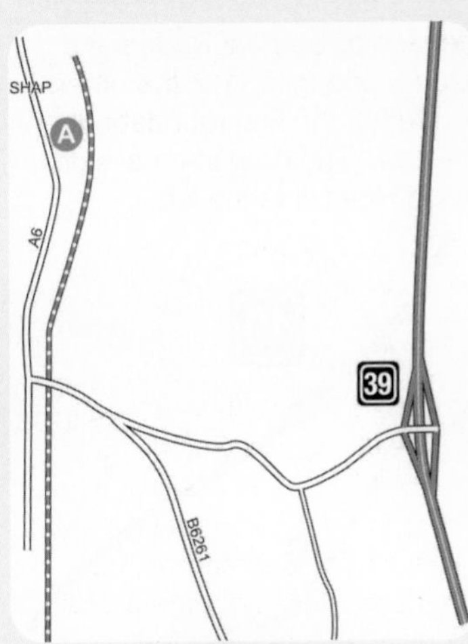


An easy junction. Picnics on a fine day.

**Places of interest**
Shap Abbey EH – 3 miles

## Ⓐ The Greyhound Hotel

Satnav
**CA10 3PW**

Main Street, Shap, Cumbria
01931 716 474
www.greyhoundshap.co.uk
info@greyhoundshap.co.uk

**Orders for food:** Daily: Noon to 2.00pm and 6.00pm to 9.00pm. Sundays: Noon to 2.30pm and 6.00pm to 9.00pm.

££

Apparently Bonnie Prince Charlie spent a night on his way south in 1745. It has been taken over by the previous lessee of the Cross Keys in Tebay. It serves good local lamb and fresh fish. For those spending the night beware of the main railway just behind.

For the Gate Inn take the road to Eamont Bridge and turn right on the Tirril road for one mile. For the others take the A66 to Keswick. Left at the first roundabout on the A592 and right to Stainton. The King's Arms is on the right and the Brantwood Hotel is to the left.

**Places of interest**

Dalemain (15thC and 19thC) – 3 miles 
The Toffee Shop, Penrith – 1 mile

## 

## Ⓐ The Gate Inn

Satnav
**CA10 2LF**

Old Road, Yanwath, Cumbria
01768 862 386
www.yanwathgate.com
enquiries@yanwathgate.com

**Orders for food:** Daily: Noon to 2.30pm and 6.00pm to 9.00pm.

££

A privately owned pub-cum-restaurant dating from 1683, which was originally a toll gate, in a quiet secluded lane with whitewashed exposed stone walls. It has a dining room and bar, as well as outside seating. It has been awarded the Cumbrian Dining Pub of the Year for the past five years.

## Ⓑ Kings Arms

Satnav **CA11 0EP**

The Green, Stainton, Cumbria
01768 862 778

www.kingsarmspub.com
info@kingsarmspub.com

**Orders for food**: Mondays to Fridays: Noon to 2.00pm and 6.00pm to 9.00pm. Saturdays and Sundays: Noon to 9.00pm.

££

A family run 18th-century rural pub provide an extensive menu of homemade and vegetarian dishes. Friendly welcome and you get what you see. Outside seating on hot days.

## Ⓒ Brantwood Country Hotel

Satnav **CA11 0EP**

Main Street, Stainton, Cumbria
01768 862 748
www.brantwoodhotel.co.uk
enquries@brantwoodhotel.co.uk

**Orders for food:** Daily: Noon to 2.15pm and 6.00pm to 8.45pm.

£££

A family-owned hotel and restaurant with a large garden. A comfortably furnished house with oak beams and log fires and a friendly welcome.

For the Crown Hotel take either road to Wetheral, which is 2 miles from the junction. Follow signs to the station.

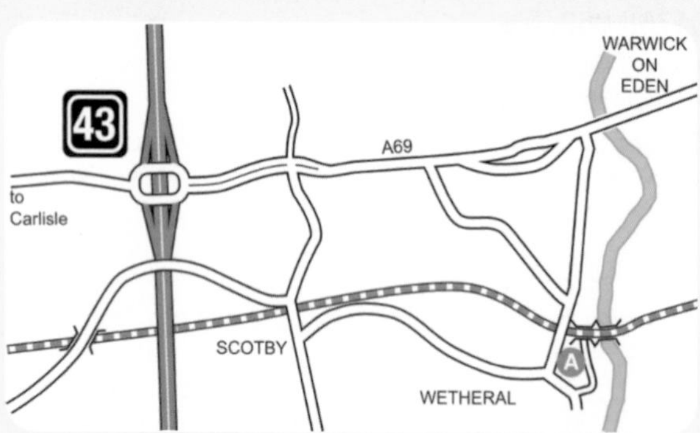


**Places of interest**

Carlisle Castle and Cathedral – 3 miles

## Ⓐ Crown Hotel

Satnav
**CA4 8ES**

Station Road, Wetheral, Cumbria
01228 561 888
www.crownhotelwetheral.co.uk
info@crownhotelwetheral.co.uk

**Orders for food:** Daily: Noon to 2.00pm and 6.00pm to 9.00pm.

££/£££

The Crown Hotel dates back to the old coaching days and is now a modern and efficient country hotel. Waltons Bar is an ideal place for a quick meal with a friendly welcome. A large garden for fresh air and an indoor swimming pool.

From the Junction take the A689 towards Brampton. Bear left at the first roundabout. After about 2 miles turn right where signed Low Crosby. The Stag Inn will be on the left in the village.

**Places of interest** Hadrian's Turf Wall.

## Ⓐ Stag Inn

Satnav
**CA6 6QN**

Main Street, Low Crosby, Cumbria
01228 573 210
www.greyhoundshap.co.uk
info@greyhoundshap.co.uk

**Orders for food:** Monday to Friday: Noon to 2.00pm and 7.00pm to 9.00pm. Saturday and Sunday: Noon to 9.00pm

A tenanted pub of Jennings, it has been an Ale House for the past two hundred years. The low ceilings and small rooms give a feeling of timelessness. The locally grown food is cooked in a traditional manner.

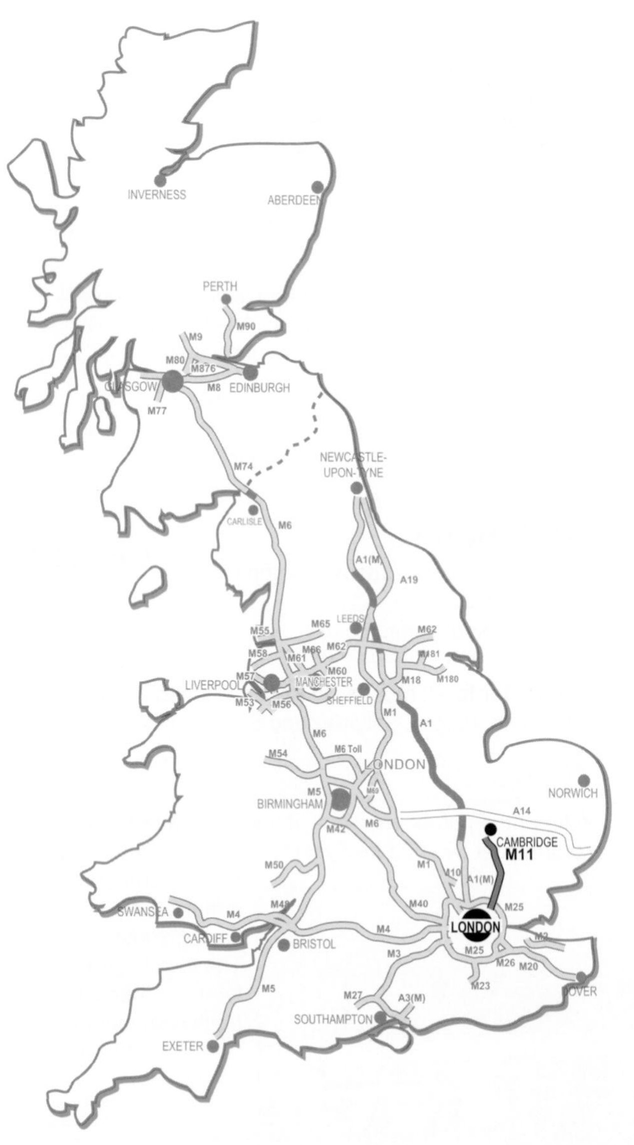
INVERNESS
ABERDEEN
PERTH
M90
M9
M80
M876
GLASGOW
M8
EDINBURGH
M77
NEWCASTLE-UPON-TYNE
M74
CARLISLE
M6
A1(M)
A19
LEEDS
M65
M55
M62
M58
M61
M66
M62
M181
M57
M60
LIVERPOOL
MANCHESTER
M18
M180
M53
M56
SHEFFIELD
M1
A1
M6
M54
M6 Toll
LONDON
M5
BIRMINGHAM
M69
NORWICH
A14
M42
M6
CAMBRIDGE
M11
M50
M1
M10
A1(M)
M48
M40
M25
SWANSEA
M4
LONDON
CARDIFF
M4
BRISTOL
M3
M25
M26
M20
M23
M5
M27
A3(M)
DOVER
SOUTHAMPTON
EXETER

# JUNCTIONS  TO 14

For those travelling to or from the Channel Tunnel it is a good alternative to the M1 as it links the M25 with the A1(M) at Huntingdon.

The southern section goes past the town of Harlow and the congestion around Stansted Airport. Once north of them, the countryside is pleasant enough and passes some attractive towns such as Saffron Walden and the imposing house of Audley End. At Duxford is the Imperial War Museum and the American Air Museum. Cambridge of course is a must for anyone who has never been there.

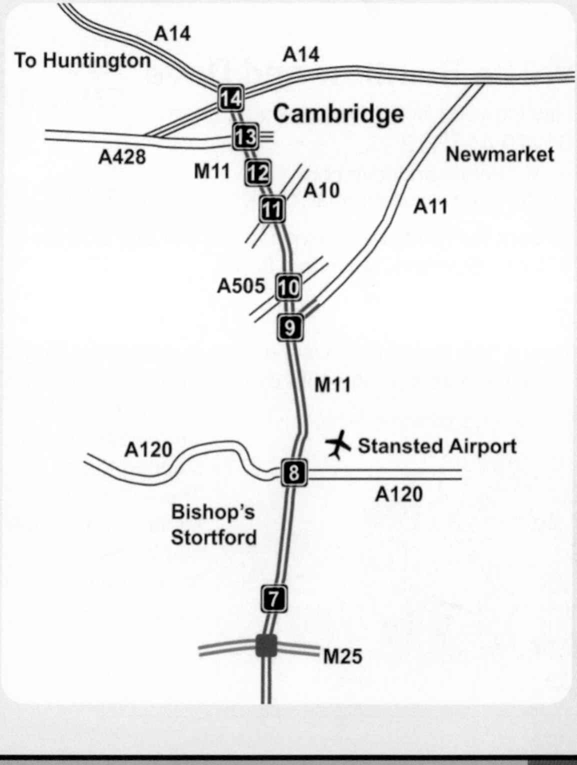

A14
To Huntington
A14
14
Cambridge
13
A428
M11
12
A10
Newmarket
11
A11
A505
10
9
M11
A120
Stansted Airport
8
A120
Bishop's
Stortford
7
M25

The roundabout is controlled by lights. Take the Chelmsford road and almost immediately turn off to the left on a small road which is marked St. Clare Hospice and Hastingwood.

## Ⓐ The Rainbow and Dove

Satnav **CM17 9JX**

Hastingwood Road, Hastingwood, Essex
01279 415 419
www.rainbowanddove.com
rainbowanddove@hotmail.co.uk

**Orders for food:** Daily: Noon to 2.30pm and 6.30pm to 9.00pm. Sundays: Noon to 4.00pm.

£

Now a free house which is a rural pub-cum-restaurant. It is said to date from the 15th century and was certainly a pub in 1645, when Cromwell's soldiers stopped there. There is outside seating in a garden and inside a roaring fire during the winter.

Construction work has been completed to cope with the increasing traffic to and from Stansted Airport. Keep going around the roundabout until you see the small turnoff for Birchanger.

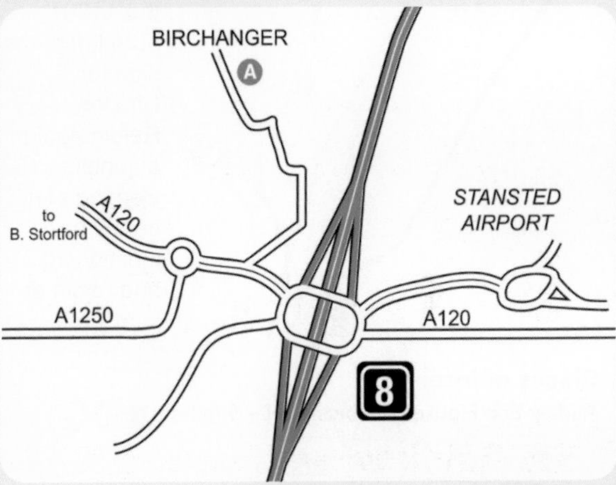


## Ⓐ The Three Willows

Satnav
**CM23 5QR**

Birchanger Lane, Birchanger, Herts.
01279 815 913
www.thompsonstiling.co.uk
thompsonstiling@gmail.com

**Orders for food:** Daily: Noon to 2.00pm and 6.00pm to 9.00pm. Sundays: Noon to 2.00pm.

££

A popular restaurant-cum-pub, with a strong cricket influence judging by the inn sign outside, and indoors as part has been designated The Oval. It specialises in fish and there are also bar meals. There is a children's playground, where they are meant to stay.

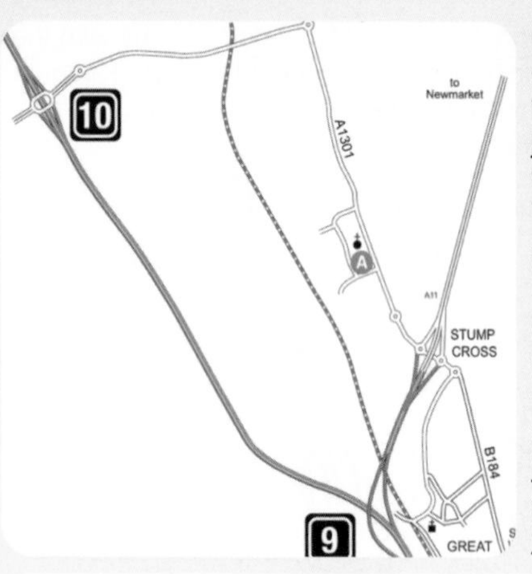


For those going North turn left at the junction with the A1301. Turn left at the sign for Hinxton. Rejoin again at junction 10. Coming south get off at junction 10 and rejoin at junction 9.

**Places of interest**

Audley End House (Jacobean) EH – 5 miles 

## Ⓐ The Red Lion

Satnav **CB10 1QY**

High Street, Hinxton, Cambs.
01799 530 601
www.redlionhinxton.co.uk
info@redlionhinxton.co.uk

**Orders for food:** Monday to Thursday: Noon to 2.00pm and 6.30pm to 9.00pm. Fridays: Noon to 2.30pm and 6.30pm to 9.30pm. Saturdays: Noon to 2.30pm and 6.30pm to 9.30pm. Sundays: Noon to 3.00pm and 6.30pm to 9.30pm.

££

A 16th-century pub in this attractive village. A well-deserved reputation for home cooking in the restaurant and bar. Friendly atmosphere and a warm welcome. There are eight guestrooms set apart.

Take the A505 towards Royston. A mile after the Imperial War Museum, turn right to Thriplow, which is an attractive village. Left at the T-Junction by the village shop.

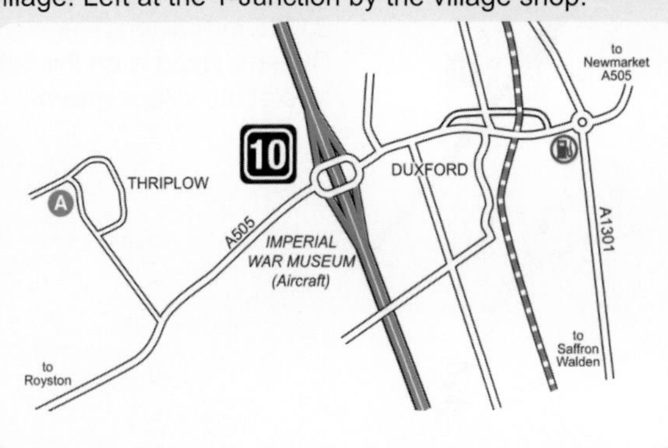


**Places of interest**

The Imperial War Museum and American Air Museum.

## Ⓐ The Green Man

Satnav **SG8 7RJ**

Lower Street, Thriplow, Herts.
01763 208 855
www.greenmanthriplow.co.uk
manager@greenmanthriplow.co.uk

**Orders for food:** Tuesday to Saturday: Noon to 2.00pm and 7.00pm to 9.00pm. Sundays: Noon to 2.00pm. Mondays: Closed.

£

Literally a locals' pub as it has just been bought out by the village. The exterior has been painted blue, to make a change from green perhaps? The interior has scrubbed floors, wooden tables and leather chairs. An impressive array of Veuve Clicquot bottles (empty) line the high shelves in both rooms.

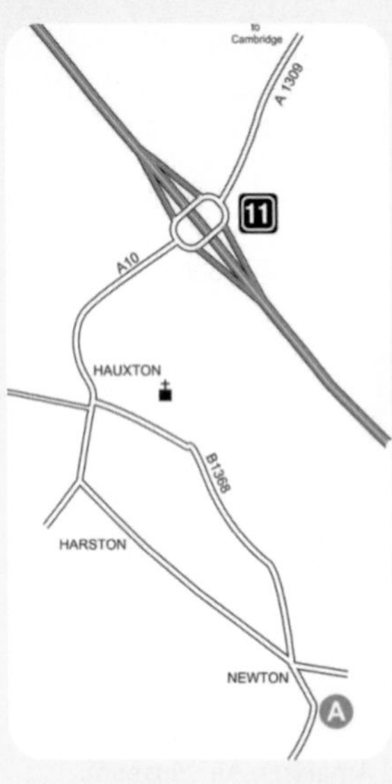


From the junction take the A10 to Royston. After about half a mile turn left onto the B1368 to Newton. The Queen's Head is on the left side of the village green.

## Ⓐ Queen's Head

Satnav
**CB22 7PG**

Fowlmere Road, Newton, Cambs.
01223 870 436

**Orders for food:** Monday to Saturday: Noon to 2.15pm and 7.00pm to 9.30pm. Sundays: Noon to 2.15pm and 7.00pm to 9.30pm.

££

A pleasant and friendly hostelry which has been in the same family ownership for 50 years. It has well-furnished dining alcoves and bars and a host of interesting mementos. Good food and a warm welcome – what more could you need?

The picturesque village of Grantchester was made famous by the First World War poet, Rupert Brooke, "… Is there honey still for tea?"

**Places of interest**
Wimpole Hall (18thC Style) NT – 6 miles 

## Ⓐ The Rupert Brooke

Satnav
**CB3 9NQ**

Broadway, Grantchester, Cambs.
01223 840 295
www.therupertbrooke.com
info@therupertbrooke.com

**Orders for food:** Tuesday to Saturday: Noon to 3.00pm and 6.00pm to 9.30pm. Sundays: Noon to 4.00pm. Closed Mondays.

Converted from a 19th-century house into a privately owned restaurant with bar areas, which has changed hands. A garden at the rear, overlooking the meadows.

## B The Green Man

Satnav **CB3 9NF**

High Street, Grantchester, Cambs.
01223 844 669
www.thegreenmangrantchester.co.uk
shaun@thegreenmangrantchester.co.uk

**Orders for food:** Mondays to Fridays: Noon to 2.30pm and 6.00pm to 9.00pm. Saturday and Sunday: Noon to 10.00pm.

A traditional pub in the centre of the village since 1510, which has been renovated with wooden floors and a bar. A garden at the rear and fires in the winter. It has changed hands.

## C The Orchard

Satnav **CB3 9ND**

Mill Way, Grantchester, Cambs.
01223 845 788
www.orchard-grantchester.com
otg@callan.co.uk

**Orders for food:** Daily: Lunches 11.am to 3.00pm. 9.30am to 5.00pm (Summer).

££

An old fashioned tea room complete with 1920s deckchairs, punts and nostalgia. You almost expect to see previous visitors such as Rupert Brooke, or John Betjeman appear from behind an apple tree. Light lunches available as well as traditional teas in and out of doors depending on the weather.

Junction 13 is easy for those coming from the south, rejoin at junction 14. For those coming from the north, get off at junction 14, but it will require a degree of map reading. However, it is well worth the effort to get to Madingley.

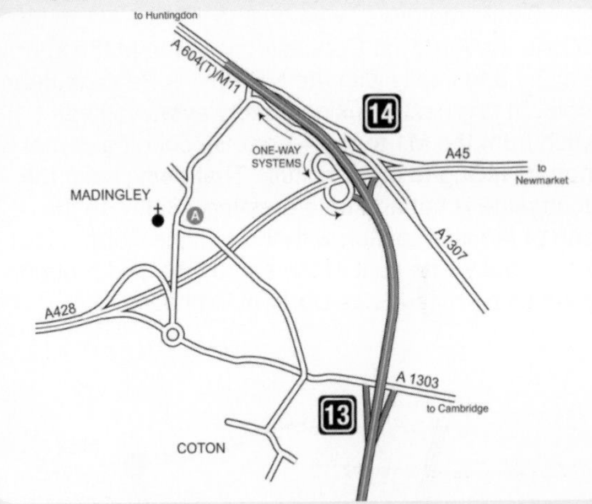


## Ⓐ The Three Horseshoes

Satnav
**CB3 8AB**

High Street, Madingley, Cambs.
01954 210 221
www.threehorseshoesmadingley.co.uk
3hs@btconnect.com

**Orders for food:** Monday to Friday: Noon to 2.00pm and 6.30pm to 9.30pm. Saturdays: Noon to 2.30pm and 6.30pm to 9.30pm. Sundays: Noon to 2.30pm and 6.30pm to 8.30pm.

£££

A privately owned pub-cum-restaurnat, which is efficient and well run. There is a restaurant and a long bar with a conservatory at the rear. It is surrounded by a pleasant garden.

# ROTHERHAM TO GOOLE

## JUNCTIONS  TO 7

This 30 mile motorway was built to link the M1 to the M62 via the A1(M) at Doncaster, with the M180 spur to Grimsby and finally with the M62 Trans Pennine near Goole. It is a useful linking motorway as you can switch from the M1 to the A1 or else cut off a corner when travelling to or from Hull. That being said, the countryside is flat and uninteresting. Selby, to the north of the intersection with the M62, is worth a visit, as the abbey was built at the same time and probably by the same masons as Durham Cathedral.

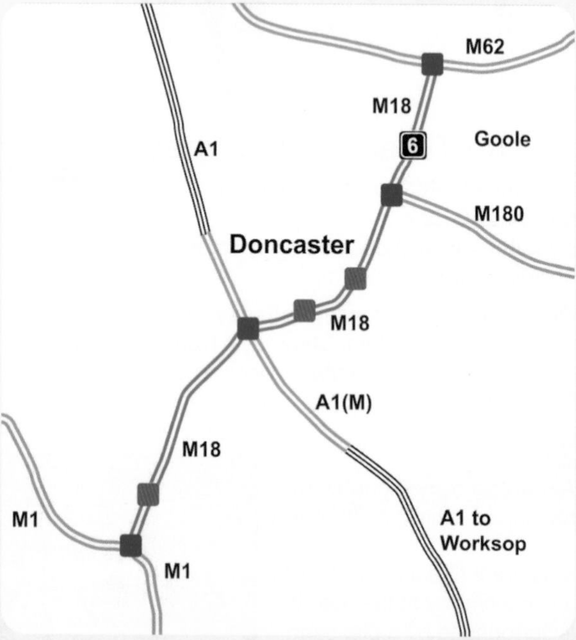

M62
M18
6
Goole
A1
M180
Doncaster
M18
A1(M)
M18
A1 to Worksop
M1
M1

This is an area of low fen land and irrigation ditches.

Waterside, where canal boats once disgorged their cargoes, was renowned for having seven pubs, but only one now remains. It is said that an Elizabethan warship was built here to harrass the Armada.

**Places of interest**

The birthplace of Thomas Crapper, the manufacturer of flushing lavatories

## Ⓐ The John Bull Inn

Satnav
**DN8 4JQ**

Waterside, Thorne, Doncaster
01405 814 677
www.the-john-bull-inn.co.uk
enquries@the-john-bull-inn.co.uk

**Orders for food:** Monday to Saturday: Noon to 8.00pm. Sundays: Noon to 4.00pm.

£

A traditional inn by the canal, where ale has been served to thirsty bargemen since the 1500s. Good real ale is still served and the food is locally sourced and home-cooked and is good value for money.

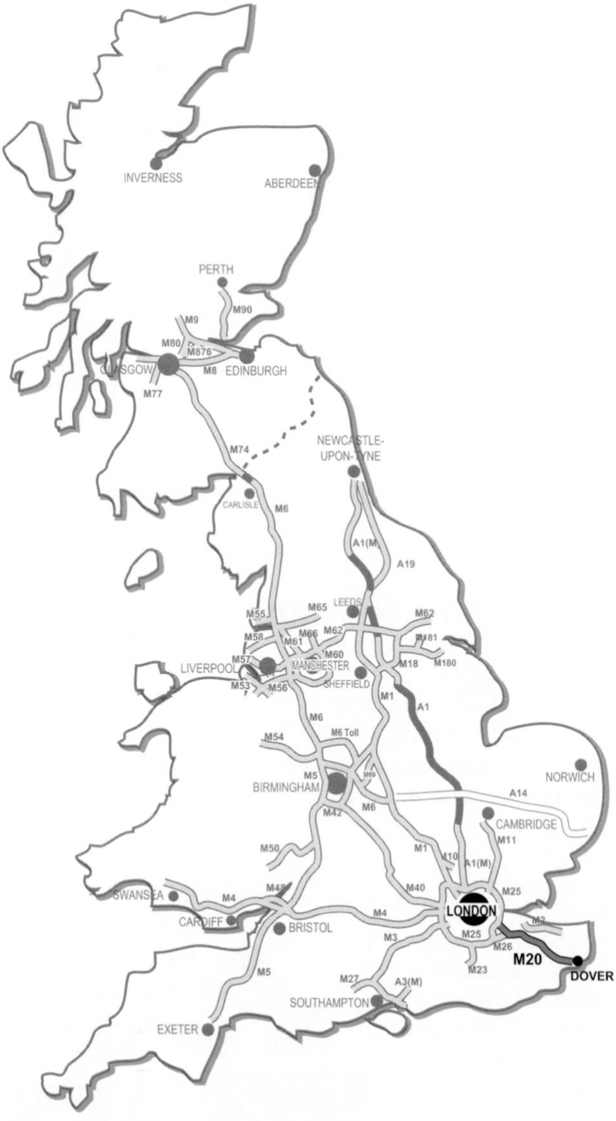

INVERNESS
ABERDEEN
PERTH
M90
M9
M80
M876
GLASGOW
M8
EDINBURGH
M77
NEWCASTLE-UPON-TYNE
M74
CARLISLE
M6
A1(M)
A19
M65
LEEDS
M55
M62
M58
M66
M61
M181
M57
M60
LIVERPOOL
MANCHESTER
M18
M180
M53
M56
SHEFFIELD
M1
A1
M54
M6 Toll
NORWICH
M5
M69
BIRMINGHAM
A14
M42
M6
CAMBRIDGE
M11
M50
M1
M10
A1(M)
M48
M40
M25
SWANSEA
M4
LONDON
CARDIFF
BRISTOL
M4
M2
M3
M25
M26
M20
M23
DOVER
M5
M27
A3(M)
SOUTHAMPTON
EXETER

## JUNCTIONS 1 TO 13

The M20, which is 40 miles long, was started in 1961 and finished twenty years later. It is the main motorway from the Channel Ports to link up directly with the M25 and the entire motorway system.

It goes through some very attractive scenery which is known as the Garden of England. There are proposals to submerge the area with new houses, so enjoy it whilst you can.

After Maidstone, with its orchards and oast houses, the M20 climbs the shoulder of the North Weald on its way to London, whilst the M26 spur continues and links up with the southern segment of the M25.

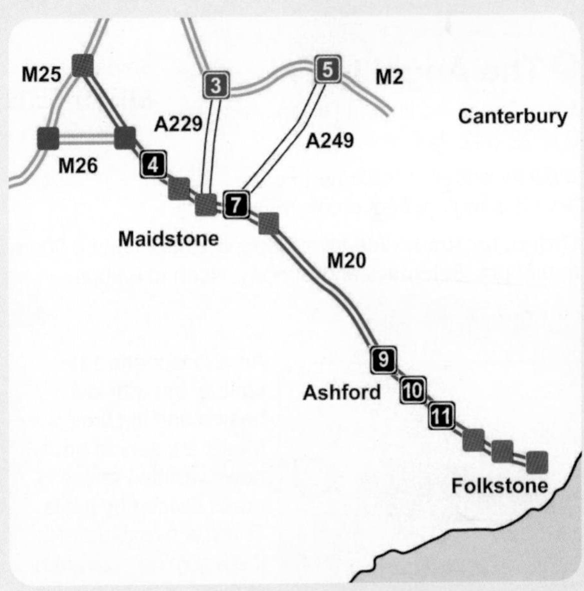

It seems a long way from the junction, but worth the journey.

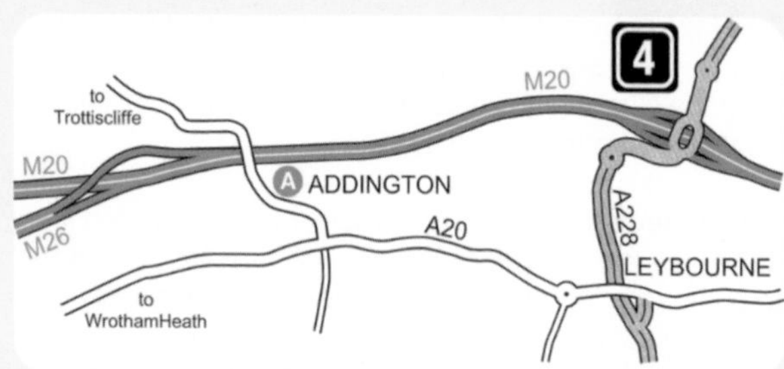


## Ⓐ The Angel Inn

Satnav
**ME19 5BB**

Main Street, Addington Green, Kent
01732 842 117

www.theangelinnaddington.co.uk
angeladdington@aol.co.uk

**Orders for food:** Weedays: Noon to 2.30pm and 6.00pm to 9.30pm. Saturdays and Sunday: Noon to 9.30pm.

An atmospheric 14th-century inn with low beams and log fires. Meals are served on hewn wooden tables in areas divided by posts. There is a restaurant in the adjoining converted stables. A large garden, and meals can be taken under a pergola.

This junction is close to Maidstone and therefore it is a more built up area. The Eurostar railtrack makes it more confusing.

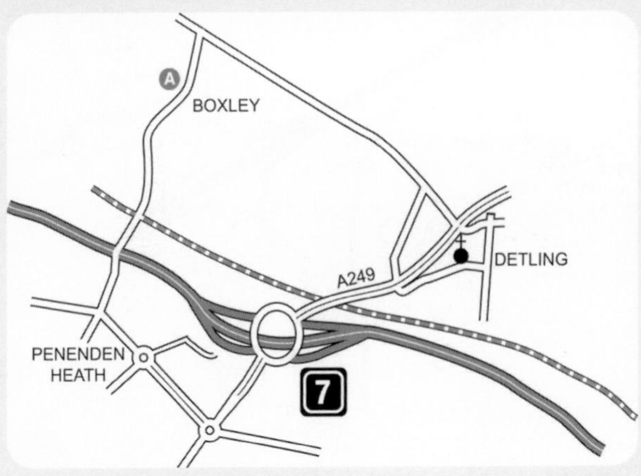


## A Kings Arms

Satnav
**ME14 3DR**

The Street, Boxley, Kent
01622 755 177
aspreylandlp@yahoo.co.uk

**Orders for food:** Daily: Noon to 2.30pm and 6.00pm to 9.00pm. Sundays: Noon to 4.00pm.

££

A traditional, family-run village pub with a cheerful atmosphere, beams and log fires. A separate dining room as well as a bar serving bar meals. A car park opposite and a large garden at the rear with a heated patio. Well behaved dogs and children welcomed. Under new management.

Not quite as easy as it looks but persevere with the roundabouts. Just before the dual carriageway becomes a single road, the Hare and Hounds will be on the right.

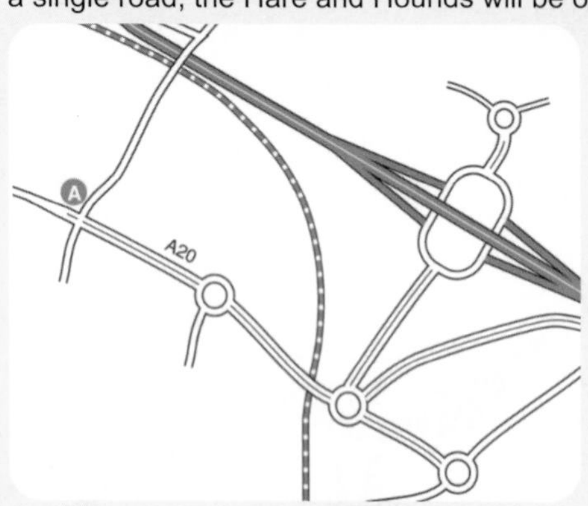


## A Hare and Hounds

Satnav **TN25 4NR**

Maidstone Road, Ashford, Kent
01233 621 760
www.thehareandhoundsashford.com
hare.andhounds@live.co.uk

**Orders for food:** Mondays to Fridays: Noon to 3.00pm and 5.30pm to 9.00pm. Saturdays: Noon to 9.00pm. Sundays: Noon to 4.00pm

££

Once an 18th century wayside inn it has been brought up to date and has a friendly welcome and a cheerful atmosphere. There is a menu of home cooked food together with a range of wines and beers. There is outside seating at the front if you want to see who is who but the beer garden at the back offers quiet seclusion where dogs are welcome.

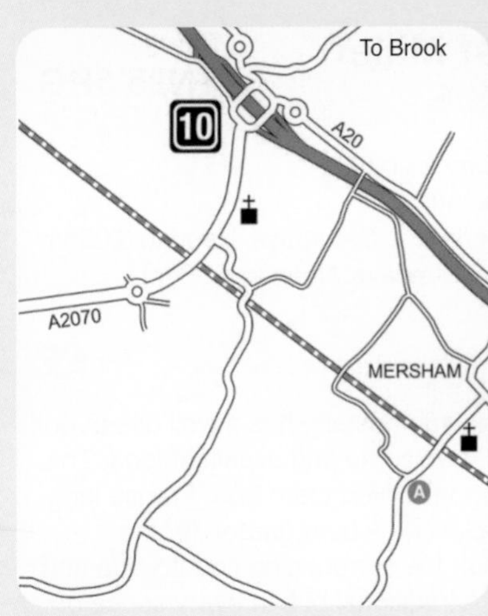


At the junction, turn north and join the A20 to Folkestone. After a mile, turn right to Mersham. Go through the village and turn right over a bridge and the Farrier's Arms will be on the left. For the Honest Miller take twisty road to Brook and Hastingleigh.

## A Farrier's Arms

Satnav
**TN25 6NU**

The Forstal, Mersham, Kent
01233 720 444
www.thefarriersarms.com
info@thefarriersarms.com

**Orders for food:** Daily: Noon to 2.30pm and 6.00pm to 9.30pm. Sundays: Noon to 3.00pm, no evening meals

££

It has been there from 1606 onwards and has survived happily until recently when it had to be saved by the villagers clubbing together to buy it. It is therefore truly a locals' pub. It is also a friendly place with low beams, outdoor seating in a large garden at the back and a good atmosphere. A tribute to communal enterprise.

## Ⓑ The Honest Miller

Satnav
**TN25 5PG**

The Street, Brook, Kent.
01233 812 303
www.thehonestmillerbrook.co.uk
gslthompson@yahoo.com

**Orders for food:** Tuesdays to Saturdays: Noon to 3,00pm and 6.00pm to 9.00pm. Sundays: Noon to 4.00pm. Mondays: Closed.

££

Built in 1609, this family run hostelry has a well deserved reputation for a friendly welcome and excellent food. This was proved when my son arrived there from France long after the kitchen was closed! A beer garden for the summer with views over the surrounding countryside and log fires in the winter. A traditional pub in every sense of the word especially for those coming from abroad.

The Eurostar track now runs alongside the motorway. Circle round to the north on the B2068 and then left to Stanford (North).

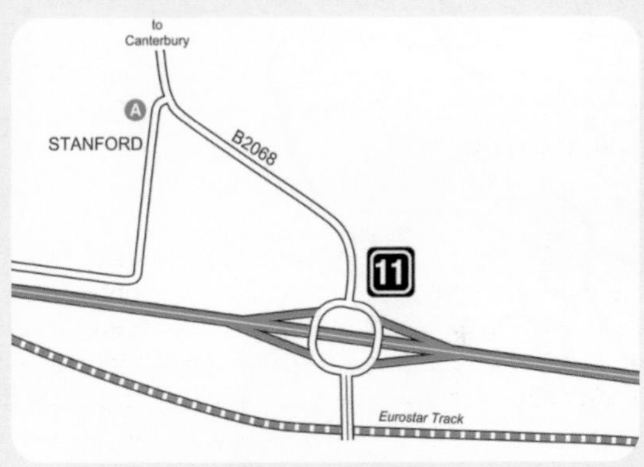


## A The Drum

Satnav
**TN25 6DN**

Stone Street, Stanford North, Kent
01303 812 125
www.thedruminn.com
thedruminn@hotmail.com

**Orders for food:** Monday to Saturday: Noon to 2.30pm and 6.00pm to 9.00pm. Sundays: Noon to 4.00pm and 6.00pm to 8.00pm.

££

It is the last hostelry before (or first after) the Tunnel. It has been a country pub for some 300 years and log fires still burn in the grates. There is a dining room and a bar for snacks, home cooking and real ales. Outside seating in the garden.

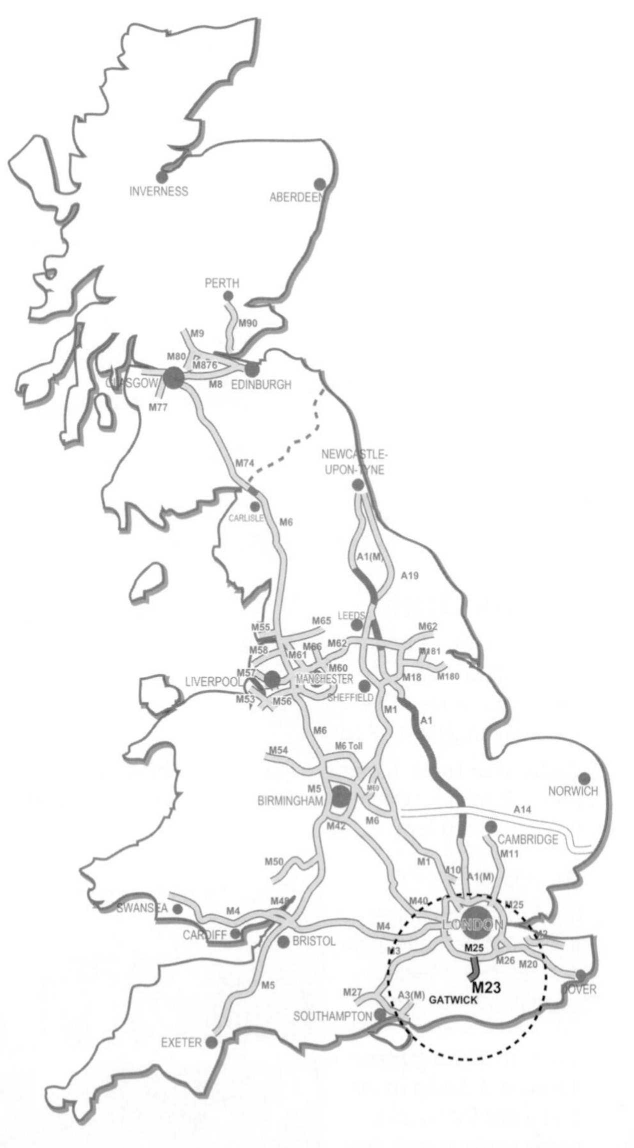
INVERNESS
ABERDEEN
PERTH
M90
M9
M80
M876
GLASGOW
M8
EDINBURGH
M77
NEWCASTLE-UPON-TYNE
M74
CARLISLE
M6
A1(M)
A19
LEEDS
M65
M55
M62
M58
M61
M66
M62
M181
M57
M60
LIVERPOOL
MANCHESTER
M18
M180
M53
M56
SHEFFIELD
M1
A1
M6
M54
M6 Toll
M5
NORWICH
BIRMINGHAM
A14
M42
M6
CAMBRIDGE
M11
M50
M1
M10
A1(M)
M40
M25
M48
SWANSEA
M4
LONDON
CARDIFF
M4
BRISTOL
M3
M25
M26
M20
M5
M27
A3(M)
M23
GATWICK
DOVER
SOUTHAMPTON
EXETER

## JUNCTIONS 7 TO 11

Built to give quick access from Gatwick Airport to London via Croydon, this 18-mile stretch took nearly four years to complete. However, the roads south of Croydon are so congested that many motorists driving from London prefer to head west to the M25 and then drive round to the M23.

Gatwick Airport started life as a racecourse in the 19th century before becoming one of the busiest airports in the UK, in spite of only having one runway.

At junction 11 it continues as the A23 to Brighton.

An easy junction as the Copthorne Hotel is on the other side of the roundabout.

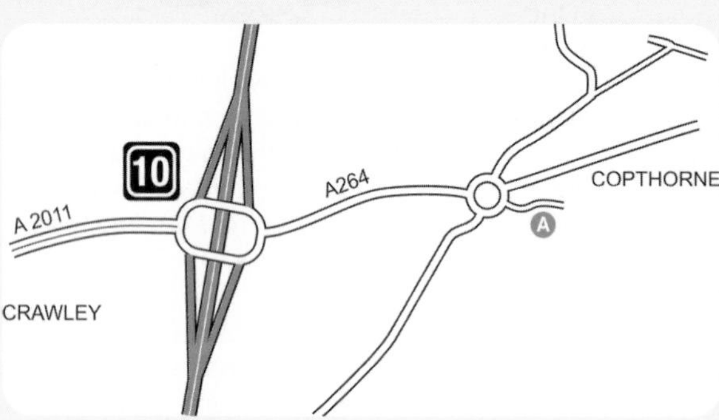


**Places of interest**

Wakehurst Place (1590) Royal Botanic Gardens – 6 miles

## Ⓐ White Swan Pub

Satnav
**RH10 3PG**

London Road, Copthorne, W.Sussex
01342 714 971
www.milleniumhotel.co.uk

**Orders for food:** Daily: 11.00am to 10.00pm.

£££

The White Swan is all that is left of the original buildings as it is now surrounded by its owner a large modern hotel complex. It has comfortable restaurant-style areas and serves food all day. In the hotel itself there is a full range of leisure activities.

This could be a difficult junction to negotiate. Head for the Pease Pottage Service Station. Go past it and take the road to the right over the motorway saying Pease Pottage. In the village the Black Swan is on the right. Do not drive into Broadfields as (like me) you will not be able to find the way out! With a name like Pease Pottage (made famous in a nursery rhyme) which was a gruel made of boiled peas and fed to passing convicts I was sure that there must be a pub in the village.

## Ⓐ The Black Swan

Satnav
**RH11 9AJ**

Horsham Road, Pease Pottage, Sussex
01293 612 261
www.blackswanpeasepottage.co.uk
blackswan.crawley@hall-woodhouse.co.uk

**Orders for food:** Mondays to Thursdays: Noon to 9.30pm. Fridays and Saturdays: Noon to 10.00pm. Sundays: Noon to 8.30pm.

££

A Hall and Woodhouse pub which is an old building but has been modernised to have large open spaces with wood and carpet flooring and a garden at the back where dogs are welcome. Nevertheless the welcome is friendly and the Independent newspaper is available to read to fill the time of day. I could not see Pease Pottage (or Pease Pudding) being featured on the menu.

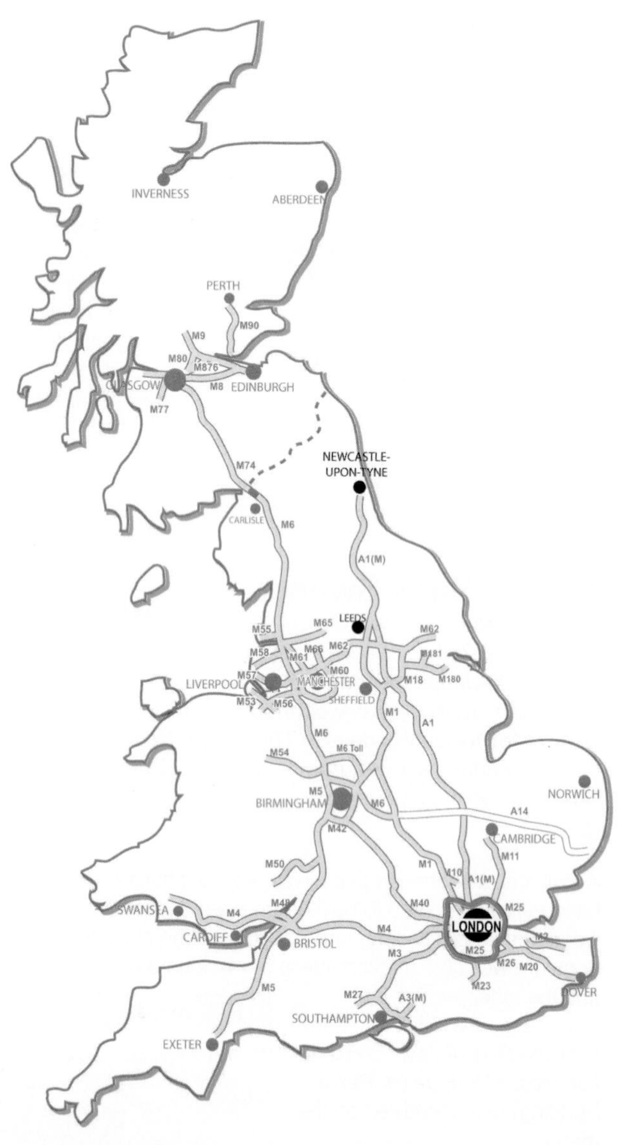
INVERNESS
ABERDEEN
PERTH
M90
M9
M80
M876
GLASGOW
M8
EDINBURGH
M77
M74
NEWCASTLE-
UPON-TYNE
CARLISLE
M6
A1(M)
LEEDS
M65
M55
M62
M58
M61
M66
M62
M181
M57
M60
LIVERPOOL
MANCHESTER
M18
M180
M53
M56
SHEFFIELD
M1
A1
M6
M54
M6 Toll
NORWICH
M5
BIRMINGHAM
M6
A14
M42
CAMBRIDGE
M11
M50
M1
M10
A1(M)
M48
M40
M25
SWANSEA
M4
M4
LONDON
CARDIFF
BRISTOL
M3
M25
M26
M20
M5
M27
A3(M)
M23
DOVER
SOUTHAMPTON
EXETER

## JUNCTIONS 1a TO 30

The idea of an orbital ring road around London was first mooted in 1905. The North Circular Road was built in the 1930s but the South Circular exists in name only.

In 1975 a decision was made to construct an integrated Orbital Ring Road, which was finally completed in 1986. It was originally intended to have more lanes, but this was deemed to be too expensive. It will now cost a fortune to upgrade it to cope with the increase in traffic.

The M25 does, however, make it easier for visitors from abroad to skirt around London and head north or west.

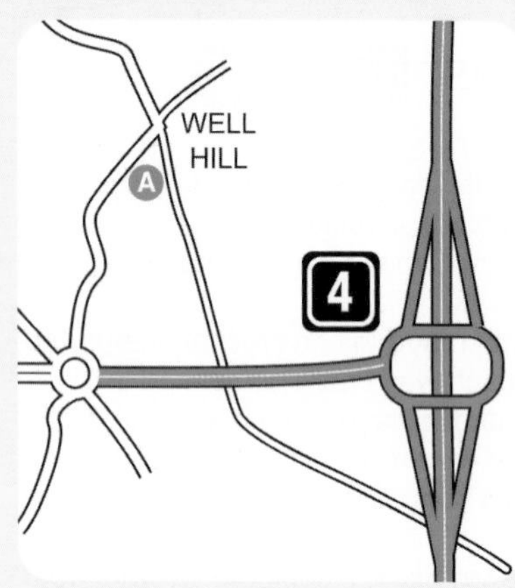


As a junction it is an easy one, but at the roundabout look out for a narrow lane signed Well Hill.

**Places of interest**

Lullingstone Castle (15thC) HHA – 2 miles 
Lullingstone Roman Villa EH – 2 miles

## Ⓐ Bo Peep Restaurant

Satnav
**BR6 7QL**

Hewitts Road, Well Hill, Kent
01959 534 457

www.thebopeep.com
kate@thebopeep.com

**Orders for food:** Monday to Thursday: Noon to 2.30pm and 6.00pm to 9.00pm. Fridays and Saturdays: Noon to 2.30pm and 6.30pm to 9.30pm.
Sundays: Noon to 5.00pm.

It has been an alehouse since 1549. It is a surprise to find somewhere so close to London and still in the middle of strawberry fields. It has a dining room and a bar for snacks. A well-kept garden and inside a friendly welcome.

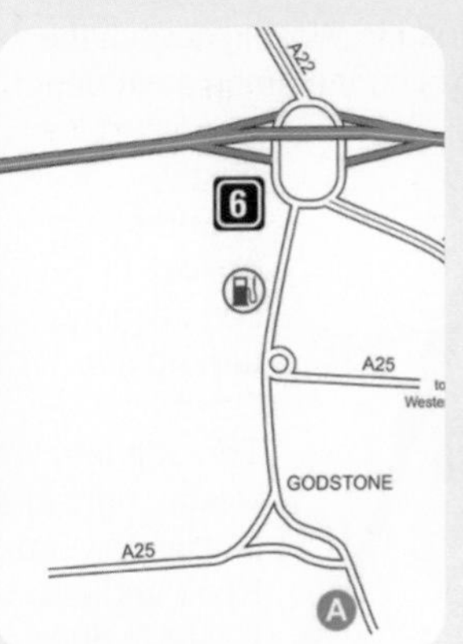


Take the B2236 to Godstone and through this attractive village. The Bell is on the right of the road as you come out.

**Places of interest**

Chartwell (Sir Winston Churchill) NT – 8 miles
Squerryes Court (17thC) HHA – 7 miles.
Quebec House (16thC) NT – 8 miles

## Ⓐ The Bell Inn

Satnav
**RH9 8DX**

High Street, Godstone, Surrey
01883 743 216
www.thebellgodstone.co.uk
enquiries@thebellgodstone.co.uk

**Orders for food:** Daily: Noon to 10.00pm.
Sundays: Noon to 9.00pm.

It has had a major makeover and is now a cheerful bustling gastro pub with friendly and efficient service.

From the junction, take the road to Woking. Left at the first roundabout and after passing the ambulance depot, turn left at the next roundabout. Almost immediately, turn right to Ottershaw. Through the village, right at a junction on Brox Road and the Castle is 500 yards on your right.

## A The Castle

Satnav
**KT16 0LW**

222 Brox Road, Ottershaw, Surrey
01932 872 373
www.the-castle-ottershaw.co.uk
johnandsue@holdfast.net

**Orders for food:** Monday to Saturday: Noon to 2.00pm and 6.30pm to 9.00pm. Sundays: Noon to 3.30pm.

££

A traditional country pub in the middle of a built up area. Owned by Punch Taverns, it nevertheless has a good atmosphere, a friendly greeting and a collection of horse harness, brasses and a newspaper of 4 September 1939 reporting the loss of a torpedoed liner for one's interest.

A fairly tortuous intersection. Head to Uxbridge on the M40 for 1.5 miles and come off at Junction 1. Go north on the A40 towards Chalfont St. Giles for 1 mile and bear right on the A412 to Rickmansworth. After 400 yards turn right to Denham. Returning, go under the motorway and rejoin the M40 via two roundabouts and then onto the M25.

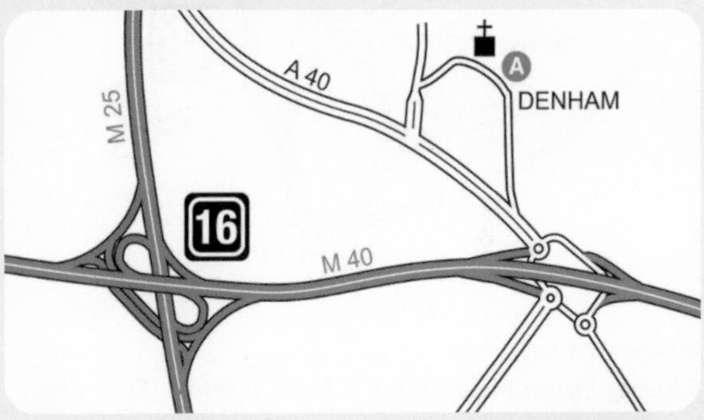


## Ⓐ Swan Inn

Satnav
**UB9 5BH**

Village Road, Denham, Bucks.
01895 832 085
www.swaninndenham.co.uk
info@swaninndenham.co.uk

**Orders for food:** Monday to Friday: Noon to 2.30pm and 6.30pm to 9.30pm (10.00pm on Fridays). Saturdays: Noon to 3.00pm and 6.30pm to 10.00pm. Sundays: Noon to 4.00pm and 6.30pm to 9.30pm.

££

The Swan is much frequented both by locals and visitors. I had a friendly welcome and dinner even after 9.30pm on a Sunday evening. The dining room is small and cosy and also serves as a meeting place. A pleasant garden for summer.

At the first crossroads look out for a sign saying Dog Kennel Road. For the Fox and Hounds and Bedford Arms continue through Chorleywood and bear to the right which is signed Chenies.

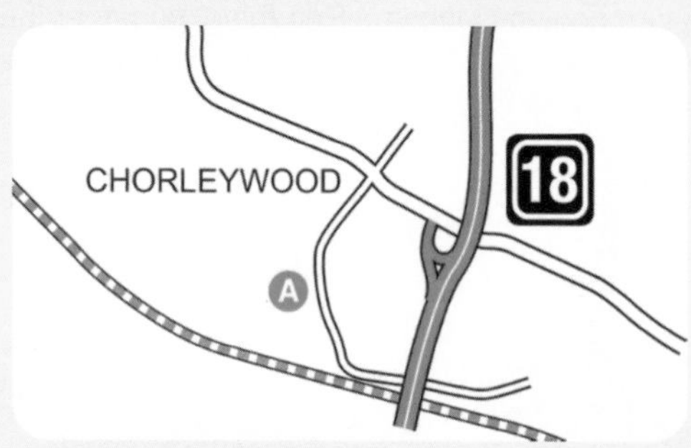


**Places of interest**

Chenies Manor House (14th & 15thC) HHA – 3 miles 

## Ⓐ The Black Horse

Satnav **WD3 5EG**

Dog Kennel Rd,Chorleywood Common,Herts.
01923 282 252

**Orders for food:** Monday to Saturday: Noon to 2.15pm and 6.30pm to 9.00pm. Sundays: Noon to 2.30pm and 4.00pm to 6.30pm.

££

A pub since the early 1800s, it now has dining areas and produces home-cooked specials by log fires in the restaurant or bar areas. There is a children's menu. Dogs have the freedom of the common.

Take the road towards St Albans but at the first roundabout bear left to Chiswell Green and then first left to Potters Crouch. The roads are narrow and not helped by the road widening of the M25 and the resultant lorry traffic. Well worth the effort.

**Places of interest**

St Alban's Abbey Church – 3 miles
Verulanium Roman City – 3 miles

## Ⓐ The Holly Bush

Satnav
**AL2 3NN**

Ragged Hall Lane, Potters Crouch, Herts.
01727 851 792
www.thehollybushpub.co.uk
info@thehollybushpub.co.uk

**Orders for food:** Monday to Tuesday: Noon to 2.00pm. Wednesday to Saturday: Noon to 2.00pm and 6.00pm to 9.00pm. Sundays: Noon to 2.30pm.

££

A 17th-century country pub covered with wisteria near a rural hamlet. It has been run by the same family for 30 years and is filled with old furniture, varnished tables, log fires and a cheerful atmosphere. Outside there is a mature garden where you can grab a moment of relaxation.

M26

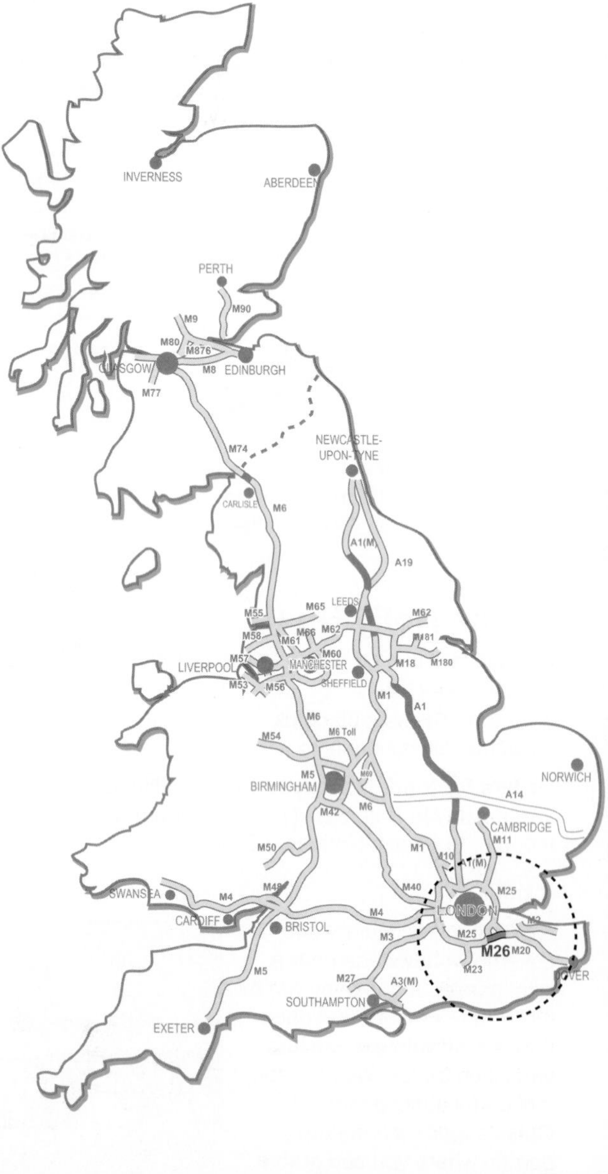

An 8 mile stretch of motorway built in 1980 to form a link from the M20 to the southern segment of the M25. Useful for those who have misread the M20 signs and find themselves on the M26 going west, as they can rejoin the M20 at Junction 2a to Wrotham.

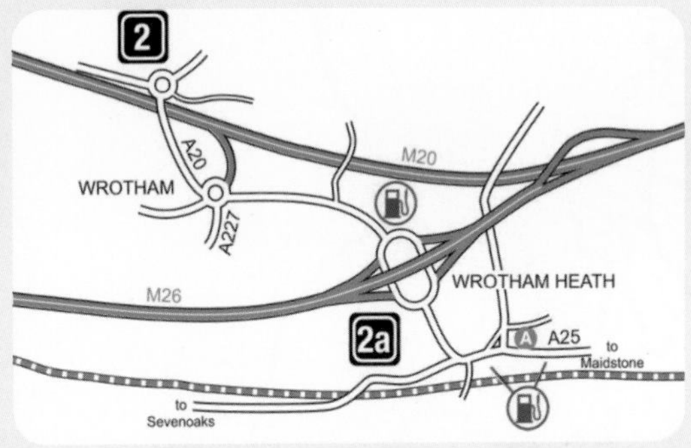


**Places of interest**

Old Soar Manor NT – 5 miles
Igtham Mote NT – 6 miles

## Ⓐ The Vineyard

Satnav
**TN15 7RU**

London Road, Wrotham Heath, Kent
01732 882 330
www.thevineyardrestaurant.co.uk
dine@thevineyard.co.uk

**Orders for food:** Daily: Noon to 10.00pm.
Mondays: Closed.

£££

A family-run restaurant, specialising in seafood with French and Italian influences. Although on the road, it is surrounded by a secluded garden and a private car park. It had changed hands.

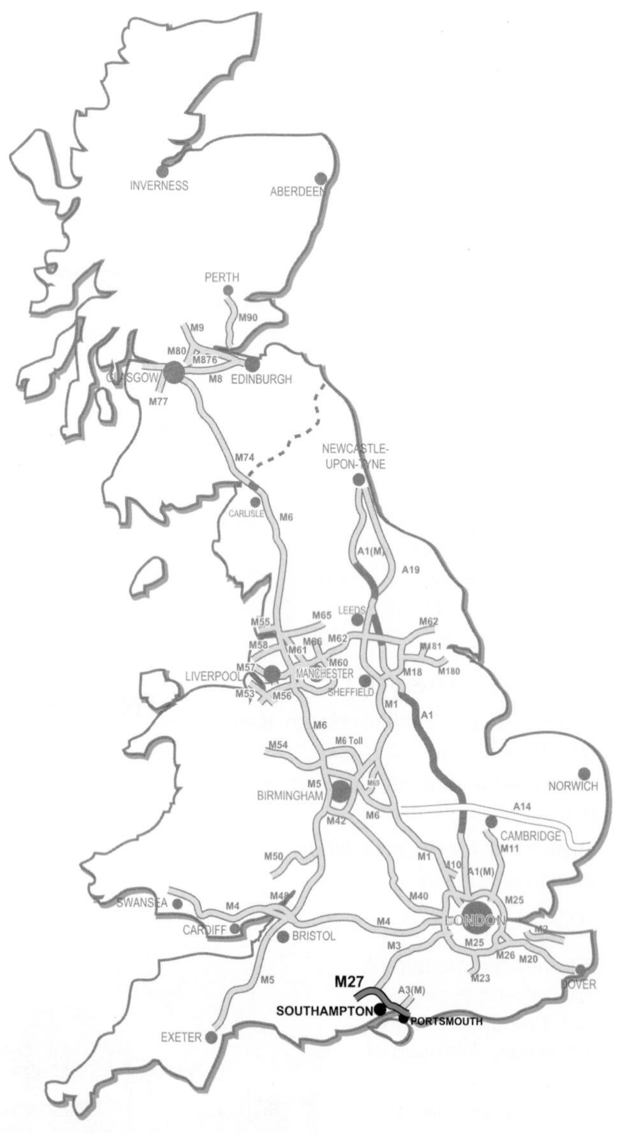
INVERNESS
ABERDEEN
PERTH
M9
M90
M80
M876
GLASGOW
M8
EDINBURGH
M77
M74
NEWCASTLE-UPON-TYNE
CARLISLE
M6
A1(M)
A19
M55
M65
LEEDS
M62
M58
M61
M66
M62
M181
M57
M60
LIVERPOOL
MANCHESTER
M18
M180
M53
M56
SHEFFIELD
M1
A1
M6
M54
M6 Toll
M5
M69
BIRMINGHAM
NORWICH
M42
M6
A14
CAMBRIDGE
M11
M50
M1
M10
A1(M)
M48
M40
M25
SWANSEA
M4
LONDON
M2
CARDIFF
M4
BRISTOL
M3
M25
M26
M20
M5
M27
A3(M)
M23
DOVER
SOUTHAMPTON
PORTSMOUTH
EXETER

## JUNCTIONS 1 TO 12

The M27, 27 miles long, was built to connect Portsmouth and Southampton with the M3. It starts or ends rather abruptly at the edge of the New Forest, but continues as a dual carriageway nearly as far as Bournemouth.

At the Portsmouth end it joins up with the A3(M) before carrying on as a dual carriageway to Chichester, Brighton and Lewes (with some breaks). It is conceivable that one day there could be a motorway along the south coast to Dover. This would help alleviate the plight of foreign visitors who, at present, have to head for London and the M25, whatever their destination.

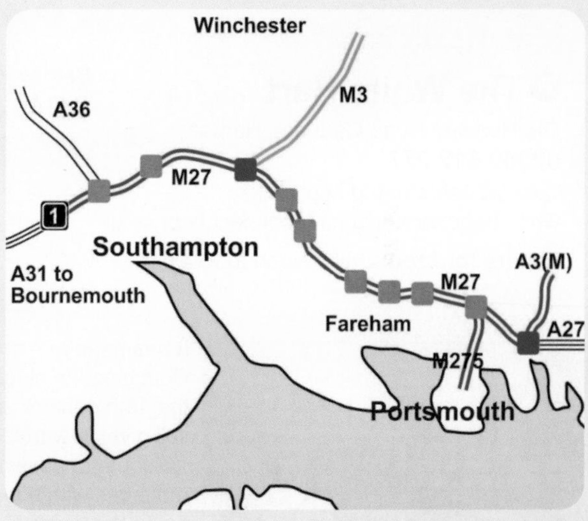

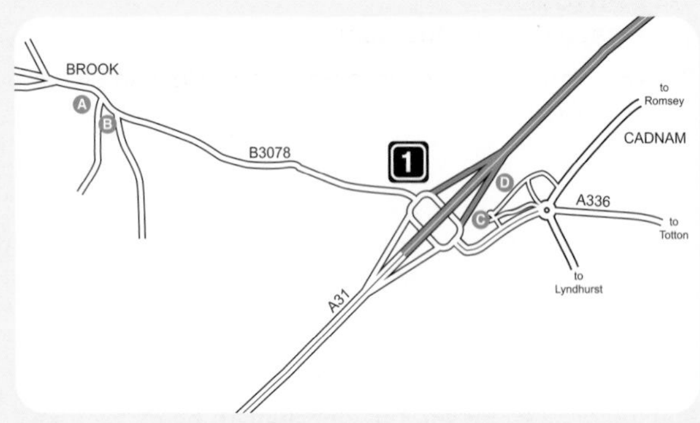


## Ⓐ The White Hart

Satnav
**SO40 2NP**

Old Romsey Road,Cadnam, Hants.
02380 812 277
www.whiteharthamp.hcpr.co.uk
white.hartcadnam@homeconnect.hcpr.co.uk

**Orders for food:** Daily: Noon to 9.00pm

££

It has been a Coaching Inn since the 16th century and still gives a warm welcome to passing motorists with a log fire in the dining room. Outside for summer days there is a secluded garden where dogs are allowed.

## B The Green Dragon

Satnav
**SO43 7HE**

Main Road, Brook, Hants.
02380 813 359
greendragon@btconnect.com

**Orders for food**: Mondays to Saturdays: Noon to 2.00pm and 7.00pm to 9.00pm. Sundays: Noon to 3.00pm.

It has been a beerhouse for the past 200 years and before that it was used by a coffin maker and before him by a wheel-wright. Now it is a cheerful, friendly place where you can have a meal in the dining areas near the bar or else in one of the smaller rooms.

## C The Bell Inn

Satnav
**CA11 0EP**

Main Road, Brook, Hants
023 8081 2214
www.bellinnbramshaw.co.uk

**Orders for food:** Mondays to Saturdays: Noon to 2.30pm and 7.00pm to 9.30pm  Sundays: Noon to 4.00pm.

It has been an hotel for the past 200 years and is still family run. There is a restaurant but quicker meals can be had in the bars. A playground and a family room are available when fathers (or mothers) are playing golf on the adjacent course. For the passing motorist there is morning coffee or afternoon tea.

M40

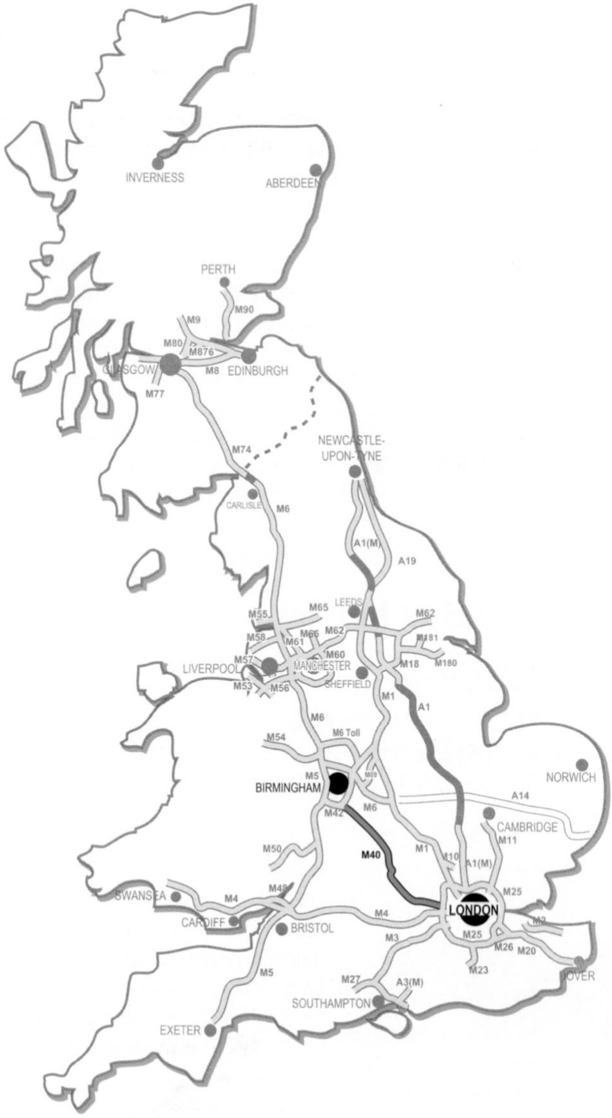

INVERNESS
ABERDEEN
PERTH
M90
M9
M80
M876
GLASGOW
M8
EDINBURGH
M77
M74
NEWCASTLE-UPON-TYNE
CARLISLE
M6
A1(M)
A19
M65
LEEDS
M62
M55
M58
M66
M61
M181
M57
M60
LIVERPOOL
MANCHESTER
M18
M180
M53
M56
SHEFFIELD
M1
A1
M6
M54
M6 Toll
M5
M69
NORWICH
BIRMINGHAM
A14
M42
M6
CAMBRIDGE
M11
M50
M40
M1
M10
A1(M)
M48
M25
SWANSEA
M4
LONDON
CARDIFF
BRISTOL
M4
M2
M3
M25
M26
M20
M5
M23
M27
A3(M)
DOVER
SOUTHAMPTON
EXETER

## JUNCTIONS 1 TO 16

The first stage to Oxford was finished in 1976, but it took fifteen years to link it to the M42. It was completed in 1991 to take the pressure off the M1 to such an extent that now it is almost as crowded.

From Uxbridge and the M25 the motorway passes through pleasant countryside before rising up to the Chiltern Escarpment. From there it descends onto the Oxfordshire Plain and continues past the market towns of Thame, Bicester and Banbury.

Chesterton Windmill is a prominent landmark on the high ground to the east of the motorway, north of Junction 12. The church nearby has original medieval wall paintings.

Beware of Junction 15 where five roads converge on the roundabout, as there could be a delay to get to Coventry.

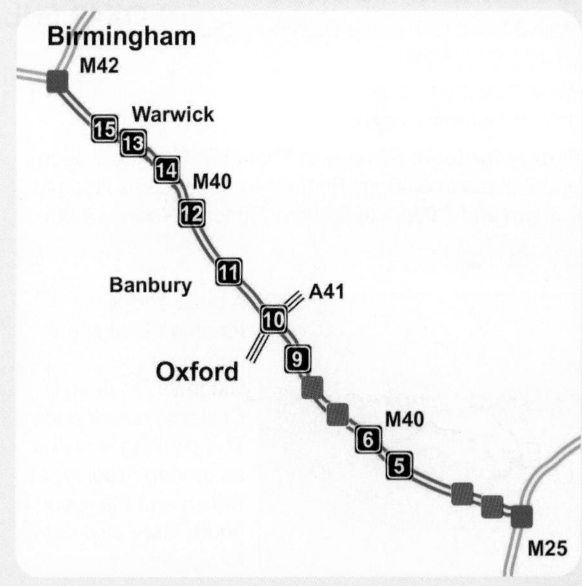

For the Fox and Hounds take the A40 towards Milton Common. After 1 mile turn left to Nettlebed. The Fox & Hounds is at Christmas Common, 4 miles down the road.

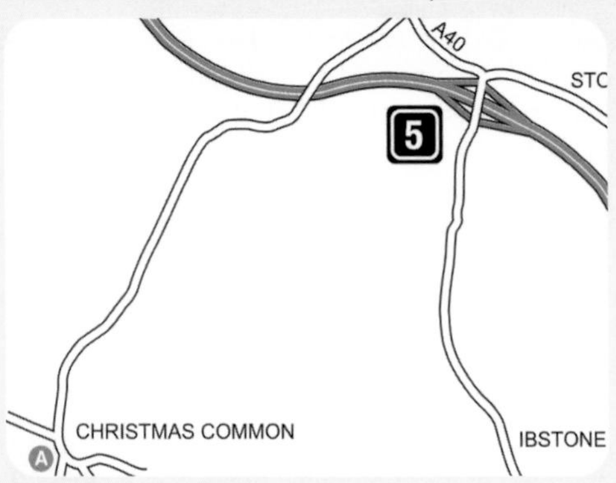


**Places of interest**

Stonor (12th, 14th & 18thC) HHA – 8 miles
West Wycombe Park (18thC) NT – 7 miles

## Ⓐ Fox and Hounds

Satnav
**OX49 5HL**

Main Street, Christmas Common, Oxon
01491 612 599
www.thetopfox.co.uk
hello@thetopfox.co.uk

**Orders for food:** Monday to Thursday: Noon to 2.30pm and 7.00pm to 9.00pm. Fridays and Saturdays: Noon to 2.30pm and 7.00pm to 9.30pm. Sunday: Noon to 4.00pm.

££

A brick-and-flint tenanted Brakspear pub, near the Ridgeway in deep Chilterns countryside. The cooking is styled as modern traditional British and the result is good. They also cater for vegans.

The road to Lewknor can be easily missed, so look out for the sign on the right. The village itself is attractive. The Cherry Tree is on the right of the road as you come into Kingston Blount.

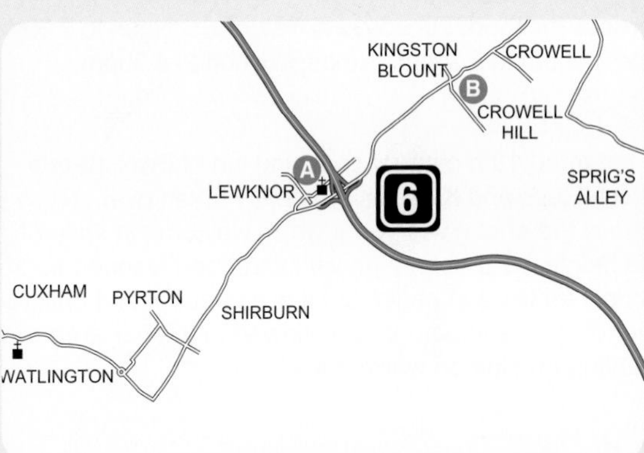


## Ⓐ Olde Leathern Bottel

Satnav
**OX49 5TW**

High Street, Lewknor, Oxon
01844 351 482
www.theleathernbottle.co.uk
juliegordon77@aol.com

**Orders for food:** Monday to Thursday: Noon to 2.00pm and 7.00pm to 9.30pm. Friday to Saturday: Noon to 2.00pm and 6.00pm to 9.30pm. Sundays: Noon to 2.30pm and 7.00pm to 9.30pm.

££

The Leathern Bottle is 450 years old and is now a pub-cum-restaurant with age-polished floors. It specialises in home cooking and serves coffee and Brakspear Traditional Ales. There is a large garden with seating.

# Ⓑ The Cherry Tree

Satnav
**OX39 4SJ**

High Street, Kingston Blount, Oxon
01844 355 966
raabooha@yahoo.com

**Orders for food:** Tuesdays to Saturdays: Noon to 2.30pm and 7.00pm to 9.30pm. Sundays: Noon to 4.30pm.

£

A tenanted 19th century coaching inn of Brakspear's which Ross and Kate have recently taken over. Ross who is the chef gives you a warm welcome in spite of his height. It is open plan with scrubbed wooden floors; simple tables and chairs but it is a cheerful and children friendly place and dogs are allowed in the bar area. Seating outside on warm days.

Take the Oxford road and after about ½ mile turn left onto the road signposted Weston-on-the-Green. This will bring you on to the B430 which ends opposite The Chequers.

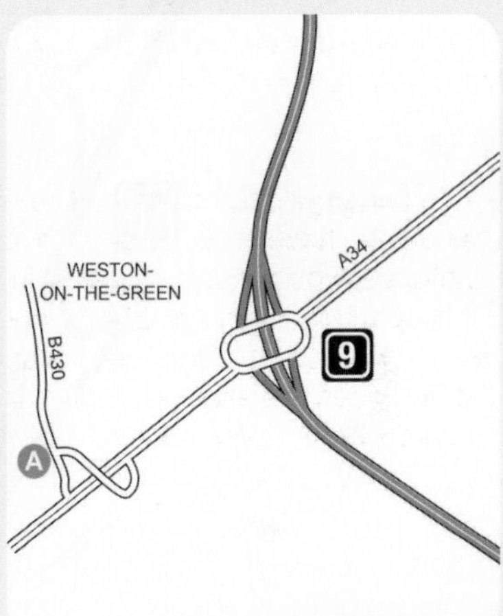


## Ⓐ The Chequers

Satnav
**OX25 3QH**

Northampton Road, Weston-on-the-Green, Oxon
01869 351 743
www.chequerswestononthegreen.co.uk

**Orders for food:** Monday to Thursday: Noon to 2.30pm and 6.00pm to 9.00pm. Fridays: Noon to 3.00pm and 6.00pm to 9.30pm. Saturdays: Noon to 9.30pm. Sundays: Noon to 4.00pm.

££

It has had a makeover, but still retains a good atmosphere with low beams, dried hops and flagged floors in the eating areas.

The Fox and Hounds is on the left in Ardley.

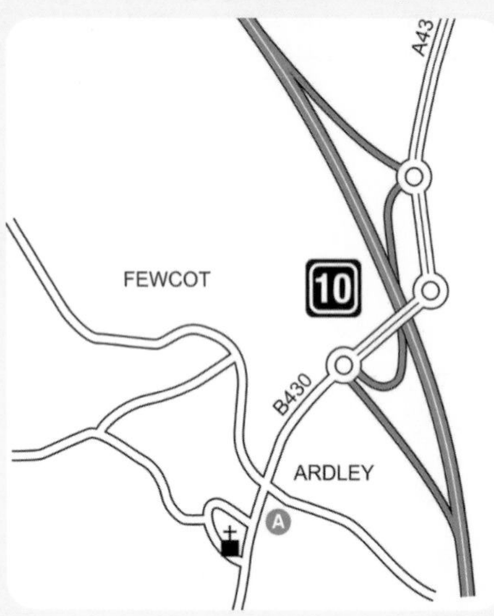


## Ⓐ Fox and Hounds

Satnav
**OX27 7PE**

Main Road, Ardley, Oxon
01869 346 883
foxandhoundsatardley@btinternet.co.uk

**Orders for food:** Weekdays: Noon to 2.30pm and 5.00pm to 9.00pm. Saturdays: Noon to 9.00pm. Sundays: Noon to 3.00pm and 5.00pm to 9.00pm.

££

An old coaching inn. It now has a restaurant but serves bar meals as well. Helpful staff who produced a good soup in quick order when I was in a hurry.

From the junction take the A361 towards Daventry. After 1 mile turn right to Chacombe. The George and Dragon is on the left as you come into the village around a bend.

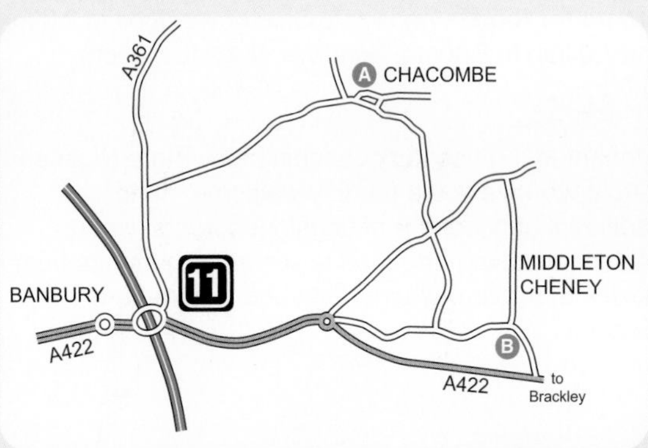


## A George and Dragon

Satnav **OX17 2JR**

Silver Street, Chacombe, Northants.
01295 711 500
www.georgeanddragon.org
thegeorgeanddragonchacombe@googlemail.com

**Orders for food:** Weekdays and Saturdays: Noon to 2.30pm and 6.30pm to 9.00pm. Sundays: Noon to 4.00pm.

££

A low-beamed inn, under new management, with a small restaurant and two dining areas, log fires and a locals' bar. The cooking is described as British traditional and they use local meat and vegetables.  Some outside seating on a patio when warm enough.

## B The New Inn

Satnav **OX17 2ND**

45 Main Road, Middleton Cheney, Oxon
01295 710 399
az@thenewinn.mc.co.uk

**Orders for food:** Mondays to Saturdays: Noon to 2.30pm and 7.00pm to 9.30pm. Sundays: Noon to 3.00pm.

££

A tenanted 17th century coaching Inn where Nigel and Carole will give you a friendly welcome. It has a traditional atmosphere of flagstoned floors, where traditional homemade food is served. There is a beer garden at the rear where dogs and children are welcome.

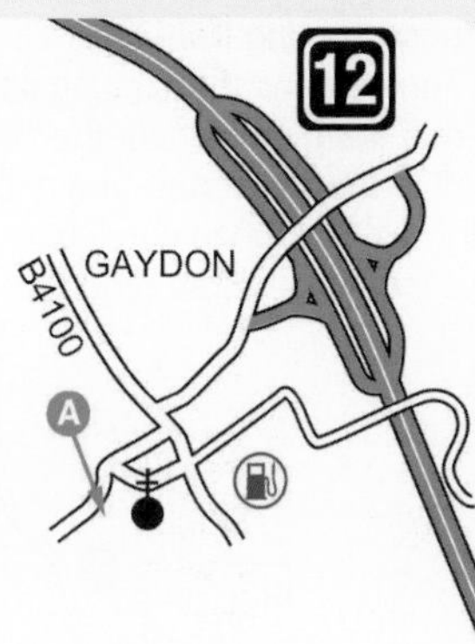


The Malt Shovel is brown-signed in the village. The windmill on the hill to the east has long been a landmark. The church in Burton Dassett is an unspoilt medieval example with original wall paintings.

Compton Verney has one of the great private art collections of this country.

**Places of interest**

Compton Verney (18thC) CVH Trust – 4 miles 
Heritage Motor Museum – 1 mile
Upton House & Gardens (17thC) NT – 9 miles
Edgehill Battlefield – 4 miles

##  The Malt Shovel Inn

Satnav
**CV35 0ET**

Church Road, Gaydon, Warks.
01926 641 221
www.maltshovelgaydon.co.uk
malt.shovel@btconnect.com

**Orders for food:** Daily: Noon to 2.00pm and 6.30pm to 9.00pm.

The owners, who used to run hotels in France, are proud to provide real food, which includes handmade meat pies and Real Ales.

This is a double Junction. For those coming from the south come off at Junction 13. Turn left and then left again to Bishops Tachbrook. To continue north cross over the motorway at Junction 13 and left at the first round-about to access the motorway at Junction 14. For those coming from the north the same will apply but in reverse order!

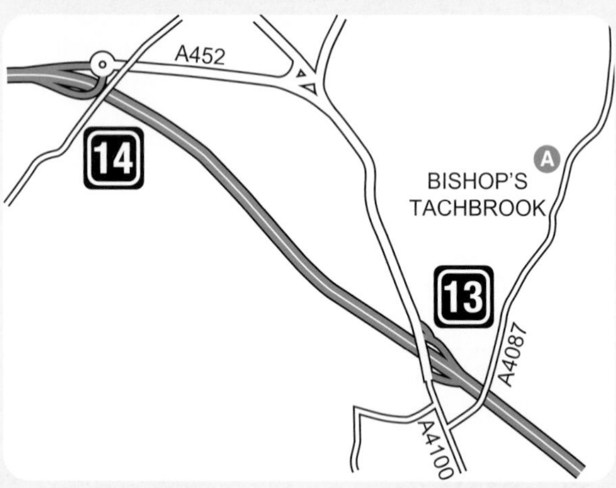


## Ⓐ The Leopard

Satnav
**CV33 9RN**

Oakley Wood Road, Bishops Tachbrook, Warks.
01926 426 466
www.leopardinn.co.uk

**Orders for food:** Daily: 10.00am to 11.45am and then Noon to 9.00pm.

£££

An efficient modernised hostelry which is in the same ownership as the Swan at Whittington.
It has a bar where those in a hurry can have a sandwich and a dining room with an imaginative menu for those in a more leisurely mood.

The junction can get congested, but once on the A429 continue south. Barford is now bypassed – so follow the signs to Barford.

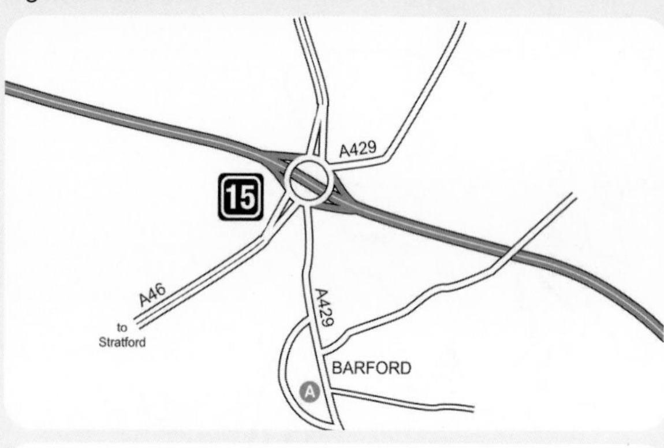


**Places of interest**

Charlecote Park (1558) NT – 7 miles 

## Ⓐ The Granville@Barford

Satnav **CV35 8DS**

Wellesbourne Road, Barford, Warks.
01926 624 236
www.granvillebarford.co.uk
info@granvillebarford.co.uk

**Orders for food:** Weekdays: Noon to 2.30pm and 6.00pm to 9.30pm. Saturdays: Noon to 9.30pm. Sundays: Noon to 5.00pm.

££

A former coaching inn, now a restaurant with a bar lounge which has been renovated with a light feminine touch. The food is locally sourced and the staff are helpful and friendly. Bar snacks are also available. A large garden with seating underneath canopies.

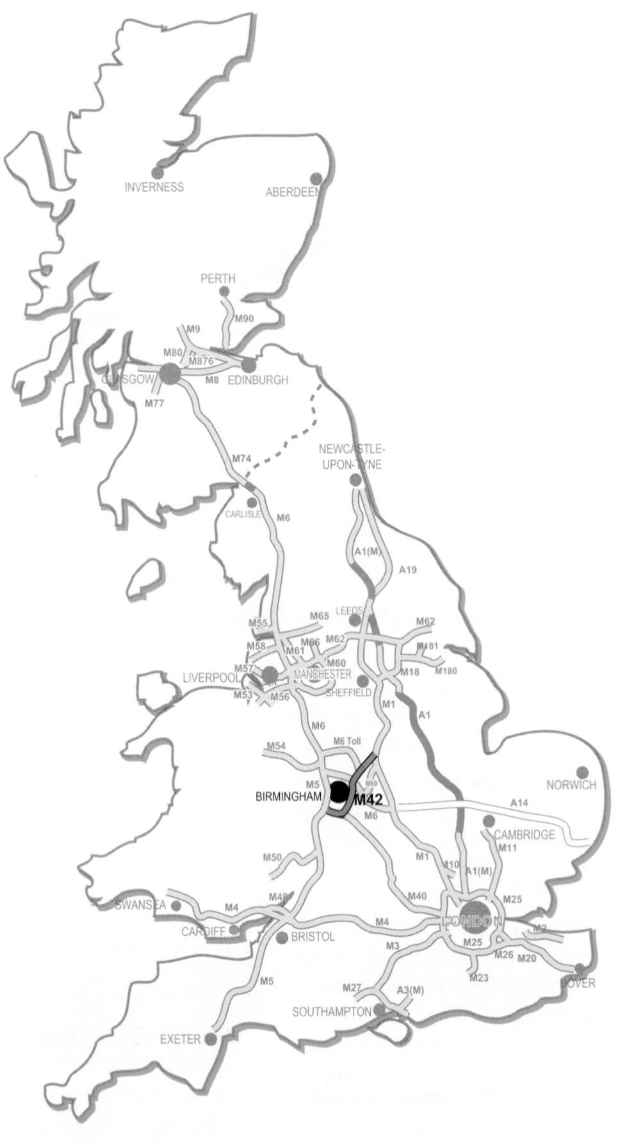
INVERNESS
ABERDEEN
PERTH
M90
M9
M80
M876
M8
EDINBURGH
M77
M74
NEWCASTLE-
CARLISLE
M6
A1(M)
A19
LEEDS
M65
M62
M55
M58
M66
M61
M181
M57
M60
LIVERPOOL
MANCHESTER
M18
M180
M53
M56
SHEFFIELD
M1
A1
M6
M54
M6 Toll
NORWICH
M5
BIRMINGHAM
M42
A14
M6
CAMBRIDGE
M11
M50
M1
M10
A1(M)
M48
M40
M25
M4
M4
BRISTOL
M3
M25
M26
M20
M23
M5
M27
A3(M)
SOUTHAMPTON
EXETER

## JUNCTIONS 2 TO 14

Completed in 1986, it might be continued as a motorway to join up with the M1 at Nottingham. It is in effect the southern and eastern part of the Birmingham Ring Road, with the M6 and the M5 completing the circuit. It is a useful link for those using the M40 and also for those who are hoping to avoid the delays at Spaghetti Junction by using the M5.

Beyond Junction 11 it continues as a dual carriageway to join the M1. The church at Breedon-on-the-Hill is a prominent landmark.

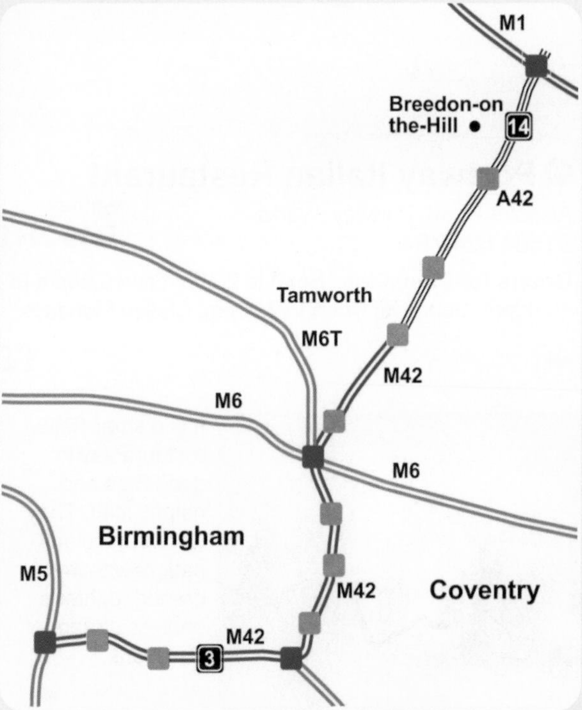

Take the A435 towards Evesham for 1 mile and then the slip road before the bridge. Return towards the motorway and the Portway is on your left.

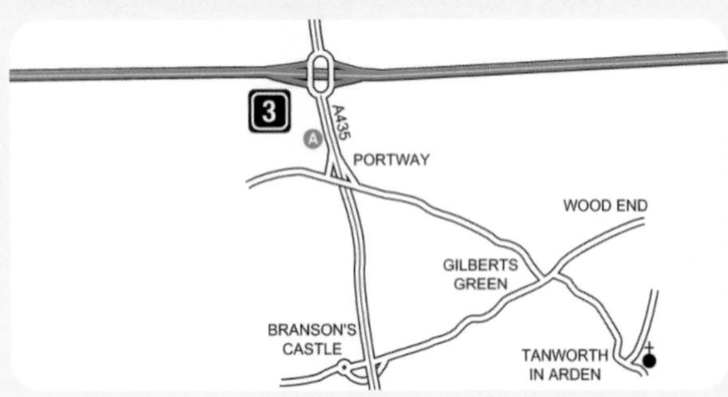


## Ⓐ Portway Italian Restaurant

Alcester Road, Portway, Warks.
01564 824 794

Satnav
**B48 7HT**

**Orders for food:** Daily: Noon to 2.30pm and 6.00pm to 10.00pm. Sundays: Noon to 2.30pm. Closed Mondays.

££

It is a small Italian restaurant with good food and helpful staff. They were particularly patient with my granddaughter's endless stream of questions.

For those driving north, take the A453 towards Castle Donington. Turn left at the T junction and head to Breedon. To continue north you will have to use the A453 to join the M1 at Junction 23a. The reverse will apply for those coming from the north.

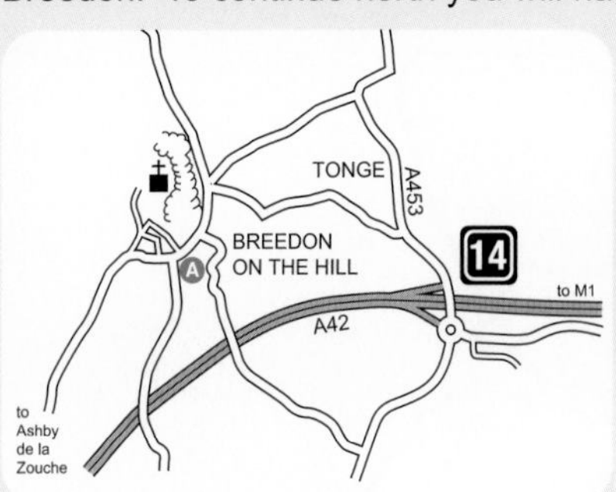


**Places of interest**

Calke Abbey(1701) NT -5miles

The Saxon Church, Breedon on the Hill - 3miles

Staunton Harold Church (!665) NT – 5 Miles

## Ⓐ The Three Horseshoes

Satnav
**DE73 8AN**

Main Road, Breedon-on-the-Hill, Derbys.
01332 695 129
www.thehorseshhoes.com
email?

**Orders for food:** Mondays to Saturdays: 11.30am to 2.00pm and 6.00pm to 9.00pm. Sundays: Noon to 3.00pm.

££

It was used by a farrier but is now a comfortable cheerful place with open spaces and lofty ceilings. The service is friendly and if need be fast but it has a restful timeless atmosphere. It also sells farm produce (and local ice-cream) over the counter as well as some useful presents.

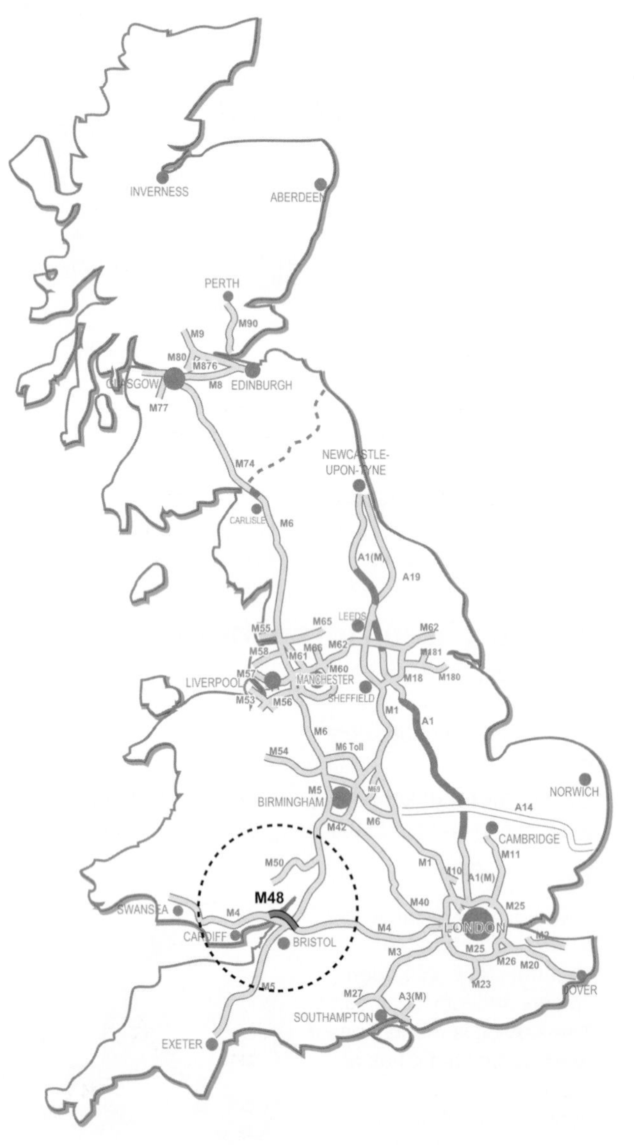
INVERNESS
ABERDEEN
PERTH
M90
M9
M80
M876
GLASGOW
M8
EDINBURGH
M77
M74
NEWCASTLE-
UPON-TYNE
CARLISLE
M6
A1(M)
A19
M65
LEEDS
M55
M62
M58
M61
M66
M62
M181
M60
M57
LIVERPOOL
MANCHESTER
M18
M180
M53
M56
SHEFFIELD
M1
A1
M6
M54
M6 Toll
M5
M69
NORWICH
BIRMINGHAM
A14
M42
M6
CAMBRIDGE
M11
M50
M1
A1(M)
M48
M40
M25
SWANSEA
M4
M4
LONDON
CARDIFF
BRISTOL
M3
M25
M26
M20
M23
M5
M27
A3(M)
DOVER
SOUTHAMPTON
EXETER

## JUNCTIONS 1 & 2

The present M48 was the M4 when the first Severn Bridge was built.

With the increase in traffic it became necessary to build another bridge further down stream which then was called the M4 and the older section was renamed the M48.

In some ways it became a backwater to the detriment, or otherwise, for the tourist trade in Chepstow but it can sometimes be quicker to take that route rather than the denser stream of traffic on the new section.

Both bridges are apt to be closed whenever there is a strong wind blowing.

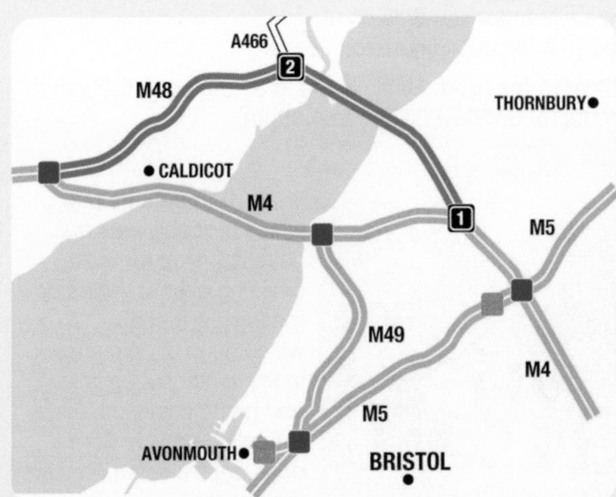

The Boars Head is just off the junction in the village of Aust. If you would like to stretch your legs you can go down to the river bank where the rotting piles of the old ferry crossing are still there.
For the White Hart take the B4461 towards Thornbury and then left in Elberton to Littleton.

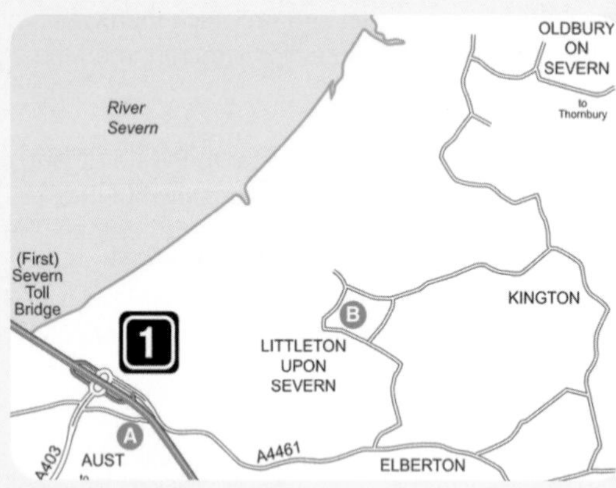


## Ⓐ Boar's Head

Satnav
**BS35 4AX**

Main Road, Aust, S.Glos.
01454 632 278
www.marstonstaverns.co.uk
boarshead.aust@marstons.co.uk

**Orders for food:** Daily: Noon to 3.00pm and 6.00pm to 9.00pm. Sundays: Noon to 4.00pm.

£

A late 18th-century pub which probably was a coaching stop for those crossing over to Wales on the ferry. A friendly welcome to all, enhanced in the winter by log fires and home cooking. There is seating outside where dogs are welcome. Beware the beams.

## B The White Hart

Satnav
**BS35 1NR**

The Village, Littleton-upon-Severn, Glos.
01454 412 275
www.whitehartbristol.com
whitehart@youngs.co.uk

**Orders for food:** Weekdays: Noon to 2.00pm and 6.30pm to 9.00pm. Saturdays: Noon to 2.30pm and 6.30pm to 9.30pm. Sundays: Noon to 8.00pm.

An old whitewashed pub on the outskirts of this small village. Small rooms with a mix of old wooden furniture. A restaurant but bar meals are available. *Petanque* in the garden for *les sportifs*. The building has an interesting scale-and-platt staircase and there is a large orchard where customers can catch some sunshine and fresh air. A large orchard for fresh air.

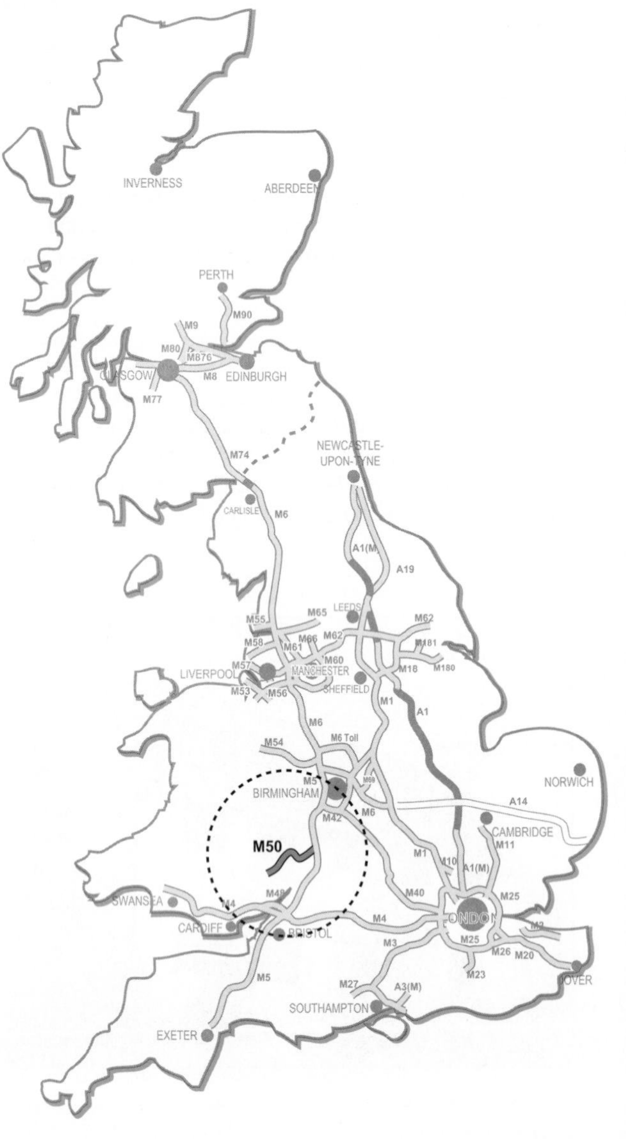
INVERNESS
ABERDEEN
PERTH
M90
M9
M80
M876
GLASGOW
M8
EDINBURGH
M77
NEWCASTLE-UPON-TYNE
M74
CARLISLE
M6
A1(M)
A19
M55
M65
LEEDS
M62
M58
M66
M61
M62
M181
M57
M60
LIVERPOOL
MANCHESTER
M18
M180
M53
M56
SHEFFIELD
M1
A1
M6
M54
M6 Toll
NORWICH
M5
M69
BIRMINGHAM
A14
M42
M6
CAMBRIDGE
M11
M50
M1
M10
A1(M)
M48
M40
M25
SWANSEA
M4
M4
LONDON
CARDIFF
BRISTOL
M2
M3
M25
M26
M20
M5
M23
M27
A3(M)
DOVER
SOUTHAMPTON
EXETER

## JUNCTIONS 1 TO 4

The M50 was one of the first motorways to be built and for some years remained in splendid isolation until joined to the M5. It was built to connect the Midlands with South Wales, but only goes as far as Ross-on-Wye, before continuing as dual-carriageway to Newport. It is also a way of driving to Wales without paying the toll charges levied on the Severn Bridges!

As well as places to eat, there are plenty of places to see not too far from the motorway. Ross-on-Wye is a market town with interesting old buildings. Nearby is picturesque Symonds Yat, where the river Wye winds through a gorge below the imposing ruins of Goodrich Castle.

To the south is the Forest of Dean, famous, amongst other things, for small family-owned coal mines which are still in private ownership.

To the west is the town of Monmouth with its medieval bridge and further on are the ruins of Raglan Castle, destroyed by Cromwell.

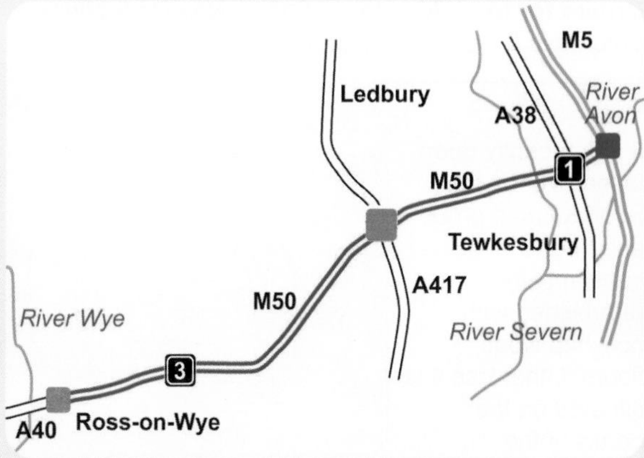

For the Jockey take A38 north to Worcester. At the junction with A4104 turn right to Pershore. Baughton is the first village you will come to and the Jockey is on the right.
For the other two in Twyning turn sharp left at the roundabout after you come off the motorway.

## Ⓐ The Fleet Inn

Satnav
**GL20 6FL**

Fleet Lane,Twyning, Glos.
01684 274 020
www.thefleetattwyning.co.uk
enquiries@thefleetattwyning.co.uk

**Orders for food:** Monday to Friday: Noon to 9.30pm.
Saturdays & Sundays: Noon to 9.00pm

££

It has recently been taken over by the Scoff & Quaff group and been substantially refurbished with polished wood floors. Otherwise it is situated on the banks of the Avonwhere you can see the ducks swim (or walk) by.

## B The Village Inn

Satnav
**GL20 6DF**

Twyning Green,Twyning, Glos.
01684 293 500
sunnybakers@yahoo.co.uk

**Orders for food:** Monday to Saturday: Noon to 2.00pm and 6.30pm to 9.00pm. Sundays: Noon to 4.00pm.

££

It was once a bakery, then a shop and Post Office, but is now a pub in this picturesque village. There is a secluded garden at the back or else you can sit outside at the front watching the world go by. It has recently changed hands so timings may alter.

The Roadmaker is on the right on the Newent road, 300 yards from the junction. For the Penny Farthing, turn left off the junction and left again to Linton. Then left to Aston Crews by the church. The Moody Cow is in Upton Bishop.

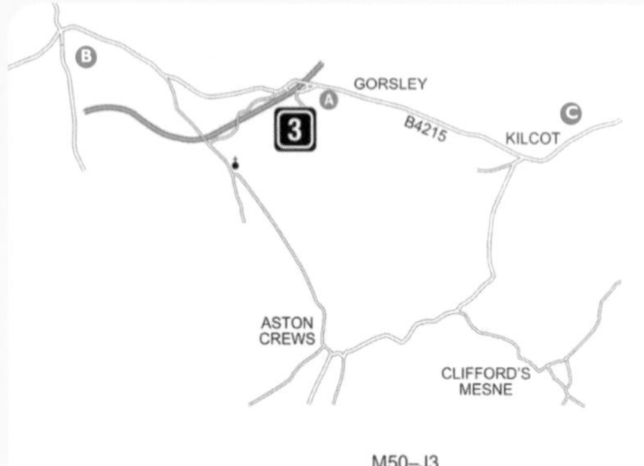


M50–J3

## Ⓐ The Roadmaker Inn

Satnav
**HR9 7SW**

Newent Road, Gorsley, Glos.

01989 720 352

www.theroadmakerinn.co.uk

info@theroadmaker.co.uk

**Orders for food:** Monday to Saturday: 11.30am to 2.30pm and 6.00pm to 10.00pm. Sundays: 11.30am to 3.30pm and 6.00pm to 9.00pm.

££

Is owned by Keschar Sherchan, an ex-Ghurka Colour Sergeant. It has been modernised and the service is discreet and friendly. The menu is half English at lunch and wholly Ghurkalese in the evening, which I thoroughly enjoyed.

## Ⓑ Moody Cow

Satnav
**HR9 7TT**

Main Road, Upton Bishop, Herefordshire.
01989 780 470
www.moodycowpub.co.uk
dawn@moodycowpub.co.uk

**Orders for food:** Tuesday to Saturday: Noon to 2.30pm and 6.00pm to 9.00pm. Sundays: Noon to 3.00pm. No lunches on Mondays.

£££

A Free House with individualistic décor. There is a fresco (as opposed to an alfresco) dining area near the bar and the main beamed dining room is in the converted barn. Outside a patio with tables and umbrellas. The food has a continental theme and is home cooked with fresh ingredients.

## Ⓒ Kilcot Inn

Satnav
**GL18 1NA**

Ross Road, Newent, Glos
01989 720 707
www.kilcotinn.com
info@kilcotinn.com

**Orders for food:** Daily: Breakfast: 7.00am to 11.30am. Lunch: Noon to 3.00pm. Teas: 3.00pm to 5.30pm. Dinner: 6.00pm to 9.00pm.

£££

Substantially rebuilt and refurbished, it was opened in June 2011 and is owned by the family who produce Weston Cider. It has an imaginative menu supplemented by home grown vegetables.  Sandwiches are however available. The four bedrooms above are new and comfortable.  Outside there is seating and a rose garden. Pay heed to the notice "Duck yer Nut"

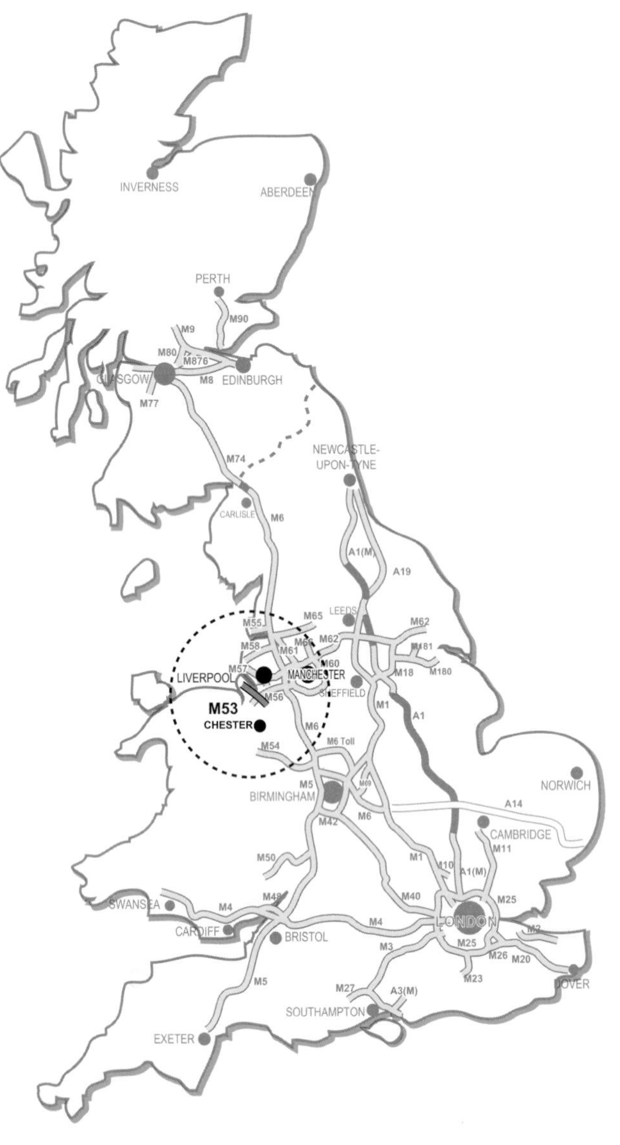
INVERNESS
ABERDEEN
PERTH
M90
M9
M80
M876
GLASGOW
M8
EDINBURGH
M77
M74
NEWCASTLE-UPON-TYNE
CARLISLE
M6
A1(M)
A19
M65
LEEDS
M55
M62
M58
M61
M60
M57
LIVERPOOL
MANCHESTER
SHEFFIELD
M181
M18
M180
M56
M53
CHESTER
M1
A1
M6
M54
M6 Toll
M5
M69
BIRMINGHAM
NORWICH
A14
M6
M42
CAMBRIDGE
M11
M50
M1
M10
A1(M)
M40
M25
SWANSEA
M48
M4
CARDIFF
BRISTOL
M4
LONDON
M2
M3
M25
M26
M20
M23
M5
M27
A3(M)
SOUTHAMPTON
DOVER
EXETER

## JUNCTIONS 1 TO 12

This short 12-mile stretch of motorway is interesting as it passes through the densely industrialised area of Ellesmere Port as well as some pleasant wooded countryside. Port Sunlight is the home of soap and the Leverhulme house and art collection. There are apparently more millionaires in the Wirral than elsewhere in the UK excluding the London area!

At the other end of the motorway is Chester, still a walled city with medieval buildings and once the home base of the Roman XX (Victrix) Legion.

Take the B5137 from the junction towards Heswall. A mile after Brimstage bear to the right and after another mile turn right at the T-junction to Barnston. The Fox and Hounds does not do evening meals. The Ship, which is part of the same group, has 6 bedrooms and does breakfasts as well as evening meals.

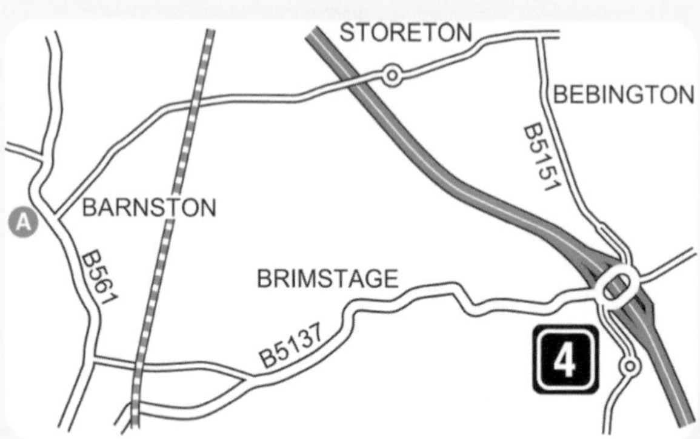


## Ⓐ Fox and Hounds

Satnav
**CH61 1BW**

Barnston Road, Barnston, Wirral
0151 648 7685
www.the-fox-hounds.co.uk
info@the-fox-hounds.co.uk

**Orders for food:** Weekdays: Noon to 2.30pm (lunches only). Sundays: Noon to 2.30pm. No evening meals.

Built in 1911 it is a well-ordered place with a dining area, a snug and a large bar area for bar meals. An eye-catching collection of 85 brass ashtrays, 115 horse brasses, police helmets and 30 flying ducks will keep you occupied or diverted whilst ordering.

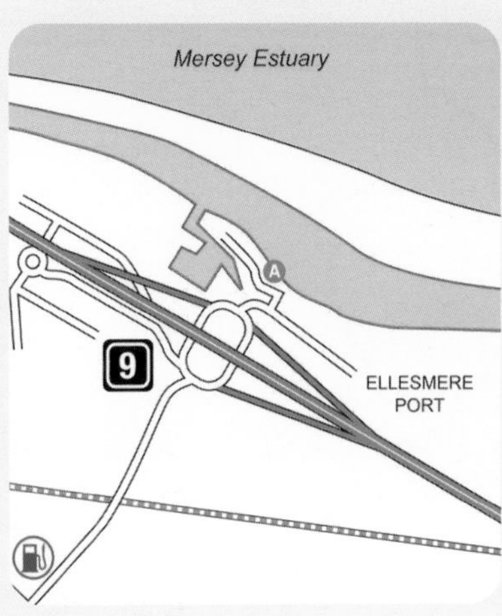


Just follow the signs to the Boat Museum, which is well worth a visit.

**Places of interest**

The Boat Museum

## Ⓐ Jabula Restaurant

Satnav **CH65 4FW**

South Pier Road, Ellesmere Port, S.Wirral
01513 551 163
www.jabularestaurant.co.uk
jabulainfo@btconnect.com

**Orders for food:** Daily: Noon to 2.30pm and 5.30pm to 9.00pm. Closed on Mondays.

£

A large airy eating area. It specialises in contemporary South African cooking such as springbok, ostrich or crocodile, served by friendly South African staff.

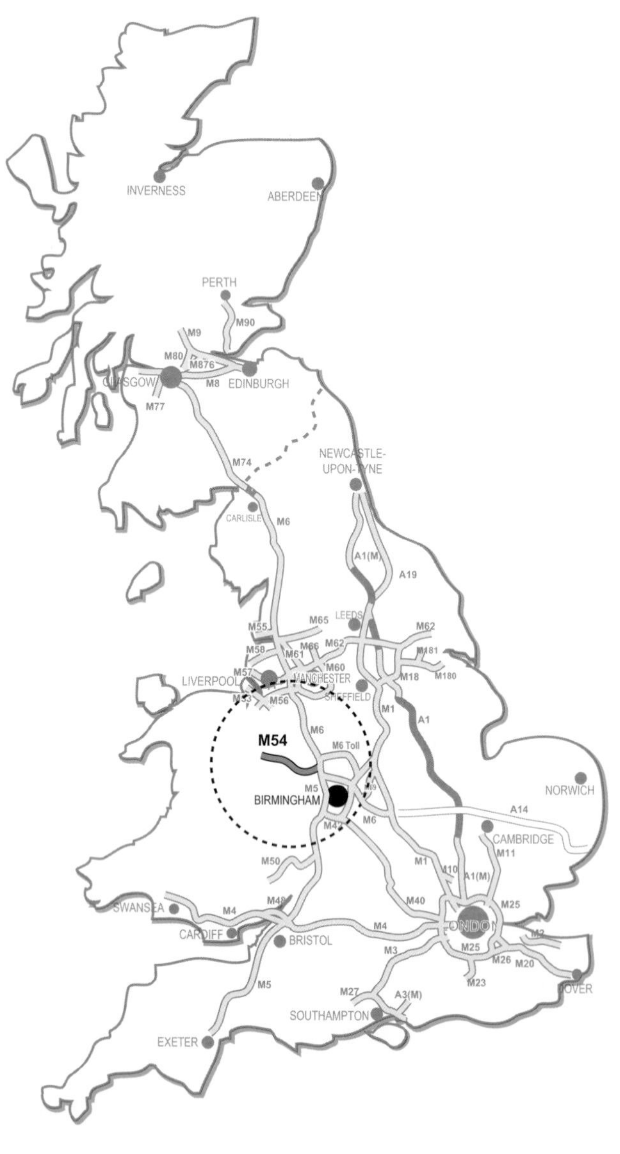
INVERNESS
ABERDEEN
PERTH
M90
M9
M80
M876
GLASGOW
M8
EDINBURGH
M77
M74
NEWCASTLE-UPON-TYNE
CARLISLE
M6
A1(M)
A19
M65
LEEDS
M55
M62
M58
M61
M66
M62
M181
M57
M60
LIVERPOOL
MANCHESTER
M18
M180
M53
M56
SHEFFIELD
M1
A1
M6
M54
M6 Toll
M5
BIRMINGHAM
M69
NORWICH
A14
M42
M6
CAMBRIDGE
M11
M50
M1
M10
A1(M)
M48
M40
M25
SWANSEA
M4
LONDON
M2
M4
CARDIFF
BRISTOL
M3
M25
M26
M20
M5
M27
M23
A3(M)
DOVER
SOUTHAMPTON
EXETER

## JUNCTIONS 1 TO 7

A 23-mile stretch of motorway which was opened in 1975 to link Birmingham to Shrewsbury and Wales. Beyond Telford it has been upgraded to dual carriageway to the other side of Shrewsbury. After coming off the M6 it passes through pleasant farming countryside until the much vaunted Telford New Town, which is typical of 1960s planning – interminable tree-lined roads and roundabouts with sparse signing.

The countryside around is well worth a visit. The Ironbridge Gorge is the cradle of modern industry. Close by is medieval Much Wenlock with its Priory. To the west of Telford rises the Wrekin and the ruins of the Roman administrative town of Viroconium, now Wroxeter, with the ruins of its massive public baths. Shrewsbury itself is one of the most attractive county towns in England with a wealth of old buildings.

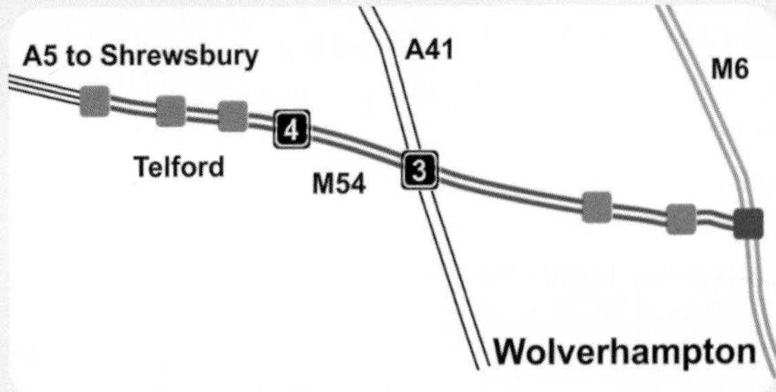

Take the dual carriageway A41 towards Wolverhampton.

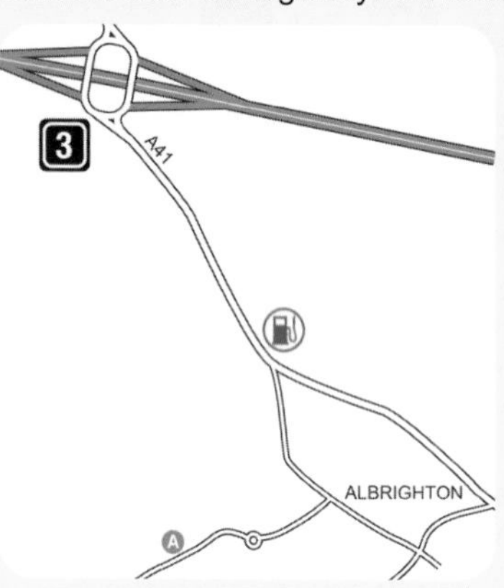


After 1.5 miles there is a road bearing right to Albrighton (if you miss it there is another one further on). After the railway bridge there is a road to the right through a housing estate. After a roundabout the grounds of the rose nursery will be evident to the right.

**Places of interest**

Weston Park (1671) HHA – 4 miles 
Boscobel House (17thC) EH – 4 miles
Lilleshall Abbey EH – 11 miles
Air Museum, Shifnal – 1 mile

## Ⓐ David Austin Roses

Satnav **WV7 3HB**

Bowling Green Lane, Albrighton, Shrops.
01902 376 334
www.davidaustinroses.com
plantcentre@davidaustinroses.com

**Orders for food:** Daily: 9.30am to 4.30pm.

Many of you will have bought his world-famous roses but did you also know that you can have an excellent light lunch while pondering the future layout of your garden? Even I found myself selecting the odd rose tree to buy.

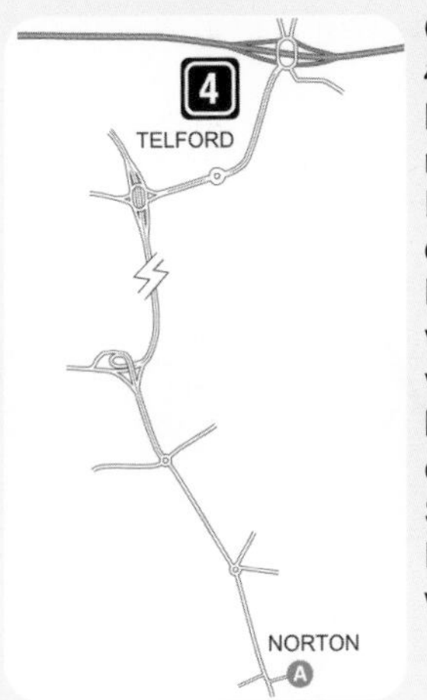


Come off the M54 at Junction 4 and take the A442 to Bridgnorth. Norton is about 8 miles to the south.

If you want an evening meal or a bed for the night the Hundred House Hotel is good value for money and is in the village. For those wanting a longer stay there are 3 holiday cottages on the bank of the Severn. Details from the Apley Farm Shop or www.apleyholidaycottages.co.uk

**Places of interest**

Ironbridge Gorge and museum – 5 miles

## Ⓐ Apley Farm Shop

Satnav
**TF11 9EF**

Stockton Buildings, Norton, Shropshire
01952 730 345
www.apleyfarmshop.co.uk
enquiries@apleyfarmshop.com

**Orders for food:** Monday to Saturday: 9.30am to 5.00pm. Sundays: 10.00am to 3.00pm.

££

A recently opened Farm Shop in a converted old dairy complex which is privately owned and sells its own produce. There is a separate café in the old cheese dairy which serves breakfasts and light lunches as well as teas. There is also a childrens' playbarn with suitable refreshments. A friendly welcome in a picturesque and genuinely rustic setting.

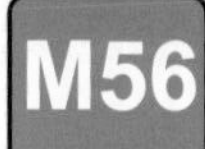

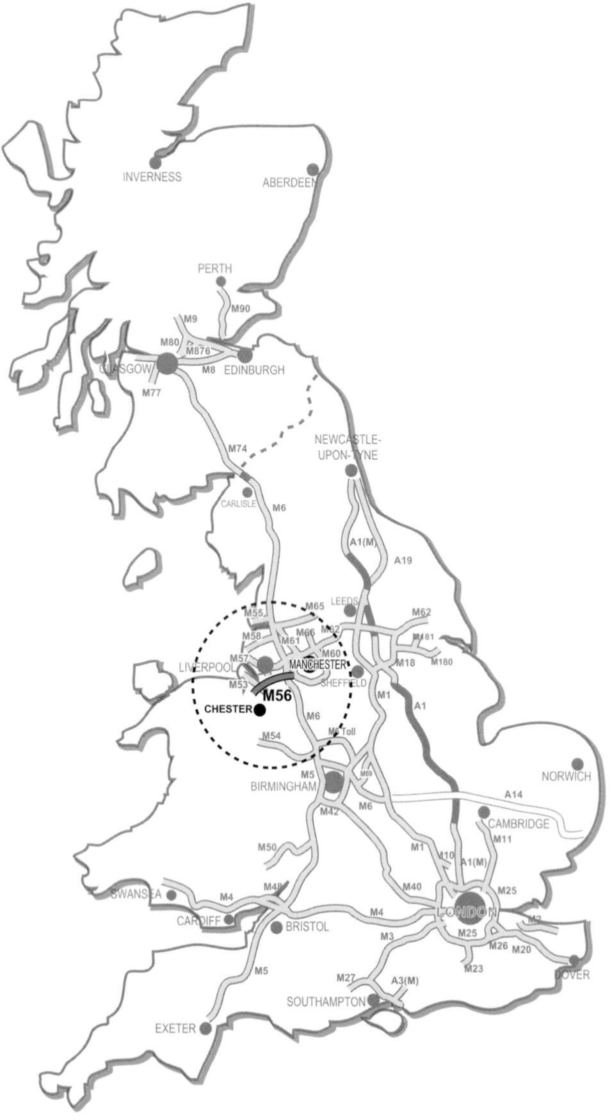
INVERNESS
ABERDEEN
PERTH
M90
M9
M80
M876
GLASGOW
M8
EDINBURGH
M77
NEWCASTLE-
UPON-TYNE
M74
CARLISLE
M6
A1(M)
A19
M65
LEEDS
M55
M62
M58
M66
M61
M181
M60
M57
LIVERPOOL
MANCHESTER
M18
M180
M53
SHEFFIELD
M56
CHESTER
M1
A1
M6
M54
M6 Toll
M5
M69
NORWICH
BIRMINGHAM
A14
M42
M6
CAMBRIDGE
M11
M50
M1
A1(M)
M48
M40
M25
SWANSEA
M4
LONDON
M4
CARDIFF
BRISTOL
M2
M3
M25
M26
M20
M5
M23
M27
A3(M)
DOVER
SOUTHAMPTON
EXETER

## JUNCTIONS 1 TO 16

Some 37 miles long, it connects Manchester with the commuter areas of Cheshire as well as Chester and North Wales beyond. It is not particularly attractive, especially when coming out of Manchester past the airport. However once over the intersection with the M6 (a complicated junction, badly signed) it gets slightly better. At the end of the motorway it continues into Wales as a dual carriageway.

The historic city of Chester was once the base of the Roman XX (Victrix) Legion. It still has its medieval walls and was where the dramatist and architect Sir John Vanbrugh grew up.

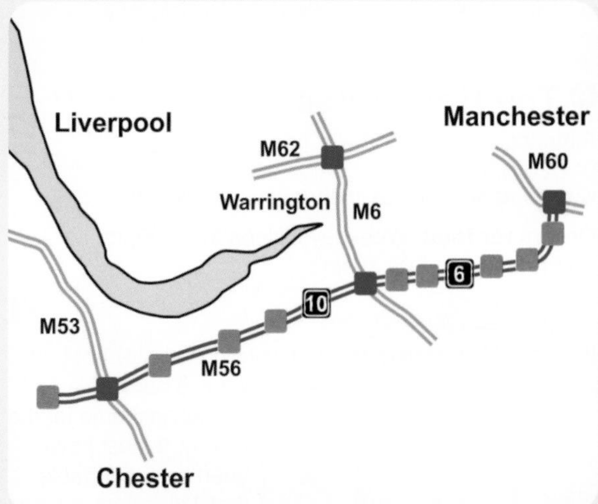

From the junction take the A538 towards Wilmslow. After the tunnel and underneath the Manchester Airport runway, the Honey Bee will be on your left.

## Ⓐ The Honey Bee

Satnav
**SK9 4LT**

Altrincham Road, Morley, Ches.
01625 526 511
www.vintageinn.co.uk/thehoneybeewilmslow

**Orders for food:** Weekdays: Noon to 10.00pm.
Sundays: Noon to 9.30pm.

££

It started life privately as Oversley House until about 1950 when it became a residential home for the elderly. It must have been so comfortable that it was then converted into the Oversley House Hotel before assuming its present mantle as a comfortable inn.

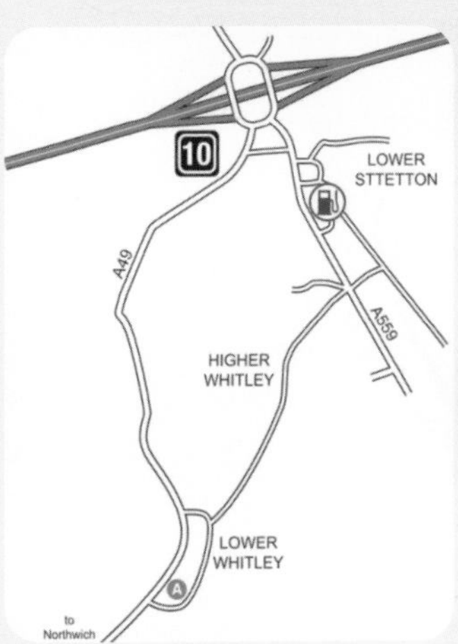


The Chetwode Arms is three miles south on the A49. Take a sharp left beyond the outskirts of Lower Whitley.

**Places of interest**
Arley Hall (19thC) HHA – 6 miles
Belmont Hall Pte - 6 miles

## Ⓐ Chetwode Arms

Satnav
**WA4 4EN**

Street Lane, Lower Whitley, Ches.
01925 730 203
www.chetwodearms.org
info@chetwodearms.co.uk

**Orders for food:** Weekdays: 5.30pm to 9.00pm. Saturdays: 12.30pm to 9.00pm. Sundays: 12.30 to 5.30pm.

£££

A brick-built former coaching inn. It exudes the charm and hospitality of a bygone age in the three former bar parlours with open fires. The co-owner is Austrian so from time to time you may be lucky to have *Schnitzel*. Otherwise you will have to be more than content with the high quality of the duck.

# M61

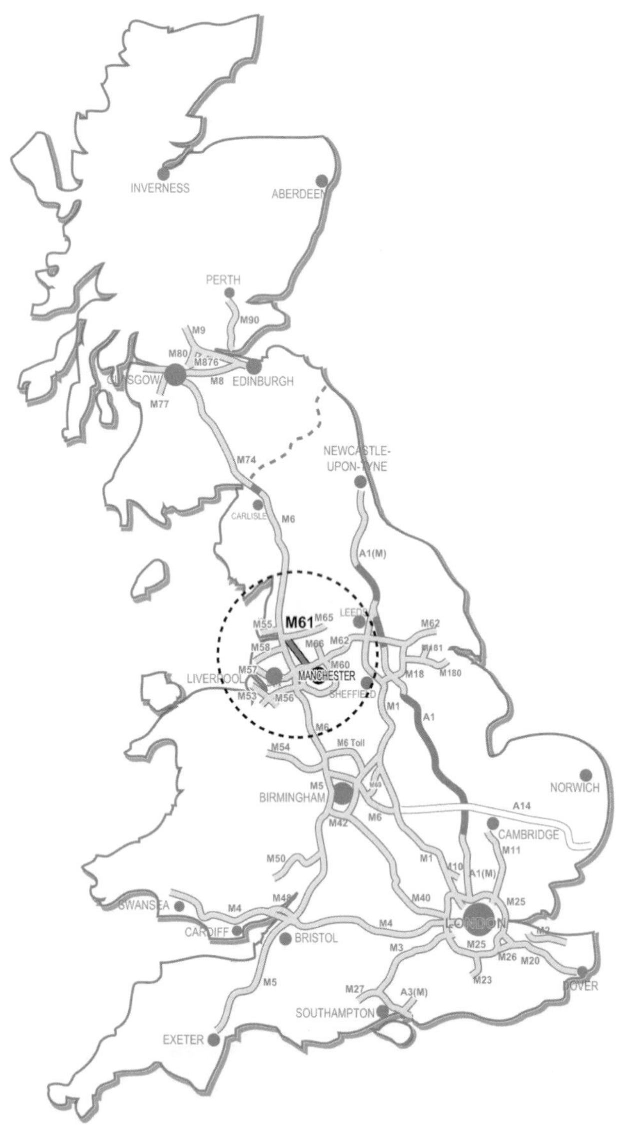

INVERNESS
ABERDEEN
PERTH
M90
M9
M80
M876
GLASGOW
M8
EDINBURGH
M77
M74
NEWCASTLE-UPON-TYNE
CARLISLE
M6
A1(M)
M61
M65
LEEDS
M55
M62
M58
M66
M62
M181
M60
M57
MANCHESTER
M18
M180
LIVERPOOL
M53
M56
SHEFFIELD
M1
A1
M6
M6 Toll
M54
M5
BIRMINGHAM
M69
NORWICH
A14
M42
M6
CAMBRIDGE
M11
M50
M1
M10
A1(M)
M48
M40
M25
SWANSEA
M4
LONDON
CARDIFF
M4
BRISTOL
M3
M25
M2
M26
M20
M23
M5
M27
A3(M)
DOVER
SOUTHAMPTON
EXETER

## JUNCTIONS  TO 9

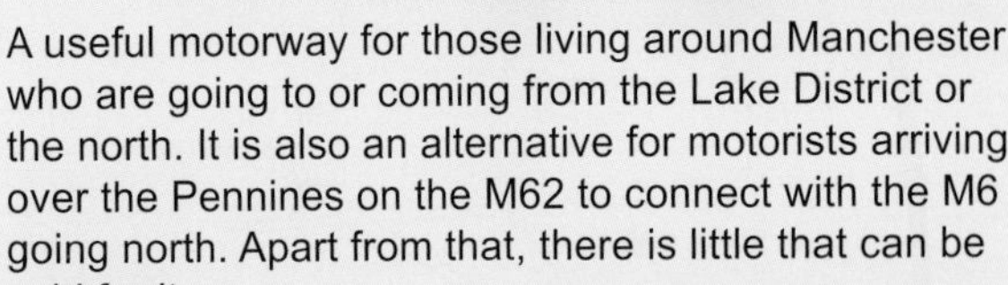

A useful motorway for those living around Manchester who are going to or coming from the Lake District or the north. It is also an alternative for motorists arriving over the Pennines on the M62 to connect with the M6 going north. Apart from that, there is little that can be said for it.

About the only redeeming feature is the sight of the Pennines to the east looming over the outer suburbs of Manchester and Bolton. The place names in the area, such as Whittle-le-Woods or Bottom o' the' Moor have a certain charm.

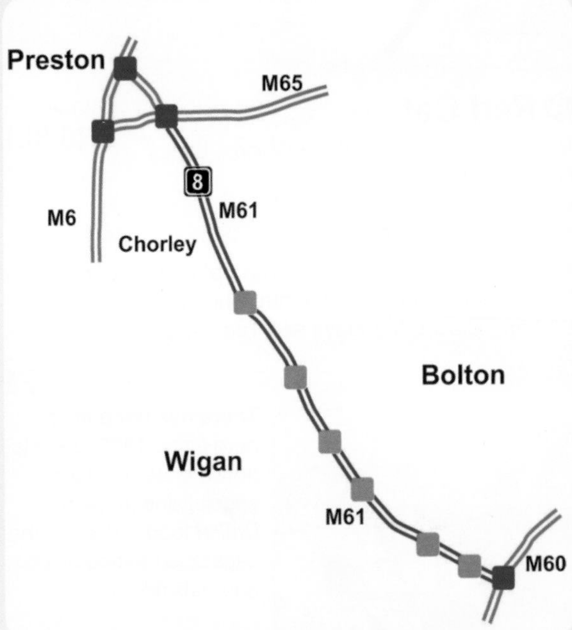

The Red Cat requires concentration as you have to drive past it and then come round behind it. The Dressers Arms is further on the right.

## Ⓐ Red Cat

Satnav
**PR6 8LL**

Blackburn Road, Whittle-le-Woods, Lancs.
01257 263 966
www.theredcat.co.uk
enquiries@theredcat.co.uk

**Orders for food:** Wednesday to Saturday: Noon to 2.00pm and 6.00pm to 9.30pm. Sundays: Noon to 6.00pm. Closed Mondays and Tuesdays.

££

There has been an inn here since 1805 and it is now a cheerful place, specialising in modern British food served in the flagstoned eating areas and outside.

## B The Dressers Arms

Satnav
**PR6 8HD**

Briers Row, Wheelton, Lancs.
01254 830 041
www.dressersarms.co.uk
info@dressersarms.co.uk

**Orders for food:** Monday to Saturday: Noon to 9.00pm.
Sundays: Noon to 8.00pm

A free house which is reputedly the friendliest pub in Lancashire, with home cooking and real ales. It has a dining room and bar serving specialities such as wild boar and venison. Beware the low door when leaving!

# M62

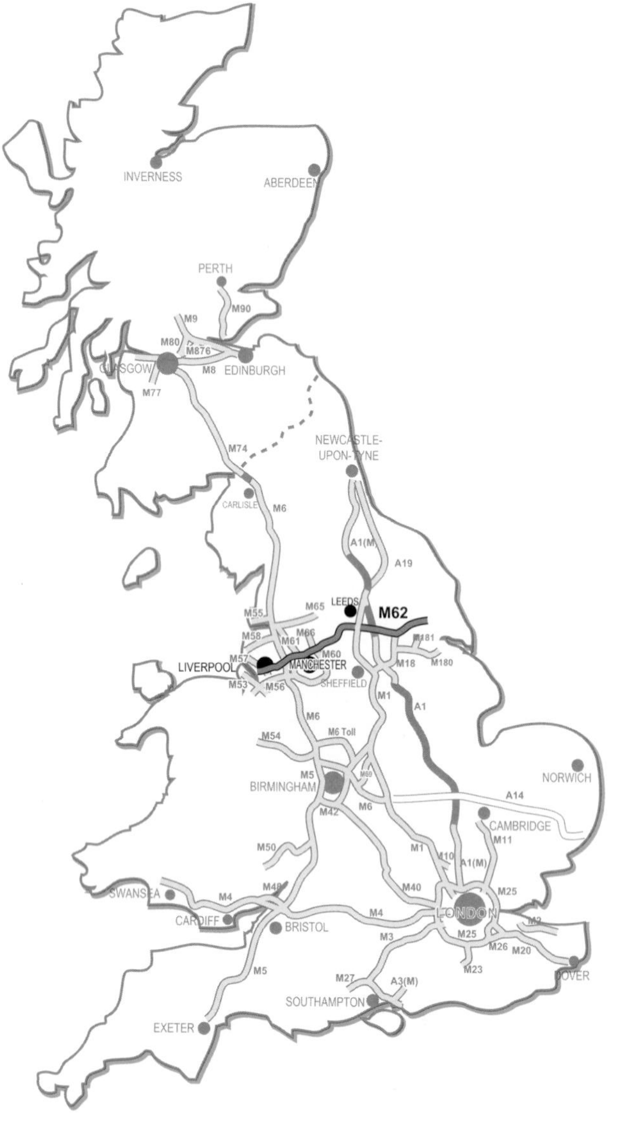
INVERNESS
ABERDEEN
PERTH
M90
M9
M80
M876
GLASGOW
M8
EDINBURGH
M77
NEWCASTLE-UPON-TYNE
M74
CARLISLE
M6
A1(M)
A19
M65
LEEDS
M62
M55
M58
M61
M66
M181
M57
M60
LIVERPOOL
MANCHESTER
M18
M180
M53
M56
SHEFFIELD
M1
A1
M6
M54
M6 Toll
NORWICH
M5
BIRMINGHAM
A14
M42
M6
CAMBRIDGE
M11
M50
M1
A1(M)
M25
M40
SWANSEA
M4
M48
LONDON
M4
CARDIFF
BRISTOL
M3
M25
M26
M20
M23
M5
M27
A3(M)
DOVER
SOUTHAMPTON
EXETER

## JUNCTIONS 1 TO 38

One of the few motorways which run laterally across the country. It is 108 miles long and was completed in 1976 to link the ports of Liverpool and Hull. It does not lend itself to gastronomic feasts.

It is divided into two sections.

# LIVERPOOL TO HUDDERSFIELD

## JUNCTIONS 6 TO 24

This part, from Liverpool to beyond Manchester, is not pretty. However, once past Junction 21, it climbs up into the Pennines and Junction 22, which at 1221 ft (372m) is the highest point of any motorway in the UK. It could be a remote spot for picnics near the top. The motorway then descends into the industrial areas of Huddersfield and Bradford.

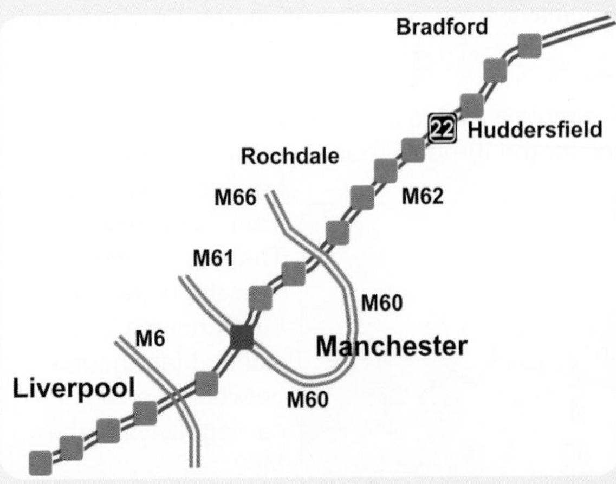

Junction 22 is the highest junction in the country and is 1221 feet or 372 metres above sea level. Take the A672 towards Ripponden. The Turnpike is about three miles on the left of the road. The views are stunning, marred only by the street lights along the motorway.

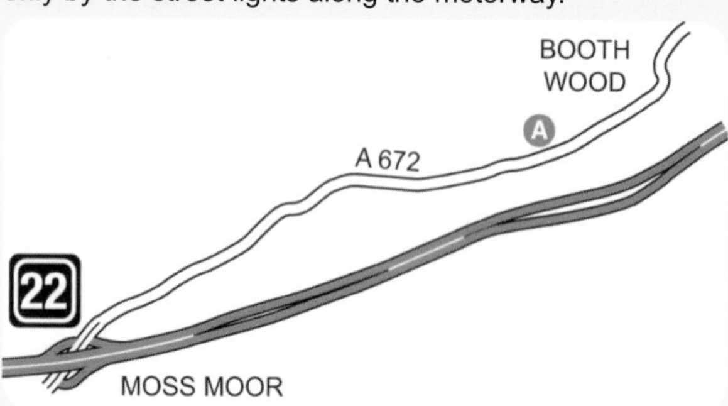


## Ⓐ The Turnpike

Satnav
**HX6 4QT**

Oldham Road, Rishworth, W.Yorks.
01422 822 789
www.turnpikeinn.com
bookit@turnpikeinn.com

**Orders for food:** Monday to Friday: Noon to 9.00pm. Saturdays: Noon to 10.00pm. Sundays: Noon to 8.00pm.

£

A simple wayside pub, which may have been the toll for the turnpike road. Apart from bar meals, breakfast can be had from 9.00am onwards. There is a good view over the reservoir to the Pennines and the isolated farmhouse between the two carriageways of the M62.

# LEEDS TO HULL

## JUNCTIONS 25 TO 38

Not the most attractive part of England as it passes through the industrial areas south of Leeds. However, once past the intersection with the A1(M) and the famous Ferrybridge Power Station, the surroundings become more rural, excepting the odd slag heap or power station. It is flat and level and full of drainage ditches and fens.

The M62 crosses over the Ouse at Goole with views over the surrounding countryside. The tower of the Minster at Howden is impressive and the inland port of Goole, made visible by the cranes, is to the south.

The motorway ceases just short of Brough, an old Roman town which was the ferry point for those crossing over the Humber in those days. It continues as a dual carriageway to Hull and the ferry terminals for Rotterdam and Zeebrugge.

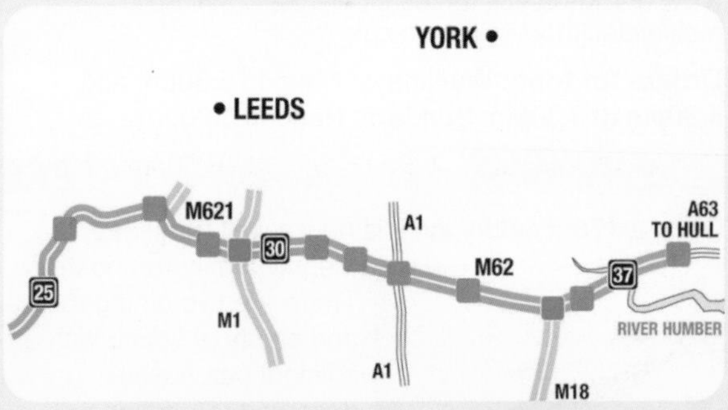

Take the road to Brighouse. After less than half a mile there is a road to the right. Up the hill and bear to the left. The Black Horse is on the left.

## Ⓐ The Black Horse Inn

Satnav
**HD6 4HJ**

Towgate, Clifton, W.Yorks.
01484 713 862
www.blackhorseclifton.co.uk
mail@blackhorseclifton.co.uk

**Orders for food:** Weekdays: Noon to 2.30pm and 5.30pm to 9.30pm. Sundays: Noon to 8.00pm.

£££

Once a 17th-century inn it is now a well-furnished, friendly family-run hostelry. There are two dining rooms and plenty of space with an efficient bar. A well-deserved reputation for comfort and ease in this part of the world.

The Three Horse Shoes is easy to find as it is on the right just over the first roundabout of the A642 on the way to Leeds.

## Ⓐ Three Horse Shoes

Satnav
**LS26 8JU**

16 Leeds Road, Oulton, W.Yorks
0113 282 2370
www.threehorseshoesoulton.co.uk
info@threehorseshoesoulton.co.uk

**Orders for food:** Daily: 11.30am to 9.00pm.
Sundays: Noon to 8.00pm.

A popular place, especially for those living nearby. It has won Best Pub for Flowers in Yorkshire for the past three years and the hanging baskets are a wonder to behold. Friendly and quick service even though the place may be full of folk.

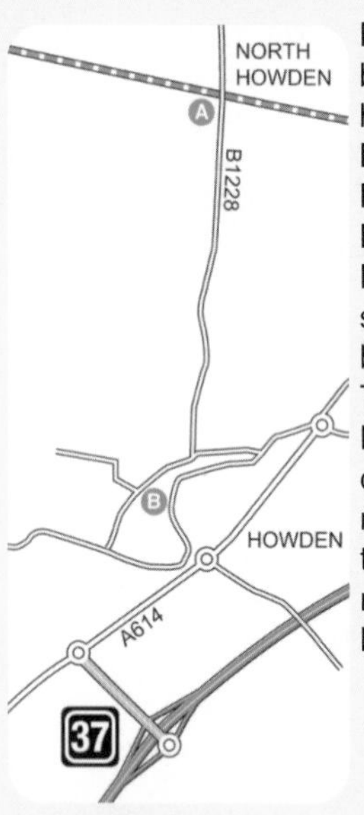


Howden was once famous for being one of Europe's largest horse fairs and where the Bishop of Durham's Summer Palace was situated. With the Dissolution of the Monasteries Howden declined and until some thirty years ago it had become a one horse town. Thanks to the generosity of the Monument Trust the Great Hall of the Palace was rescued and restored and since then the town has become a picturesque market town again dominated by the Minster.

## Ⓐ Wellington Hotel

Satnav
**DN14 7JG**

31 Bridgegate, Howden, Yorks
01430 430 258
wellingtonhotel@rocketmail.com

**Orders for food:** Weekdays: Noon to 2.00pm and 6.00pm to 9.00pm. Saturdays and Sundays: Noon to 3.00pm.

A local hotel owned by Old Milll Brewery in Snaith. I stayed there many years ago and it is a simple honest-to-goodness Yorkshire hostelry. It still serves that vanishing species of food - the sandwich at lunch for those in a hurry.

*The Minster at Howden.*

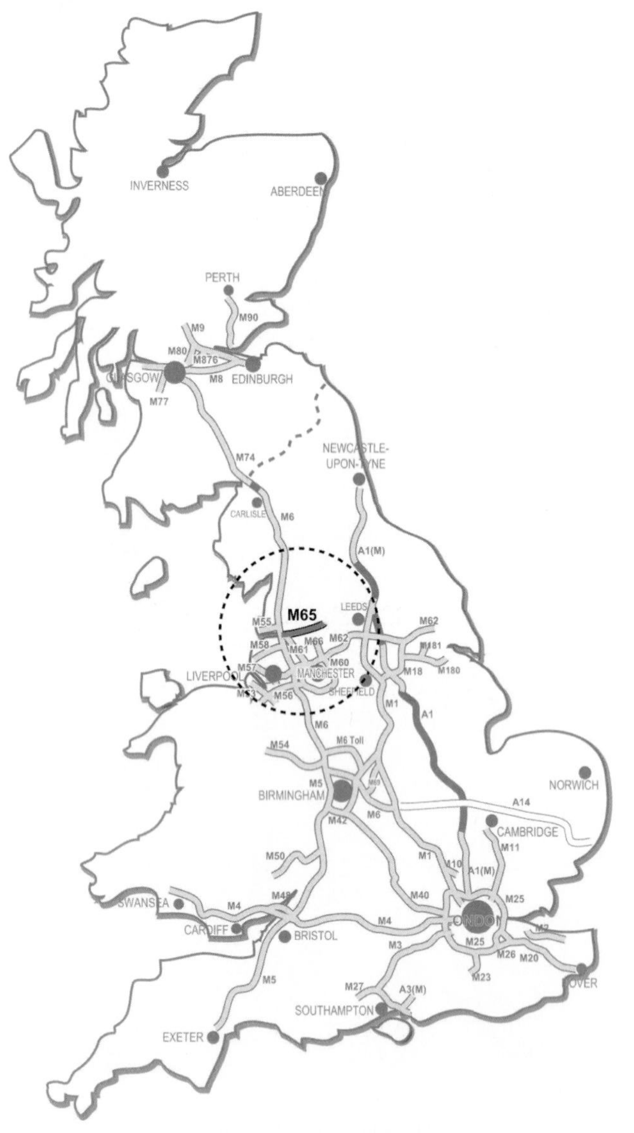
INVERNESS
ABERDEEN
PERTH
M90
M9
M80
M876
GLASGOW
M8
EDINBURGH
M77
M74
NEWCASTLE-UPON-TYNE
CARLISLE
M6
A1(M)
M65
LEEDS
M55
M62
M58
M61
M66
M181
M57
M60
LIVERPOOL
MANCHESTER
M18
M180
M53
M56
SHEFFIELD
M1
A1
M6
M54
M6 Toll
M5
BIRMINGHAM
M69
NORWICH
A14
M42
M6
CAMBRIDGE
M11
M50
M1
M10
A1(M)
M48
M40
M25
SWANSEA
M4
M4
CARDIFF
BRISTOL
M3
M25
M26
M20
M23
M5
M27
A3(M)
SOUTHAMPTON
EXETER

## JUNCTIONS 1 TO 27

For many years the M65 was a short isolated stretch from Blackburn to Colne. It has now been continued to link up with the M6 at Preston.

There is not much to say about it except that you are driving through the last remaining vestiges of the Lancashire cotton industry with huge palatial factories of Italianate architecture. The comforting sight of the Pennines visible on both sides of the motorway is welcome.

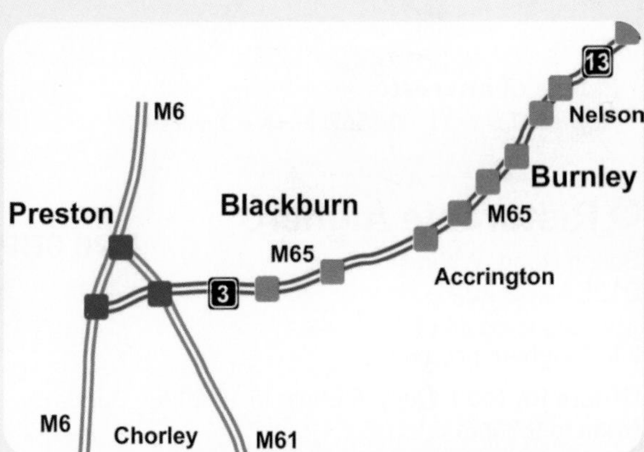

The roundabout at the end of the slip-road could be confusing.

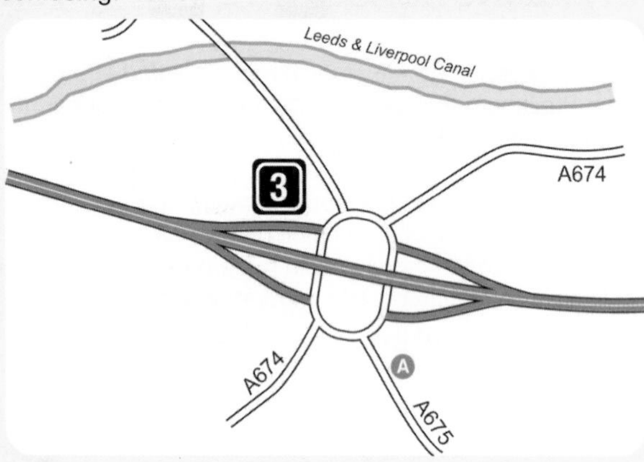


**Places of interest**

Hoghton Tower (1100-1565) HHA – 3 miles 

## Ⓐ Ristorante Alghero

Satnav
**PR6 8BP**

Bolton Road, Withnell, Lancs.
01254 202 222
www.algheros.co.uk
info@algheros.co.uk

**Orders for food:** Daily: 6.00pm to 10.00pm. Sundays: Noon to 9.30pm.

£££

As the name implies, this is a Sardinian restaurant which has a good local reputation and a friendly atmosphere.

As you come off the motorway to Barrowford the Thatch and Thistle is on your left.

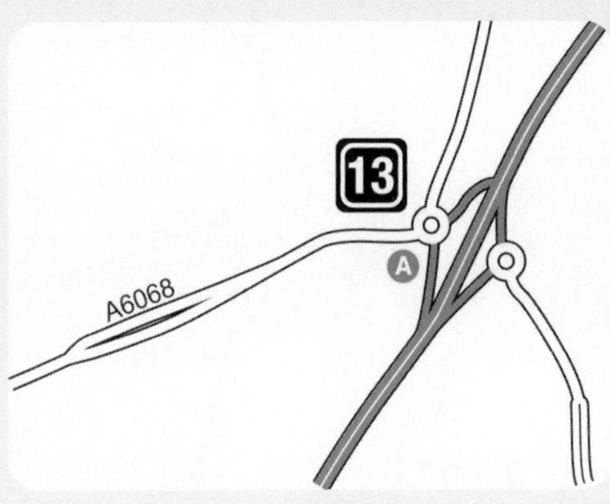


## Ⓐ Thatch and Thistle

Satnav
**BB9 7TZ**

Surrey Road, Nelson, Lancs.
01282 615 215
4890@greeneking.co.uk

**Orders for food:** Daily: 11.00am to 9.00pm.

££

A modern thatched roadhouse which has an American flavour. Large open areas for eating, a pool table for amusement and open (gas) fires for warmth. The welcome is friendly and the staff were very helpful to me.

M66

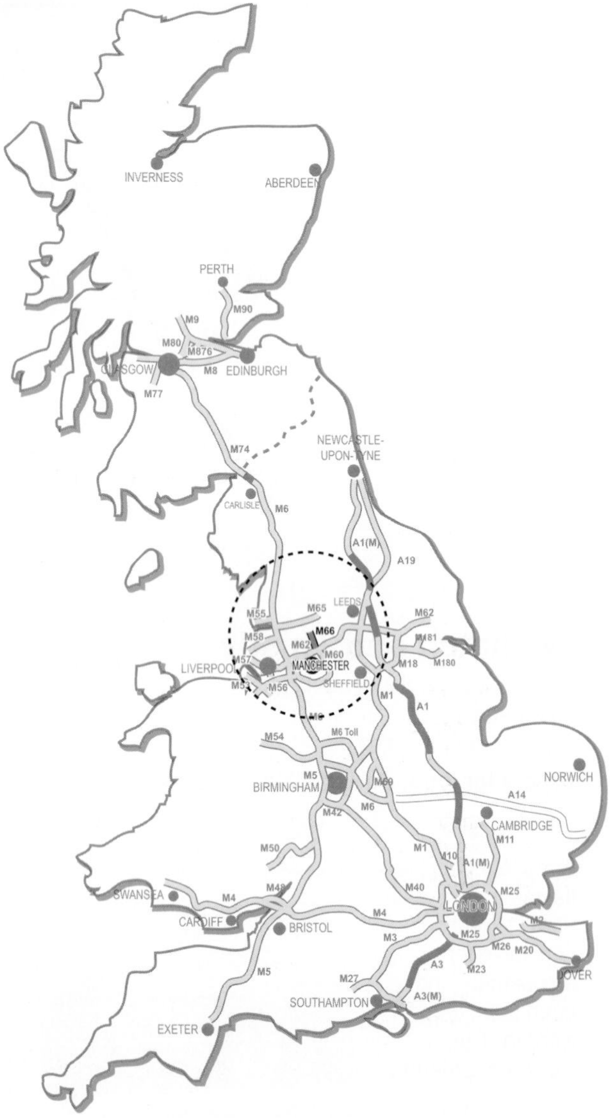

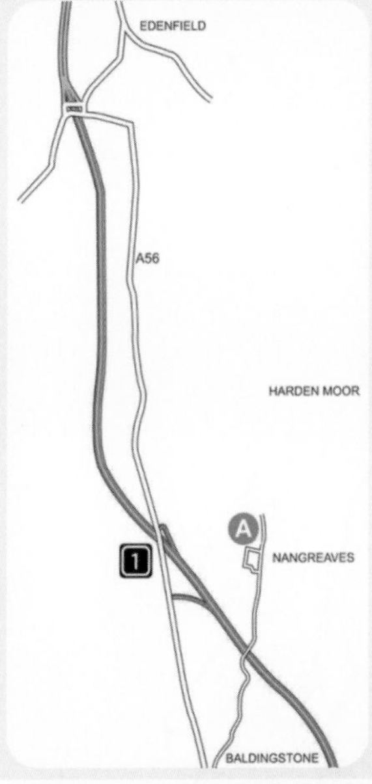


Going North come off at the Junction and left on the A56 to Bury. After 1½ miles turn left at the traffic lights and take the Old Road up the hill to Nangreaves which is a cobbled road throughout. The Lord Raglan is to the left as you get to the top of the hill, which is a dead end. To continue North drive up the A56 to Edenfield.

Driving south, you will have to get off at Edenfield and rejoin the M66 at Junction 1.

## A The Lord Raglan

Satnav **BL9 6SP**

Mount Pleasant, Nr Bury, Lancs.
0161 764 6680
www.lordraglannangreaves.co.uk

**Orders for food:** Monday to Thursday: Noon to 2.00pm and 6.00pm to 9.00pm Fridays. Noon to 2.00pm and 5.00pm to 9.00pm. Saturdays: Noon to 9.00pm. Sundays: Noon to 8.00pm.

£

It is aptly named Mount Pleasant as you will find yourself on top of the hills in rural Lancashire with a view of moorland and the Pennines. It has been in the same family for three generations so it has a cheerful atmosphere with a friendly staff. The menu and the moorland airmake for a pleasant stopover.

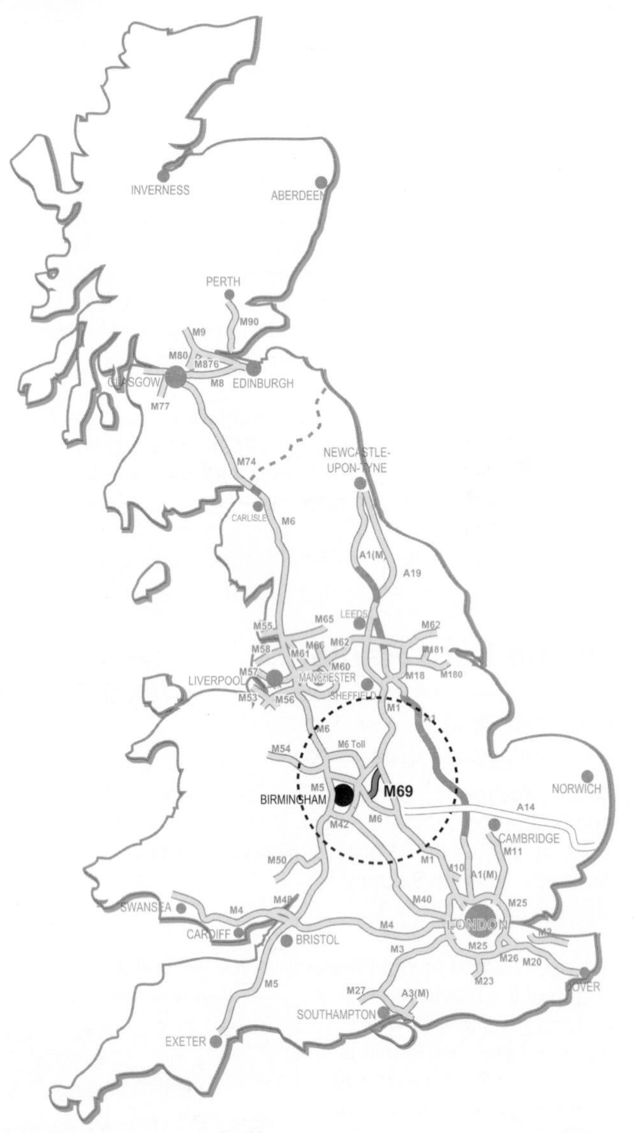
INVERNESS
ABERDEEN
PERTH
M90
M9
M80
M876
GLASGOW
M8
EDINBURGH
M77
M74
NEWCASTLE-
UPON-TYNE
CARLISLE
M6
A1(M)
A19
M65
LEEDS
M55
M62
M58
M66
M62
M181
M61
M60
M57
LIVERPOOL
MANCHESTER
M18
M180
M53
M56
SHEFFIELD
M1
A1
M6
M6 Toll
M54
M5
BIRMINGHAM
M69
NORWICH
A14
M42
M6
CAMBRIDGE
M11
M50
M1
M10
A1(M)
M48
M40
M25
SWANSEA
M4
M4
LONDON
CARDIFF
BRISTOL
M3
M25
M2
M26
M20
M23
M5
M27
A3(M)
DOVER
SOUTHAMPTON
EXETER

## JUNCTIONS 1 TO M1

The motorway was built in the mid 1970s to give direct access between Coventry and Leicester. It is comparatively little used so is useful to those who use the M1 or M40 as a means of driving north or south.

The junction with the M1 is rather abrupt as a result of a decision at the time not to make it into a proper clover-leaf exit as the volume of traffic would not warrant the expense. It will now be very expensive to reverse the decision.

The building of the motorways has had the curious effect of isolating corners of the countryside to create rural areas of calm, such as the part around Bosworth Field ("…my kingdom for a horse"), which has now been proved to be in the wrong place!

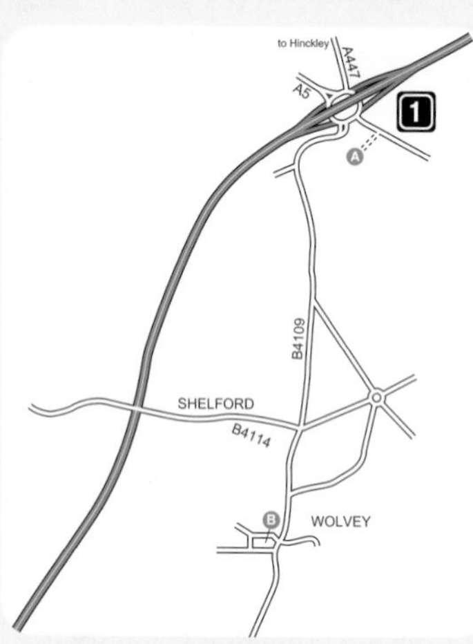


Pretty straightforward for Barnacles Restaurant. For the Blue Pig take the Wolvey Road. In the village there is a modern pub and a post office on the right and a sharp turning just beyond it. Turn right and the Blue Pig is down the road on the left.

**Places of interest**

Bosworth Battlefield (1485) – 8 miles

## A Barnacles Restaurant

Satnav **LE10 3JA**

Watling Street, Hinckley, Warks.
01455 633 220
www.barnaclesrestaurant.co.uk
enq@barnaclesrestaurant.co.uk

**Orders for food:** Mondays: 6.30pm to 9.00pm. Tuesdays to Fridays: Noon to 2.00pm and 6.30pm to 9.00pm. Saturdays: 6.00pm to 9.30pm. Sundays: Noon to 3.30pm.

£££

A privately owned restaurant in pleasant grounds with a lake. It specialises in fish and there is a separately owned fish shop next to the restaurant. Dogs are not welcomed and there are no special facilities for children.

## The Blue Pig

Satnav
**LE10 3LG**

Hall Road, Wolvey, Leics.
01455 220 256
www.thebluepigpub.co.uk
enquiries@thebluepig.co.uk

**Orders for food:** Tuesday to Saturday: Noon to 2.00pm and 6.00pm to 9.00pm. Mondays: Noon to 2.00pm. Sundays: Noon to 4.00pm.

££

An old coaching inn dating from the 15th century with exposed masonry walls and low beams with quips such as "Now Good Digestion wait on Appetite & Health on Both". There is a restaurant and a bar serving home cooked specials and real ales. It has recently come under new management so advisable to telephone beforehand to check.

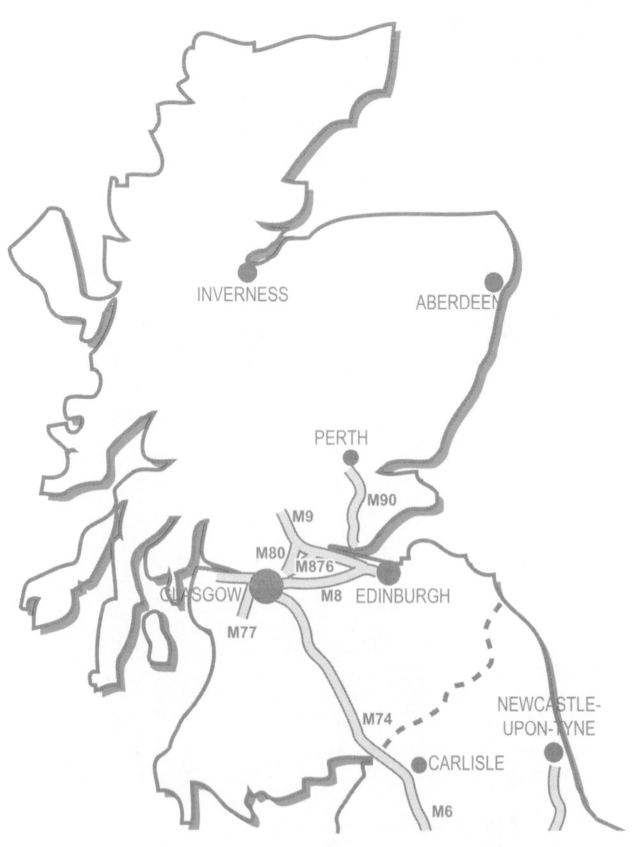
INVERNESS
ABERDEEN
PERTH
M90
M9
M80
M876
GLASGOW
M8
EDINBURGH
M77
M74
NEWCASTLE-
UPON-TYNE
CARLISLE
M6

# SCOTLAND

Scotland may extend a warm welcome to visitors and even Sassenachs, but the motorway user gets the impression that the Scots have forgotten the art of hospitality to the passing traveller.

Part of this impression may be due to the fact that the new motorways, except for the M74, do not follow the old coaching routes.

There are some excellent exceptions to the rule, but there were a lot of places which did not come up to scratch. On the M8 for example, from Edinburgh to Glasgow, there is only one single place worthy of being mentioned, but that is too difficult to find.

The most tedious aspect of the Scottish motorways is the system of linked junctions. It might save money, but it generates unnecessary driving on minor roads.

# M9

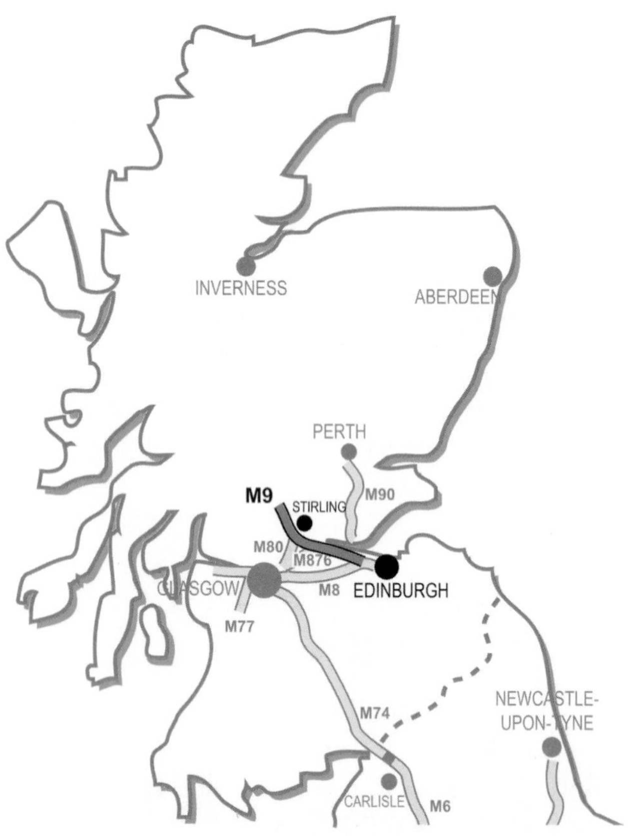

INVERNESS
ABERDEEN
PERTH
M9
STIRLING
M90
M80
M876
GLASGOW
M8
EDINBURGH
M77
M74
NEWCASTLE-
UPON-TYNE
CARLISLE
M6

# EDINBURGH TO STIRLING M9

## JUNCTIONS  TO 11

Starting near the Airport it passes through agricultural country and past old shale heaps.

You then drive past the impressive ruins of Linlithgow Palace, which was admired even by the French princesses who were married to Scottish kings. It was burnt in 1745 during the Jacobite Rebellion and has been roofless ever since. There are rumours that parts could be re-roofed.

The motorway ends north of the equally impressive Stirling Castle, the favourite refuge for the Scottish kings, which was remodelled by James V and is a fine example of Renaissance architecture.

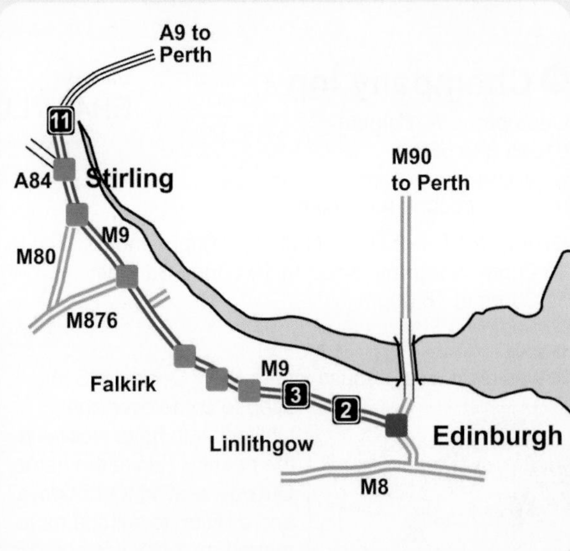

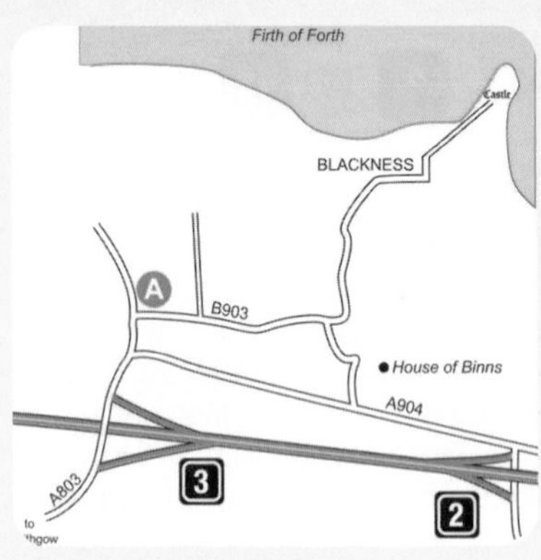


Like most of the junctions these are linked together, depending upon the direction of travel. There are alternative places in Linlithgow to suit most requirements.

**Places of interest**

Hopetoun House (1699 & 1721) HHA – 4 miles 
The House of the Binns (17thC) NTS – 1 miles
Blackness Castle (14th & 16thC) HS – 3 miles
Linlithgow Palace (Burnt 1746) HS – 2 miles

# A Champany Inn

Satnav
**EH49 7LU**

Champany, W. Lothian
01506 834 532
www.champany.com
reception@champany.com

**Orders for food:** Daily: Noon to 2.00pm and 6.30pm to 10.00pm. Saturday: Noon to 10.00pm. Sunday: 12.30am to 10.00pm.

£££

It was once a farmhouse where Mary Queen of Scots used to come over from Linlithgow to have picnics in the country, hence the name. Outside seating for hot days and a Bistro to suit the more hurried motorist. It is noted for Aberdeen Angus beef.

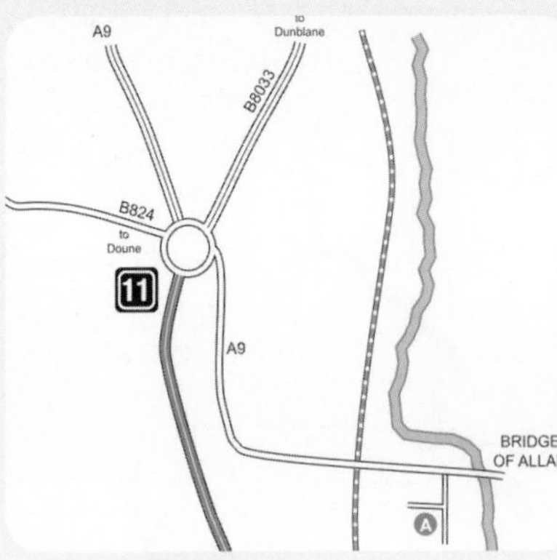


After coming off the roundabout, drive towards the outskirts of the Bridge of Allan. Turn right just before the bridge with a high wooded bluff on the other side of the river. The Inn is to the right.

**Places of interest**

Doune Castle (14thC) HS – 3 miles
Stirling Castle (13thC & Renaissance) HS – 5 miles
Argyll's Lodging (17thC) HS – 5 miles
The Wallace Monument – 2 miles

## A The Old Bridge Inn

Satnav
**FK9 4JA**

Inverallen Road, Bridge of Allen, Stirlings.
01786 833 335
www.oldbridgeinn.co.uk

**Orders for food:** Daily: Noon to 2.30pm and 6.00pm to 9.00pm. Closed Mondays.

££

The Inn was originally surrounded by mills and by Willie's brewery. The interior has been stripped out to make a larger area with rough stone walls and timber panelling to form a comfortable restaurant/bar, where local fish and salmon from the Tay is also served. The thoughtful owners provided me with a newspaper in case I needed an excuse not to converse with my talkative neighbours. A bell from a Glasgow church is used to signal last orders.

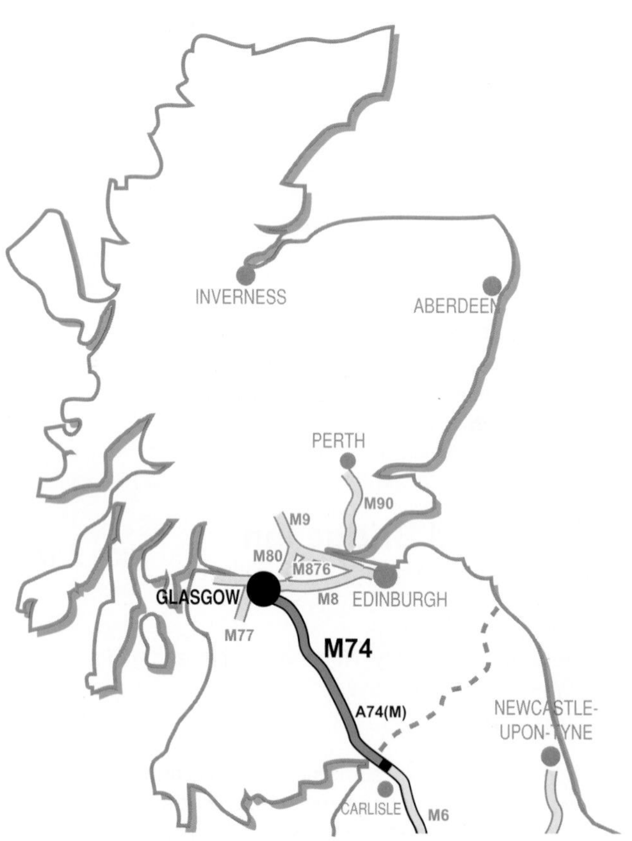
INVERNESS
ABERDEEN
PERTH
M90
M9
M80
M876
GLASGOW
M8
EDINBURGH
M77
M74
A74(M)
NEWCASTLE-UPON-TYNE
CARLISLE
M6

## JUNCTIONS 4 TO 22

The A74 has now been rebuilt to motorway standard throughout.

North of Junction 13 it is the M74, but south to the Border it is still the A74(M).

Between Scotland and England the section of dual carriageways has been upgraded so that the M6 now goes as far as the border.

There is almost nowhere south of Glasgow where you can stop to find a decent meal. However, there are some impressive buildings to see such as Bothwell Castle, Chatelherault, Cadzow Castle and Craigneathen.

The town of Moffat off Junction 15 is interesting and has a variety of places to eat and sleep.

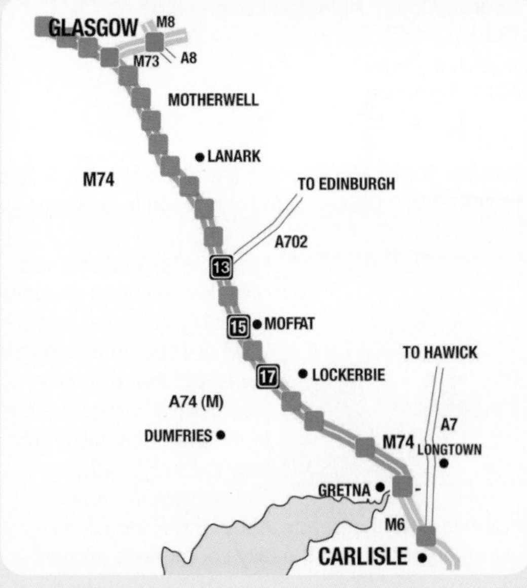

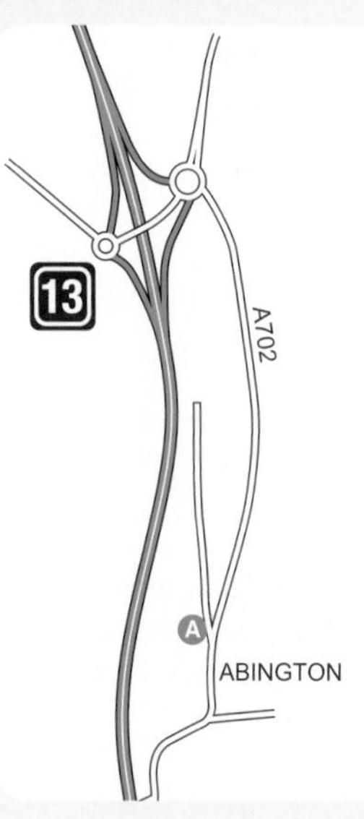


Drive into Abington from the junction. The hotel is to your right as you come into the village.

## Ⓐ The Abington Hotel

Satnav
**DG10 9HF**

78 Carlisle Road, Abington,Lanarkshire
01864 502 467
www.ab-hotel.com
info@ab-hotel.com

**Orders for food:** Monday to Saturdays: Noon to 2.30pm and 5.30pm to 9.00pm. Sundays: Noon to 3.00pm.

Mr and Mrs McBride now own the hotel and gave me a friendly welcome and a hot bowl of soup on a cold day. I was told that Emperor Napoleon III sat on the chair in the entrance hall on his way to the Eglington Tournament in 1834.

Abington is near the headwater of the River Clyde so you can stretch your legs in the hilly countryside around.

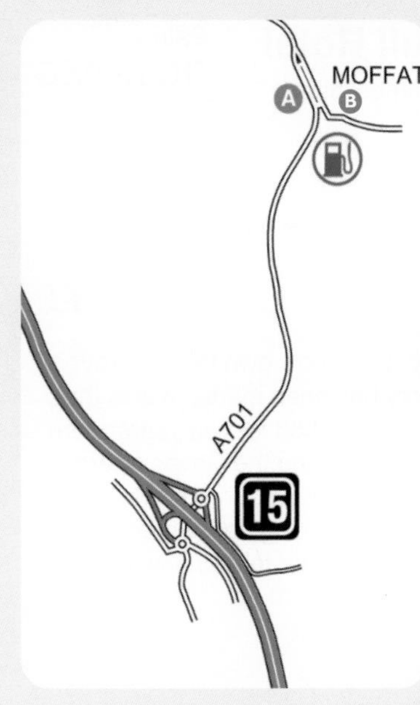


Moffat is an interesting market town and worth the detour to see it. The Café Ariete was suggested by a reader but there are many other places in the town such as the Rumblin Tum, the Buccleugh Arms or the more up-market Moffat House Hotel.

## Ⓐ Café Ariete

Satnav
**DG10 9HF**

10 High Street, Moffat, Dumfriesshire
01683 220 313

**Orders for food:** Daily: 9.00am to 5.00pm.

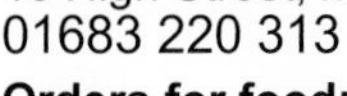

As the name suggests, it is a café which has good coffee, ice cream and cakes made on the premises, as well as a range of fillings for baps and also freshly made sandwiches. There is proper soup for colder days. A friendly welcome and a cheerful atmosphere.

## Ⓑ The Black Bull Hotel

Satnav **DG10 9EG**

Churchgate, Moffat, Dumfriesshire.
01683 220 206
www.blackbullmoffat.com
nicky@blackbullmoffat.com

**Orders for food:** Daily: 9.00am to 9.00pm

Alasdair Rankin and Nicky Long now own this ex-drovers hotel where Scottish history has been made. It was the headquarters of Claverhouse in 1683 for two years when he was given the task of suppressing the Covenanters- hence his nickname of Bloody Clavers. In addition to history there is a restaurant and a long bar named after Robert Burns who etched a poem on the window in 1791.

An easy junction, you can see the hotel from the motorway.

**Places of interest**

Lochmaben Castle (15thC) HS – 4 miles

## Ⓐ Dryfesdale Hotel

Satnav
**DG11 2SF**

Nr. Lockerbie, Dumfriesshire
01576 202 427
www.dryfesdalehotel.co.uk
reception@dryfesdalehotel.co.uk

**Orders for food:** Daily: Noon to 2.00pm and 6.00pm to 9.00pm. Sundays: Noon to 2.00pm and 6.00pm to 8.00pm.

£££

The house was built in the late 17th century as the Manse and was converted into a hotel in the early 1900s. It has a restaurant and a bar catering for lunches and dinners, and bar meals are available for those in a hurry. Telephone beforehand.

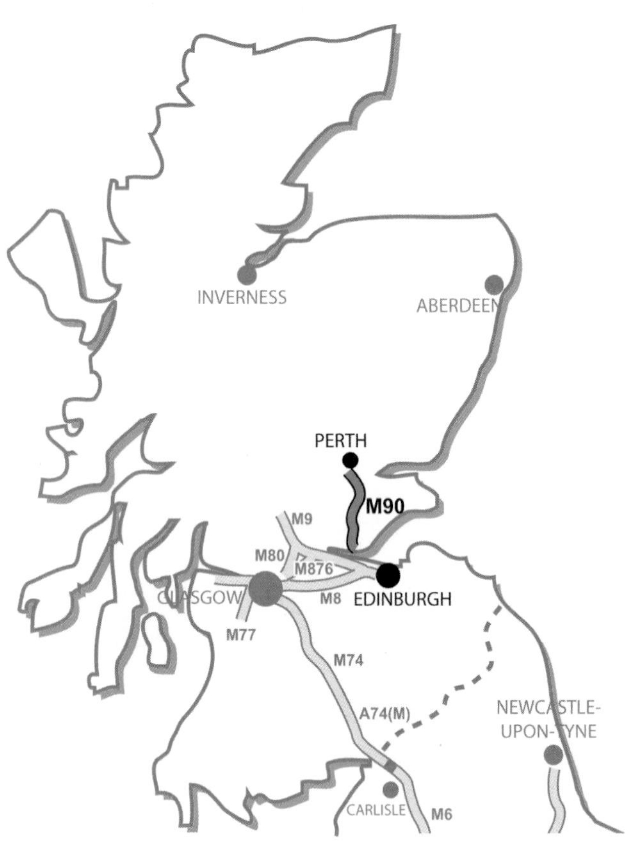
INVERNESS
ABERDEEN
PERTH
M90
M9
M80
M876
GLASGOW
M8
EDINBURGH
M77
M74
A74(M)
NEWCASTLE-UPON-TYNE
CARLISLE
M6

## JUNCTIONS 1 TO 11

An interesting motorway which starts at the Forth Road Bridge and passes Loch Leven, where Mary Queen of Scots was imprisoned. Further on, the motorway passes Glenfarg and then drops down to the Bridge of Earn. Beyond Moncrieffe Hill are the outskirts of Perth and towards the north the distant outline of the Highlands can be seen.

On the way, there are castles such as Huntingtower and Elcho to be seen and to the east is Abernethy, where William the Conqueror took the personal submission of the Scottish King Malcolm Canmore in 1072.

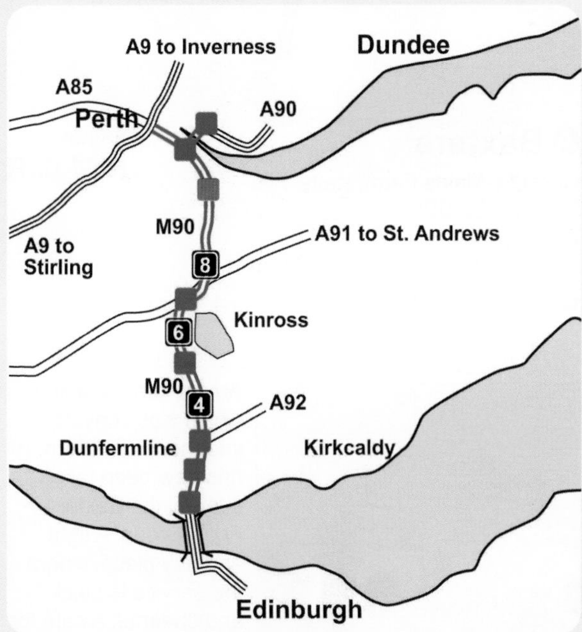

You can see Baxters from the motorway when coming from the south.

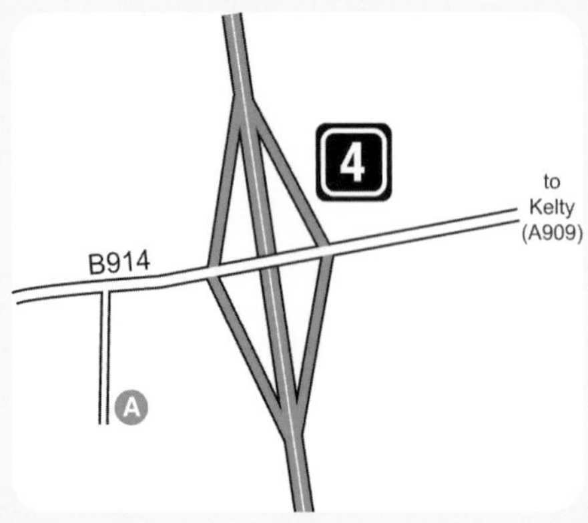


## Ⓐ Baxters

Satnav
**KY4 0JR**

Cocklaw-Mains Farm, Kelty, Fife
01383 832 020
www.baxters.co.uk
natalierichardson@baxters.co.uk

**Orders for food:** Daily: 9.00am to 4.15pm.

An old farm steading which was converted into the Butterchurn. It has now been taken over by the Baxters Food Group. A light and airy place, where the service is quick and cheerful. A café for those in a hurry and a food shop where Baxters' world famous range of food products can be bought.

The private road to The Grouse and Claret is opposite the Esso Filling Station. If it is full, there are at least four good hotels in Kinross.

**Places of interest**

Loch Leven Castle (14thC) HS – 2 miles
Kinross House Garden (17thC) HHA – 1 mile

## Ⓐ Grouse and Claret

Heatheryford, Kinross
01577 864 212
www.grouseandclaret.com
grouseandclaret@lineone.net

Satnav
**KY13 0NQ**

**Orders for food:** Daily: Noon to 2.00pm and 6.30pm to 9.00pm. Sundays: No evening meals. Mondays: Closed.

££

A surprisingly peaceful spot, with a large garden looking onto a small loch. An imaginative menu, combining Scottish ingredients with an Eastern twist, in a comfortable restaurant with a bar.

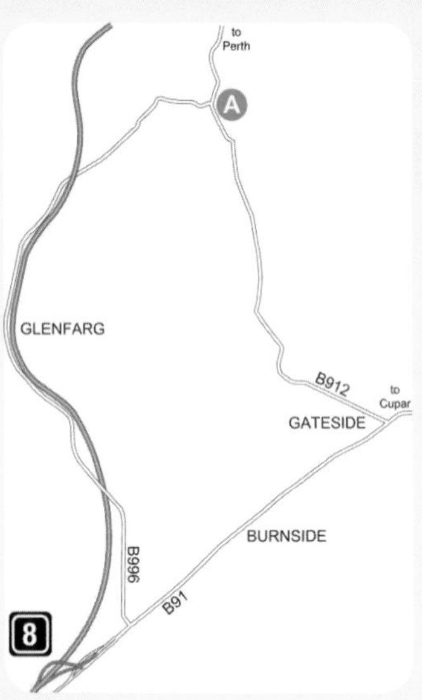


Those of us who had to endure the twisting road by Glenfarg before the advent of the motorway will remember the Bein Inn. The old road the B996 is still there but access is from Junction 8 or else, at the bottom, at Junction 9.

## Ⓐ The Bein Inn

Satnav
**PH2 9PY**

Main Road, Glenfarg, Perthshire
01577 830 216
www.beininn.com
enquiries@beininn.com

**Orders for food:** Daily: Noon to 9.00pm in summer. In winter: Noon to 2.30pm and 5.00pm to 9.00pm.

££

Set in a tree-covered dip by the old road it was well known to those travelling north or south. It is now family-owned and father and son have made it into an efficient, well-run hotel with a good reputation for food. A cheerful atmosphere made so by the helpful staff.

# Notes

# Notes

| Name | Motorway | Junction | Page |
|---|---|---|---|
| **England & Wales** | | | |
| Abington Hotel | M74 | 13 | 278 |
| Alghero | M65 | 3 | 262 |
| Angel View | A1 | 65 | 37 |
| Angel | M20 | 4 | 186 |
| Apley Farm Shop | M54 | 4 | 243 |
| Barnacles | M69 | 1 | 268 |
| Bay Horse | M6 | 33 | 163 |
| Belgian Arms | M4 | 8/9 | 102 |
| Bell | M25 | 6 | 199 |
| Bell Hotel | M27 | 1 | 208 |
| Bell Inn | M5 | 13 | 130 |
| Bell Inn | M6 | 12 | 152 |
| Bell Inn Hotel | A1 | 16 | 9 |
| Bird in Hand | M4 | 48 | 121 |
| Black Bull | M74 | 15 | 280 |
| Black Horse | A1 | - | 31 |
| Black Horse | M5 | 19 | 134 |
| Black Horse | M25 | 18 | 202 |
| Black Horse | M62 | 25 | 256 |
| Black Swan | M23 | 11 | 195 |
| Bliss Tearoom | M1 | 16 | 72 |
| Blue Ball | M5 | 30 | 145 |
| Blue Bell | A1 | - | 21 |
| Blue Pig | M69 | 1 | 269 |
| Bo Peep | M25 | 4 | 198 |
| Boars Head | M48 | 1 | 228 |
| Bowl Inn | M5 | 16 | 133 |
| Brantwood Hotel | M6 | 40 | 169 |
| Bridgwater | A1 | 56 | 35 |
| Bull | M4 | 18 | 116 |
| Bush | M3 | 9 | 99 |
| Canalside Craft | M6 | 33 | 162 |
| Carpenters Arms | M1 | 12 | 68 |
| Carrington Arms | M1 | 14 | 70 |
| Castle | M25 | 11 | 200 |
| Caunton Beck | A1 | - | 18 |
| Chequers | A1 | 42 | 23 |
| Chequers | M1 | 19 | 76 |
| Cherry Tree | M40 | 6 | 214 |
| Chestnut Horse | M3 | 9 | 98 |

# Alphabetical Index


| Name | Motorway | Junction | Page |
|---|---|---|---|
| Chetwode Arms | M56 | 10 | 247 |
| Chiseldon House | M4 | 15 | 111 |
| Cock | A14 | 25 | 51 |
| Compass Tavern | M5 | 24 | 139 |
| County | A1 | 59 | 36 |
| Crab & Lobster | A1 | 49 | 28 |
| Crooklands Hotel | M6 | 40 | 164 |
| Cross Keys | M6 | 38 | 165 |
| Crown | A1 | 17 | 11 |
| Crown | M4 | 18 | 115 |
| Crown Hotel | M6 | 43 | 170 |
| Crown Inn | A1 | 48 | 26 |
| Crown & Cushion | M3 | 4a | 94 |
| Crown & Punchbowl | A14 | 34 | 54 |
| David Austin Roses | M54 | 3 | 242 |
| Diggers Rest | M5 | 30 | 146 |
| Dressers Arms | M61 | 8 | 251 |
| Drum | M20 | 11 | 191 |
| ElmTree | M1 | 29 | 81 |
| Falcon | A1 | 17 | 12 |
| Falcon | M1 | 24 | 80 |
| Farriers Arms | M20 | 10 | 189 |
| Field Head Hotel | M1 | 22 | 79 |
| Fleet Inn | M50 | 1 | 232 |
| Fox | A1 | 9 | 3 |
| Fox & Hounds | A1 | 46 | 24 |
| Fox & Hounds | A1 | - | 29 |
| Fox & Hounds | M40 | 5 | 212 |
| Fox & Hounds | M40 | 10 | 216 |
| Fox & Hounds | M53 | 4 | 238 |
| French Horn | M1 | 12 | 69 |
| Frombridge Mill | M5 | 13 | 131 |
| Gate Inn | M6 | 40 | 168 |
| General Tarleton | A1 | 48 | 27 |
| George Brasserie | A1 | - | 7 |
| George Inn | A14 | 18 | 49 |
| Greendale | M5 | 30 | 146 |
| Green Dragon | M27 | 1 | 209 |
| Green Man | M11 | 10 | 177 |
| Green Man | M11 | 12 | 180 |
| Greyhound | A1 | - | 32 |
| Greyhound | M1 | 20 | 28 |

| Name | Motorway | Junction | Page |
|---|---|---|---|
| Greyhound | M6 | 39 | 167 |
| Hankridge Arms | M5 | 25 | 140 |
| Hardwick Inn | M1 | 29 | 82 |
| Hare | A14 | 3 | 45 |
| Hare restaurant | M4 | 14 | 108 |
| Hare & Hounds | A1 | - | 5 |
| Hare & Hounds | M20 | 9 | 188 |
| Harrow Inn | M2 | 5 | 89 |
| Hit or Miss | M4 | 17 | 112 |
| Hobnails Inn | M5 | 9 | 128 |
| Hole in the Wall | A14 | 35 | 55 |
| Honest Miller | M20 | 10 | 190 |
| Honey Bee | M56 | 6 | 246 |
| Italian Orchard | M6 | 32 | 160 |
| Jabula Restaurant | M53 | 9 | 239 |
| Jack In the Green | M5 | 29 | 144 |
| Jackson Stops | A1 | - | 13 |
| John Bull | M18 | 6 | 183 |
| Jolly Huntsman | M4 | 17 | 114 |
| Kennedys | M6 | 38 | 166 |
| Kilcot Inn | M50 | 3 | 235 |
| King Willam IV | A14 | 27 | 52 |
| Kings Arms | M20 | 7 | 187 |
| Langley Hall Inn | M4 | 13 | 106 |
| Leathern Bottle | M2 | 1 | 88 |
| Lion Hotel | A1 | - | 6 |
| Littleton Arms | M6 | 12 | 152 |
| Lord Raglan | M66 | 1 | 265 |
| Malt Shovel | M40 | 12 | 219 |
| Manor Farm Shop | M1 | 19 | 77 |
| Merry Harriers | M5 | 26 | 141 |
| Moody Cow | M50 | 3 | 235 |
| Moorings | M1 | 18 | 73 |
| Mussel & Crab | A1 | - | 19 |
| Nags Head | A1 | 50 | 30 |
| Neeld Arms | M4 | 17 | 113 |
| New Inn | M4 | 17 | 113 |
| New Inn | M40 | 11 | 218 |
| Nobody Inn | M5 | 31 | 147 |
| Norton Dog | A14 | 47 | 58 |
| Oad Street Centre | M2 | 5 | 90 |
| Old Chequers | M5 | 6 | 125 |

# Alphabetical Index


| Name | Motorway | Junction | Page |
|---|---|---|---|
| Old House at Home | M3 | 5 | 95 |
| Old Leathern Bottle | M40 | 6 | 213 |
| Old Oak Tree | A19 | - | 63 |
| Old Post Office | M1 | 38 | 84 |
| Olde Punchbowl | A1 (M) | 48 | 27 |
| Olde Red Lion | M4 | 13 | 105 |
| Old Well | M5 | 27 | 143 |
| Olive Branch | A1 | - | 14 |
| Orchard | M11 | 12 | 180 |
| Oswalds | A19 | - | 62 |
| Overstone | A14 | 9 | 46 |
| Pheasant | A14 | 15 | 48 |
| Pheasant | M4 | 14 | 107 |
| Plough | M4 | 15 | 110 |
| Portway Restaurant | M42 | 3 | 224 |
| Prince of Wales | M4 | 37 | 120 |
| Priory | M5 | 19 | 135 |
| Puriton Inn | M5 | 23 | 138 |
| Queens Head | M11 | 11 | 178 |
| Queen Inn | M3 | 7 | 96 |
| Rainbow & Dove | M11 | 7 | 174 |
| Red Cat | M61 | 8 | 250 |
| Red House | M4 | 14 | 106 |
| Red Lion | A3 | 1 | 40 |
| Red Lion | M1 | 18 | 74 |
| Red Lion | M2 | 7 | 91 |
| Red Lion | M11 | 9 | 176 |
| Reindeer | A1 | - | 17 |
| Rising Sun | M4 | 27 | 119 |
| Roadmaker | M50 | 3 | 234 |
| Robin Hood | A3 | 2 | 41 |
| Robin Hood | M5 | 5 | 124 |
| Rupert Brooke | M11 | 12 | 179 |
| Ship | A14 | 58 | 59 |
| Shoulder of Mutton | A1 | 56 | 34 |
| Silks on the Downs | M4 | 15 | 111 |
| Smoker | M6 | 19 | 156 |
| Snooty Fox | A14 | 12 | 47 |
| Stag | M6 | 44 | 171 |
| Stanwick Arms | A1 | 56 | 35 |
| Stilton Cheese | A1 | 16 | 10 |
| Sun Inn | M3 | 7 | 97 |

# Alphabetical Index


| Name | Motorway | Junction | Page |
|---|---|---|---|
| Swan | A14 | 2 | 44 |
| Swan  Hotel | M1 | 47 | 85 |
| Swan | M4 | 11 | 103 |
| Swan | M5 | 7 | 126 |
| Swan Inn | M25 | 16 | 201 |
| Thatch & Thistle | M65 | 13 | 263 |
| Three Horseshoes | A1 | 9 | 4 |
| Three Horseshoes | M11 | 13/14 | 181 |
| Three Horseshoes | M42 | 14 | 225 |
| Three Horseshoes | M62 | 30 | 257 |
| Three Tuns | A14 | 28 | 53 |
| Three Tuns | A19 | - | 64 |
| Three Willows | M11 | 8 | 175 |
| Tiger | A1 | 47 | 25 |
| Tollgate | M4 | 18 | 116 |
| Turnpike | M62 | 22 | 254 |
| Village Inn | M50 | 1 | 233 |
| Vineyard | M26 | 2a | 205 |
| Volunteer | M4 | 12 | 104 |
| Walter de Cantalupe | M5 | 7 | 127 |
| Welby Arms | A1 | - | 16 |
| Wellington Arms | M62 | 37 | 258 |
| Wheatsheaf | M4 | 23a | 118 |
| White Cottage | M5 | 22 | 137 |
| White Hatr | M27 | 1 | 209 |
| White Hart | M48 | 1 | 229 |
| White Horse | A14 | 42 | 56 |
| White Lion | M6 | 16 | 154 |
| White Lion | M6 | 27 | 159 |
| White Swan | A1 | 34 | 20 |
| White Swan | M23 | 10 | 194 |
| Windmill | M6 | 19 | 157 |
| Zest Restaurant | M6 | 17 | 155 |

| Name | Motorway | Junction | Page |
|---|---|---|---|
| **SCOTLAND** | | | |
| Abington Hotel | M74 | 13 | 278 |
| Baxters | M90 | 4 | 284 |
| Bein Inn | M90 | 8 | 286 |
| Black Bull | M74 | 15 | 280 |
| Café Ariete | M74 | 15 | 279 |
| Champany Inn | M9 | 2/3 | 274 |
| Dryfesdale | M74 | 17 | 281 |
| Grouse & Claret | M90 | 6 | 285 |
| Old Bridge Hotel | M9 | 11 | 275 |

# Index by Motorways

## England and Wales


### A1(M)

9 Fox
9 Three Horseshoes
- Hare & Hounds
- Lion Hotel
- George Brasserie
16 Bell Inn
16 Stilton Cheese
17 Crown
17 Falcon
- Jackson Stops
- Olive Branch
- Caunton Beck
- Mussel & Crab
- Blue Bell
34 White Swan
42 Chequers
46 Fox & Hounds
47 Tiger
48 Crown
48 General Tarleton
48 Olde Punch Bow
49 Crab & Lobster
50 Fox & Hounds
50 Nags Head
51 Green Dragon
- Black Horse
- Greyhound
56 Shoulder of Mutton
56 Stanwick Arms
56 Bridgewater Arms
59 The County
65 Angel View Inn

### A3(M)

1 Red Lion
2 Robin Hood

### A14

2 The Swan
3 The Hare
9 Overstone
12 Snooty Fox
15 Pheasant
18 George Inn
25 The Cock
27 King William IV
28 Three Tuns
34 Crown & Punchbowl
42 White Horse
47 Norton Dog
58 The Ship

### A19

- Oswalds
- Oak Tree
- Three Tuns
- Spotted Cow

### M1

12 Carpenters Arms
12 French Horn
14 Carrington Arms
16 Olde Sun
16 Bliss Tearoom
16 White Hart
18 The Moorings
18 Red Lion
19 Chequers
19 Manor Farmshop
20 Greyhound
22 Field House Hotel
24 Falcon
29 Elm Tree
29 Hardwick Inn
38 Old Post Office
47 Swan Hotel

# Index by Motorways


**M2**

1 Leather Bottle
5 Harrow Inn
5 Oad Street Centre
7 Red Lion

**M3**

4a Crown & Cushion
5 Old House at Home
7 Queen Inn
7 Fox Inn
9 Chestnut Horse
9 Bush Inn

**M4**

8/9 Belgian Arms
11 Swan
12 Volunteer
13 Olde Red Lion
13 Langley Hall Inn
13 Red House
14 Pheasant
14 Hare Restaurant
15 Plough
15 Chiseldon House
15 Silks on the Downs
17 Hit or Miss
17 New Inn
17 Neeld Arms
17 Jolly Huntsman
18 The Crown
18 Tollgate
18 Bull

**M4 Wales**

23a Wheatsheaf
27 Rising Sun
37 Prince of Wales
48 Bird In Hand

**M5**

5 Robin Hood
6 Old Chequers
7 Swan
7 Walter de Cantelupe
7 Talbot
9 Hobnails
13 Bell Inn
13 Frombridge Mill
14 Anchor Inn
16 Bowl Inn
19 Black Horse
19 Priory
22 White Cottage
23 Puriton Inn
24 The Compass
25 Hankridge Arms
26 Merry Harriers
27 Globe Inn
27 Old Well Garden Centre
29 Jack in the Green
30 Blue Ball Inn
30 Diggers Rest
30 Greendale Farmshop
31 Nobody Inn

**M6**

12 The Granary
12 Bell Inn
12 Littleton Arms
16 White Lion
17 Zest Restaurant
19 The Smoker
27 Corner House
27 White Lion
32 Italian Orchard
33 Canalside Craft Centre
33 Bay Horse
36 Crooklands Hotel

**M6 (cont)**
38 Crossed Keys
38 Old School Tearoom
38 Kennedys Fine Chocolates
39 Greyhound
40 Gate Inn
40 Kings Arms
40 Brantwood Hotel
43 Crown Hotel
44 Stag Inn

**M11**
7 Rainbow & Dove
8 Three Willows
9 Red Lion
10 Green Man
11 Queens Head
12 Rupert Brooke
12 Orchard
12 Green Man
13/14 Three Horseshoes

**M18**
6 John Bull

**M20**
4 Angel
7 Kings Arms
9 Hare & Hounds
10 Farrier's Arms
10 Honest Miller
11 Drum

**M23**
10 White Swan
11 Black Swan

**M25**
4 Bo Peep
6 Bell Inn
11 Castle
16 Swan
18 Black Horse
21a Holly Bush

**M26**
2a Vineyard

**M27**
1 Bell Hotel
1 Green Dragon
1 White Hart

**M40**
5 Fox & Hounds
6 Olde Leathern Bottel
6 Cherry Tree
9 Chequers
10 Fox & Hounds
11 George & Dragon
11 New Inn
12 Malt Shovel
13/14 The Leopard
15 The Granville

**M48**
1 Boars Head
1 White Hart

**M50**
1 Fleet Inn
1 Village Inn
3 Roadmaker
3 Kilcot Inn
3 Moody Cow

**M53**
4 Fox & Hounds
9 Jabula Restaurant

**M54**
3 David Austin Roses
4 Apley Farm Shop

**M56**
6 Honey Bee
10 Chetwode Arms

**M61**
8 Red Cat
8 Dressers Arms

**M62**
22 Turnpike
25 Black Horse
30 Three Horseshoes
37 Wellington

**M65**
3 Alghero Restaurant
13 Thatch & Thistle

**M66**
1 Lord Raglan

**M69**
1 Barnacles
1 Blue Pig

## Scotland

**M9**
2/3 Champany Inn
11 Old Bridge Inn

**M74**
13 Abingdon Hotel
15 Black Bull Hotel
15 Café Ariete
17 Dryfesdale Hotel

**M90**
4 Baxters
6 Grouse & Claret
8 Bein Inn

# Places of Interest Index

**A1**

| | | |
|---|---|---|
| - | Shuttleworth Collection - 2m | 01767 627927 |
| 16 | Peterborough Cathedral - 4m | |
| 17 | Elton Hall & Gdns HHA - 3m | 01832 280468 |
| 45 | Bramham Park HHA - 2m | 01937 846000 |
| 48 | Isurium Roman Town - 2m | |
| | Newby Hall HHA - 8m | 01423 322583 |

**A3(M)**

| | | |
|---|---|---|
| 2 | Stansted Park HHA - 1m | 02392 413432 |

**A14**

| | | |
|---|---|---|
| 2 | Lamport Hall HHA - 4m | 01604 686272 |
| | Kelmarsh Hall HHA - 4m | 01604 686543 |
| | Cottesbrooke Hall & Gdns HHA - 8m | 01604 505808 |
| 12 | Lyveden New Bield NT - 7m | 01832 205358 |
| 42 | Ickworth House NT - 3m | 01284 735720 |

**M1**

| | | |
|---|---|---|
| 13 | Woburn Abbey HHA - 5m | 01525 290333 |
| 14 | Bletchley Park Pte - 6m | 01908 640404 |
| 15 | Stoke Park Pavillions Pte - 4m | 01604 862172 |
| 19 | Stanford Hall HHA - 2m | 01788 861540 |
| 29 | Hardwick Hall EH - 2m | 01246 850430 |
| | Bolsover Castle EH - 1m | 01246 822844 |
| | Sutton Scarsdale Hall EH - 1m | 01246 822400 |
| | Chatsworth HHA - 15m | 01246 582204 |
| | Haddon Hall HHA - 17m | 01629 812855 |
| 37 | Cannon Hall, Barnsley MBC - 2m | 01226 790427 |

**M3**

| | | |
|---|---|---|
| 4A | Napoleon III's Mausoleum, Farnborough Pte - 3m | |
| | Airborne Forces Museum - 4m | |
| 5 | Old Basing House, Hants C.C. - 5m | 01256 467294 |
| 7 | The Grange EH - 8m | 01424 775705 |

# Places of Interest Index

| | | |
|---|---|---|
| **M4** | | |
| 8/9 | Dorney Court HHA - 5m | 01628 604638 |
| 11 | Stratfield Saye HHA - 5m | 01256882694 |
| 11 | Silchester (site of Calleva Atrebartum) - 7m | |
| 12 | Engelfield House Garden HHA - 3m | 0118 9302504 |
| | Basildon Park NT - 7m | 0118 9843040 |
| 14 | Ashdown House NT - 9m | 01793 762209 |
| 17 | Bowood House HHA - 6m | 01249 812102 |
| | Lacock Abbey NT - 7m | 01249 730459 |
| | Corsham Court HHA - 9m | 01249 701610 |
| 18 | Dyrham Park NT - 2m | 01179 372501 |
| | Horton Court NT - 5m | 01179 372501 |
| **M5** | | |
| 5 | Hanbury Hall NT - 4m | 01527 821214 |
| 9 | Tewkesbury Abbey - 1m | |
| 13 | Frampton Court Pte - 3m | 01452 740267 |
| | Wildfowl Ctre (Slimbridge) - 5m | 01453 891900 |
| 23 | Glastonbury Abbey - 13m | |
| 24 | Maunsel House HHA - 7m | 01278 661076 |
| 25 | Hestercombe Gdns HHA - 4m | 01823 413923 |
| 26 | Cothay Manor & Gdns HHA - 4m | 01823 672283 |
| 27 | Knightshayes Court NT - 6m | 01884 257381 |
| **M6** | | |
| 17 | Little Moreton Hall NT - 6m | 01260 272018 |
| 18 | Capesthorne Hall HHA - 11m | 01625 861221 |
| 19 | Arley Hall & Gdns HHA - 5m | 01565 777353 |
| | Tatton Park NT - 3m | 01625 374400 |
| | Tabley House - Univ. of M'chstr - 2m | 01565 750151 |
| 35 | Leighton Hall HHA - 3m | 01524 734474 |
| 36 | Levens Hall & Gdns HHA - 4m | 01539 560321 |
| | Sizergh Castle NT - 5m | 01539 560951 |
| 38 | Roman Fort, Low Borrowbridge - 3m | |
| 39 | Shap Abbey EH - 3m | |

**M6**

40 Dalemain HHA - 3m 01768 486450
The Toffee Shop, Penrith - 1m 01768 862008
41 Hutton-in-the-Forest HHA - 3m 01768 484449
43 Carlisle Castle and Cathedral - 3m
44 Hadrian's Turf Wall - 4m

**M11**

9 Audley End EH - 5m 01799 522842
10 Imperial War Museum - 1m 01223 835000
12 Wimpole Hall NT - 6m 01223 206000

**M20**

8 Leeds Castle Pte - 2m 01622 765400
Stoneacre House NT - 3m 01622 863247

**M23**

10 Wakehurst Place RBG Kew - 6m 01444 894066

**M25**

4 Lullingstone Castle HHA - 2m 01322 862114
Lullingstone Roman Villa EH - 2m 01322 863467
6 Chartwell NT - 8m 01732 868381
Squerryes Court HHA - 7m 01959 562345
Quebec House NT - 8m 01732 868381
18 Chenies Manor House HHA - 3m 01494 762888
21A St Alban's Abbey - 3m
Verulamium Roman City - 3m 01727 751810

**M26**

2A Old Soar Manor NT - 5m 01732 810378
Ightham Mote NT - 6m 01732 810378

**M27**

1 The Rufus Stone - 1m
Broadlands House Pte - 7m 01794 529750

**M40**

5 Stonor HHA - 8m 01491 638587
West Wycombe Park NT - 7m 01494 513569

**M40**

12 Compton Verney CVH Trust - 4m 01926 645500
Heritage Motor Museum - 1m 01926 641188
Upton House NT - 9m 01295 670266
Edgehill Battlefield - 4m
15 Charlecote Park NT - 7m 01789 470277

**M42**

14 The Saxon Church, Breedon-on-the-Hill - 3m
Calke Abbey NT - 5m 01332 863822
Staunton Harold Church NT - 5m 01332 863822

**M48**

2 Chepstow Castle EH - 2m 01291 624065
Tintern Abbey EH - 8m 01291 689251
Caerwent (Silures Roman Town) - 5m
Offa's Dyke - 5m

**M50**

1 Tewkesbury Abbey - 3m 01684 850959
2 Eastnor Castle HHA - 5m 01531 633160

**M54**

3 Weston Park HHA - 4M 01952 852100
Boscobel House EH - 4m 01902 850244
Air Museum, Shifnal 01902 376200
Lilleshall Abbey EH - 11m 01216 256820
4 Ironbridge Gorge - 5m 01952 435900

**M56**

10 Arley Hall HHA - 6m 01565 777353
Belmont Hall Pte - 6m 01606 891235

**M65**

3 Hoghton Tower HHA - 3m 01254 852986

**M69**

1 Bosworth Battle Field - 8m

## Scotland

### M9

| Junction | Place | Telephone |
|---|---|---|
| 2/3 | Hopetoun House HHA - 4m | 0131 3312451 |
| | The House of Binns NTS - 1m | 01506 834255 |
| | Blackness Castle HS - 3m | 01506 834807 |
| | Linlithgow Palace HS - 2m | 01506 842896 |
| 11 | Doune Castle HS - 3m | 01786 841742 |
| | Stirling Castle HS - 5m | 01786 450000 |

### M9

| Junction | Place | Telephone |
|---|---|---|
| 11 | Argyll's Lodging HS - 5m | 01786 431316 |
| | The Wallace Monument - 2m | 01786 472140 |

### M74

| Junction | Place | Telephone |
|---|---|---|
| 17 | Lochmaben Castle HS - 4m | |

### M90

| Junction | Place | Telephone |
|---|---|---|
| 6 | Loch Leven Castle HS - 2m (by water) | 01577 862670 |
| 9 | Elcho Castle HS - 4m | 01738 639998 |
| | The Round Tower at Abernethy - 4m | |

## Reader's Suggestions

If you know of a place which should be included or if there has been a change of ownership which needs an amendment or deletion, then please let us know.

If your suggestion is included in the next edition we will send you a complimentary copy.

Your name and address.......................................................................

...............................................................................................

.........................................................................................

Telephone...........................................................................

I would suggest that the following entry be included/ amended/deleted.

Name...........................................................................

Motorway..........Junction.....Village.......................................

.................Details.........................................................

...............................................................................................

...............................................................................................

...............................................................................................

...............................................................................................

...............................................................................................

...................................................

By e-mail to **info@cheviotbooks.co.uk** or by post to

**Cheviot Books**
**Crossroads Cottage**
**Fifield**
**Oxon**
**OX7 6HD**

# Reader's Suggestions

If you know of a place which should be included or if there has been a change of ownership which needs an amendment or deletion, then please let us know.

If your suggestion is included in the next edition we will send you a complimentary copy.

Your name and address.........................................................

.........................................................................................

....................................................................................

Telephone....................................................................

I would suggest that the following entry be included/ amended/deleted.

Name.........................................................................

Motorway..........Junction.....Village........................................

.................Details...........................................................

.........................................................................................

.........................................................................................

.........................................................................................

.........................................................................................

.........................................................................................

...................................................

By e-mail to **info@cheviotbooks.co.uk** or by post to

**Cheviot Books**
**Crossroads Cottage**
**Fifield**
**Oxon**
**OX7 6HD**